Dr. Jeff Richards is an Emeritus Professor at Southampton Institute where he previously held the posts of Head of Academic Standards, Registrar, and Dean of the Social Science Faculty. His doctorate in political science was awarded by the University of Leicester.

Dr. Richards is also a free-lance academic writer, lecturer, researcher and consultant. Research interests include local political history in the 17th century, and the relationship between identity, community and nationality. He has published several papers and book chapters in these fields.

A native of Leicestershire, he now lives in Hampshire with his wife and grown up son and daughter. He enjoys soccer, cricket, the theatre, and membership of a local male voice choir.

By the same author:

Aristocrat and Regicide: The Life and Times of Thomas, Lord Grey of Groby (1623 - 1657)

New Millennium, London 2000

The Siege and Storming of Leicester

(MAY 1645)

by

Jeff Richards

New Millennium

292 Kennington Road, London SE11 4LD

British Library Cataloguing in Publication Data.
A catalogue record for this book is available
from the British Library.

Printed by Watkiss Studios Ltd. Biggleswade, Beds
Issued by New Millennium*
ISBN 1 85845 340 2
*An imprint of The Professional Authors' & Publishers' Association

To Mark and Caroline

This book is also dedicated to the people of Leicester and Leicestershire generally; but especially to the supporters of Leicester City Football Club, 'The Foxes', Leicester Rugby Football Club, 'The Tigers', and Leicestershire County Cricket Club, 'The Leicestershire Foxes'.

ACKNOWLEDGEMENTS

This book owes much to the advice, assistance and support of others. In particular I am indebted to the following people: -

Melanie Blake, Courtauld Institute of Art, University of London
Roger Burdell, Old Manor Hotel, Loughborough
Kate Burrows, Groby Old Hall & Cropston
Paul and Yolanda Courtney
Jane Cunningham, Courtauld Institute of Art, University of London
Robert Dimsdale
John Holling
Helene Kelly, Leicester City Museums Service
James Kilvington, National Portrait Gallery
Alastair Laing, Adviser on Pictures and Sculpture, National Trust
Joyce Mills, Living History Unit, Arts & Leisure, Leicester City Council
Anthony Squires
Joan Stevenson
also, David Ramsey of Groby for material and illustrations used both here and in *Aristocrat and Regicide.*

and the following organisations : -

Courtauld Institute of Art, University of London
Leicester City Museum Service
Leicester City Reference Library
Leicestershire County Library Service
Leicestershire County Museums, Arts, and Records Service
Leicester City & Leicestershire County Record Office, Wigston

National Gallery
National Portrait Gallery
National Trust (The Stamford Collection, Dunham Massey)
Northamptonshire County Record Office

I would also like to record my appreciation to Sandy Harlow and Sue Fricker for word processing various stages of the original text, to Bob Moulder for illustrating the cover pictures and action drawings, and to my wife, Jan, for her on-going support.

CONTENTS

LIST OF ILLUSTRATIONS

Front cover: Equestrian portrait of King Charles I, 'in bright armour', with his army outside a town (Bob Moulder after Wenceslaus Hollar)

Back cover: The Storming of the Newarke breach (Bob Moulder)

1.   Early C18th aspect of Leicester from the north
2.   Queen Elizabeth I with Coat of Arms and Motto
3.   John Evelyn
4.   Leicester - 1610 {John Speed)
5.   C17th Map of Leicestershire (Seller)
6.   Map of West Goscote Hundred in Leicestershire
7.   King Charles I
8.   Henry Grey, 1st Earl of Stamford (circa 1638) with signature
9.   Henry Hastings - Lord Loughborough?
10. An aspect of Leicester during the Civil War, 1642-1645
11. Pass issued by Colonel Henry Grey, Governor of Leicester
12. Engraving of Henry Grey, Earl of Stamford, with insignia and signature
13. Order for demolition of the Grange Houses, with signatures
14. Thomas Grey, Lord Grey of Groby, with signature and seal
15. Sir George Booth
16. Sir Arthur Hesilrige
17. Lucy Hutchinson
18. Colonel John Hutchinson
19. Woodcut of Prince Rupert at Birmingham
20. Sir Robert Pye (Jnr) of Farringdon
21. Captain Francis Hacker

THE ILLUSTRATIONS ON THE PAGES NUMBERED
BELOW ARE REPRODUCED BY KIND PERMISSION OF
THE FOLLOWING:-

The Ashmolean Museum, Oxford 264, 267

Cambridge University 229

Paul and Yolanda Courtney 314, 322, 323, 324, 325, 329, 330, 339

Dunham Massey, The Stamford Collection (The National Trust)
photography by the Courtauld Institute of Art 67, 98, 268, 292, 293,

Leicester City Council 16, 96, 162, 263

Leicestershire Museums, Arts and Records Service 94

The Mary Evans Picture Library 287

The National Gallery, London 169

The National Portrait Gallery, London 17, 18, 66, 97, 99, 100, 101,
161, 164, 165, 166, 167, 170, 171, 172, 173, 174, 175, 176, 177, 178,
228, 266, 289, 291

Newark District Council 168

Private Collection : Roger Burdell, Loughborough 68

Private Collection : photography by the Courtauld Institute of Art.
126

The Spencer Collection, Althorp, Northants. 97, 167

Staatsbibliothek Preussischer Kulturbesitz, Berlin 203

Joan Stevenson 313, 320, 321, 333, 334, 335, 336

York City Art Gallery 227

INTRODUCTION

The significance of the siege, storming and sacking of Leicester during King Charles the First's summer campaign of 1645 has been too long neglected in studies of the English Civil War. Its consequences, leading directly to the fatally weakened state of the main royalist field army at the battle of Naseby only two weeks later, were profound for English history and constitutional development.

Contemporary chroniclers comment on, firstly, the particular ferocity of the storming and, secondly, the conspicuous courage displayed by the defenders - soldiers and civilians (particularly the townswomen); both held to be the most marked of any in the conflict between the armies of the King and the Parliament.

This account strongly takes issue with the views of recent local historians that the siege, and the disastrous sacking which followed it, was the price that Leicester had to pay for not declaring its allegiance earlier and more clearly. On the contrary it argues that the borough's clear and bold stand for the parliamentarian 'Good Old Cause' played a major, albeit hitherto overlooked, role in determining both the outcome of the first civil war and the execution of the king.

Interest in the siege and storming of Leicester arose out of research for an earlier and larger work, *'Aristocrat and Regicide - The Life and Times of Thomas, Lord Grey of Groby (1623-1657)'*, published by New Millennium, London, 2000 [1]. In the context of that biography it was only possible to deal with this particular subject briefly and the idea for this book was formed. The opportunity has also been taken to up-date and to publicise more widely some earlier works on this relatively neglected topic. As a consequence the final chapter of this book includes a number of extracts and illustrations from some relevant nineteenth century publications, i.e. those of

J.F. Hollings, *The History of Leicester during the Great Civil War* (1840) and W. Kelly, *Royal Progresses and Visits to Leicester* (1884). Also featured are some photographs, one from circa 1880 and the others from the early 1990s, which are reproduced by kind permission of both the Leicester & Leicestershire Record Office and Paul and Yolanda Courtney from their article 'A siege examined : the Civil War archaeology of Leicester' which appeared in *'Post-Medieval Archaeology'* No. 26 (1992) [2]. Other photographs and a map are reproduced by kind permission of Joan Stevenson from her book *'Leicester Through The Ages'* (1995) [3].

John Hollings, a schoolmaster, Liberal politician, and Vice President of the Mechanics Institute in Leicester, was anxious that the people of Leicester and Leicestershire be aware and proud of their historical heritage. He also wished, in particular, to draw attention to the remaining evidence of the sites of the *events* of May/June 1645, some two hundred years later, before they disappeared forever. The remains of the city walls and the walls and fortifications of the Newarke, along with the old town gates, had already been much reduced by the time of his original lecture to the Mechanics Institute in 1839 and its publication the following year. He expressed his regret at the demolition, shortly before his lecture was given, of part of the walls over which, as he put it, both the standards of the Royal Army and the Commonwealth had flown and over which so much blood had been shed. He fully realised that **"far different matters"** [in 1840, as in 2000] **"now occupy the Municipal Authorities, the citizens, and the ladies of Leicester than the defence of their hearths and homes against attacking armies"** and **"long may we avoid the evils of such civil strife"** [4]. Recent ethnic violence and civil wars around the world in our own time must lead us to endorse these sentiments.

The drawings featured in his book, reproduced in the final chapter of this one, sought to record what was left for posterity. Since that time the changes caused by the Industrial Revolution, the 'Motor Vehicle Revolution' with its new road layouts, underpasses, fly-overs, and the 'Post-Industrial Revolution' with pedestrianisation, clearance, and modernisation, have reduced the remaining physical remains and evidence from the time of the siege and storming in 1645 even more. This book in large part seeks to support John Hollings' praiseworthy efforts some one hundred and sixty years later. It was his wish that future generations of Leicester inhabitants to come would understand and appreciate the struggles and the sacrifices made by those who fought over the same ground in 1645. Fortunately much of the area central to the main events of the story of the siege and storming of Leicester has in recent years been constituted as 'Castle Park' by the County and City Councils. It covers the area of the Newarke and much of the old centre of the borough. The historical sites have been identified in an imaginative manner for the benefit of locals and tourists alike. By using the signposts provided in conjunction with the maps and photographs in this book the reader should be able to identify on the ground many of the locations mentioned in the narrative.

One of the problems which can arise from the use of source material, both primary and secondary, in historical research is that of potential confusion over names and individuals. In particular in the case of this work I have encountered a plethora of Greys and instances of mistaken identity on the part of writers past and present. It is my profound hope that I have detected all of these cases where they occur and that I have not made the same mistake. It is not easy to avoid. For one thing there appears to have been a large number of Greys in seventeenth century Leicestershire. To confuse things even more, the contemporary spelling can, and frequently does, vary from Grey to Gray to Greye. Henry Grey, first Earl of Stamford, often referred to himself by his original title (and that inherited by his eldest son Thomas) as Lord Grey. In order to attempt to reduce the confusion I shall refer to the father as 'Stamford' and the son as 'Grey of Groby' throughout this work. Also in Leicestershire, as well as Thomas's brothers Anchitel, John, and Leonard there were their relatives the Greys of Burbage. The most prominent of these were Henry Grey, Earl of Kent, and his brother, Theophilus Grey, who at one time commanded the Leicester garrison under Lord Grey of Groby's authority. Still in the same county there are references to Captain (later Colonel) Henry Grey and Edward Grey who were both officers in Lord Grey of Groby's Regiment and others of the same name who were not of the aristocratic family. This coincidence of names has sometimes led to a confusion over signatures as in the case of a military pass issued by the acting Governor of Leicester in April 1644 being incorrectly attributed to the Earl of Stamford rather than to Colonel Henry Grey [5]. Similarly, at times there appears to have been confusion between the signatures of Thomas, Lord Grey of Groby (Tho. Grey) and Theophilus Grey (Theo. Grey). The signatures of all four men, along with several others, appear on pages at the end of Chapter Three in the following text. Leicestershire at this time certainly seems to have been something of a 'grey area'! To complicate matters still further there were on the Parliamentarian side nationally Lord Grey of Wark [6], Lord Grey of Ruthin, and Lord Gray, a Scottish peer.

Throughout this work I have attempted to be consistent in the style of presentation adopted in relation to the use of quotations, dates, and references. Where quotations from contemporary seventeenth century sources are used the spelling has usually been left in the original form. Such quotations are delivered in italic script and usually in a darker type face. In all dates given the year has been taken to begin on 1 January, as it does now, and not on 25 March which was the practice in the early seventeenth century. Asterisks marked thus (*) in the end of chapter references to Nichols' *'History and Antiquities of Leicestershire'* are part of the original pagination used by Nichols and denote inserted pages.

This work draws heavily on narratives and accounts by participants in the events covered and their contemporaries. This can make things more interesting, immediate and 'real' for us; but it is not without its difficulties. Within the general problem of historiography, with its limitations of partial information, relative obscurity, confusion over individuals, uneven coverage of times and events, is the question of subjectivity and prejudice. C.V. Wedgwood, a highly respected historian who has written widely on topics during the reign of King Charles I and the Interregnum, has defined history as, **"the fragmentary record of the often inexplicable actions of innumerable bewildered human beings, set down and interpreted according to their own limitations by other human beings, equally bewildered"** [7]. This well illustrates both the fascination and the difficulty of attempting to produce an accurate account of events and the causal factors behind them.

In addition to providing a narrative compiled from the accounts of participants, I have illustrated the events by including, where possible, portraits of those involved, directly or indirectly, together with the action illustrations by Bob Moulder to 'bring to life' those troubled but interesting days in the history of Leicester.

The last chapter owes much to the archaeological research carried out by the Leicester and Leicestershire Museum Services. In particular I am grateful to Paul and Yolanda Courtney for permission to use some of the material contained in their publication referred to above, and to Joan Stevenson for the use of several photographs from her book, in this chapter.

Finally; this book aims to be of interest to readers of local history , military history, and students of the English Civil War period. It is hoped that it will appeal not only to the people of Leicester and the surrounding county of Leicestershire, but to the world beyond. I would in particular, however, echo John Hollings' hope, expressed in 1840, that **"I might safely trust for indulgence to the good sense and intelligence of those around me; ... that it would be very little to our credit, if while ... [well] versed in the history of their country ... [the people of Leicester] should ... [be] among the least able to appreciate their [own] possession."** [8]

NOTES:

1. Jeff Richards, *Aristocrat and Regicide - The Life and Times of Thomas, Lord Grey of Groby (1623-1657)* New Millennium, London, 2000.
2. Paul & Yolanda Courtney, *A Siege Examined: The Civil War Archaeology of Leicester* in *Post-Medieval Archaeology* No. 26. 1992. pp. 47-90.
3. Joan Stevenson, *Leicester Through The Ages*, Kairos Press, Leics., 1995.
4. John F. Hollings, *The History of Leicester during the Great Civil War'*, Combe & Crossley, Leicester, 1840.pp.71 & 72.
5. *Bloodie Rebellion - Leicestershire & Rutland in the Civil War* Leicestershire Museums Service - Archive Teaching Unit No. 1, Item 7., 1979.
6. John Adair, *A Life of John Hampden - The Patriot (1594-1643)* Macdonald and Jane's, London, 1976. p.221. He confuses Grey of Wark with Grey of Groby here.
7. C.V. Wedgwood, *The Historian and the World* (1942), republished in *History and Hope* - C.V. Wedgwood's collected essays.(Fontana, London, August 1989)
8. John F. Hollings, op. cit. p.73.

*"I do not care if they cut them three times more,
for they are mine enemies."*
(King Charles I)

*"Therefore saith the Lord, The Lord of Hosts,
O my people that dwellest in Zion,
be not afraid of the Assyrian:
Though he smite thee with the rod,
and lift his staff against thee ...
for yet a very little while,
and his destruction shall be accomplished."*

(*Isaiah*, Chapter 10 vs 24 & 25)

CHAPTER ONE

SEMPER EADEM ('*Always the Same*')
(Motto of the Borough of Leicester)

The position of the town up to June 1642

The beginning of the seventeenth century found Leicester a small market town of five parishes [1] with a population of approximately 3,500 people. It lay in the centre of the county of which it was the county town, like the hub in a cartwheel. The borough still possessed its open fields, its inhabitants still followed largely agricultural pursuits, and what industry and commerce there was in the town was tied closely to rural activities.

Opinions on the appearance of seventeenth century Leicester seem to have differed; but then beauty is reputed to lie in the eye of the beholder.

John Evelyn in 1654 referred to *"... the old and ragged Citty of Leicester, large and pleasantly seated, but despicably built, the chimney flues like so many smiths' forges."* [2]

Celia Fiennes describes how *"Leicester town stands on the Side of a little riseing Ground, tho' at a distance from ye adjacent hills it looks low, but its a good prospect. It has four gates, ye streetes are pretty large and well pitch'd, there are five parishes; the Market place is a Large space very handsome with a good Market Cross and town hall. Ye river Sow which runs into the rive Recke and both Empts themselves into ye Trent."* In respect of the town's churches she comments that *"St. Martin's Church .... Is one of ye biggest - there is none very big and none fine."* She adds that *"... their fewell here is but Cowdung or Coale which they are supplied with out of Warwickshire."* [3]

The whole of Leicester's prosperity and economic development appears to have been dependent upon rural or related activities. The town was, in economic terms, a place of craftsmen and small

1

shopkeepers, living by the services given to and received from the surrounding countryside. There were many links between the town and country; together they formed an integrated community.

"The town fields (almost wholly unenclosed) comprised by 1630 some 2,800 acres - an area, that is, about twenty times that of the walled town itself. Two-thirds of this arable, one third pasture. Leicester people also farmed land extensively further out, by payment of rent. Many of them kept dairies, which not only supplied their own households but also provided butter and cheese for the market. As the services of regular carriers developed, a part of this produce may well have found its way to London. There were many graziers in the town. Some of them were dairymen or craftsmen as well; others were also butchers. The largest men of this class were general farmers, growing crops for fodder and brewing, besides much hay and corn. Here was a continuing basis for employment in the town. The farmers required the services of five wage-workers each, on average, without including dairymaids and shepherds. A careful analysis of the evidence provided by wills and inventories suggests that capitalist farmers were the largest employers of labour in Leicester." [4]

In Leicester the wealthy burgesses who constituted the Corporation, which selected itself, were already beginning to assert their position against the traditional hegemony of the dominant county families. A glance at the occupations of the men who held the position of Mayor of Leicester during this period shows a predominance of merchants who made their living from meeting the needs of the town and county; they were chandlers (shopkeepers, grocers, dealers in merchandise, e.g. corn wholesalers), drapers (retailers of cloth), cordwainers (boot and shoemakers), mercers (dealers in textile fabrics and fine cloth), goldsmiths (dealers or manufacturers of gold articles and bankers), graziers (large scale farmers of sheep or cattle), and the like.

The Borough of Leicester had been granted its charter of incorporation by Queen Elizabeth in 1589. Its authority was further extended by charter in 1599. Neither charter had given the Mayor and burgesses all they had wished for. They had hoped that their town might have been made a county in its own right, as both neighbouring Coventry and Nottingham had been since the later medieval period. Leicester had been handicapped in this respect by its inclusion in the Duchy Of Lancaster and its closer connection to the Crown via John of Gaunt and the Lancastrian kings. Increased independence had been correspondingly difficult to obtain. By the Elizabethan charters there were to be, in addition to the Mayor, two Bailiffs elected by the whole Corporation, Twenty-Four 'Aldermen', and Forty-Eight members of the Common Hall or Councillors. In the words of the second charter, they were *"one body corporate and politic in fact and in name, and a perpetual community of one Mayor, two Bailiffs and the Burgesses of the Borough of Leicester, and by the same name they shall have a constant succession."* Taken together the two charters were a valuable acquisition. They strengthened the Corporation's authority over the general body of citizens and the territory of the town. They also reflected the gradual withdrawing of the ancient powers of the lords, both central and local. [5]

The Borough's badge of the ermine cinquefoil on a red shield derived from the arms of the Beaumont (or Bellemonte) Earls of Leicester. Its Latin motto, *'Semper Eadem'* ('Always The Same'), granted by Queen Elizabeth who also used it, indicated Constancy. Whether this was to be Constancy to the Tudor monarchy, any monarchy, or an unchanging faithfulness to a wider and different set of interests and convictions was soon to become a real issue.

As far as the wider county beyond the Borough of Leicester is concerned, some impression may be formed of its settlement pattern and landscape from the observations of contemporary travellers.

Richard Symonds, writing in 1645, just prior to the siege and storming of Leicester, found that *"The county of Leicester is generally champaigne pasture and erable,* [sic] *little or no waste, and small wood; some quick hedges, and the parishes stand less than one myle distant."* [6]

John Evelyn in 1654, during the Commonwealth period, described Leicestershire as *"an open, rich but unpleasant country."* Just why Evelyn found Leicestershire unpleasant is not clear, but he went on to add that *"the county is much in common."* By this he meant that the open field system or common lands in the shire had not been much enclosed at that point. Interestingly, although Evelyn regarded Leicestershire as relatively unenclosed in 1654 it should be noted that, whilst in 1607 at least one quarter of the county was enclosed, by 1640 nearly one third of all villages in the county had been entirely enclosed. [7] Evelyn also commented that *"the gentry* (are) *free drinkers."* [8] He was hardly more charitable to the small neighbouring county of Rutand and its inhabitants. He passed next on his journey through *"Uppingham, the shire-town of Rutland, pretty and well built of stone, which is a rarity in that part of England, where most of the rural parishes are but of mud, and the people living as wretchedly as in the most impoverished parts of France, which they much resemble, being idle and sluttish."* [9]

Writing towards the end of the seventeenth century Celia Fiennes, entering Leicestershire from the south-east and arriving at Leicester described the county as *"a very Rich Country - Red Land, good Corne of all sorts and grass, both fields and enclosures. You see great way upon their hills ye bottoms full of Enclosures, woods and different sort of manureing and Herbage, amongst which are placed many little towns which gives great pleasure of ye travellers to view. Ye miles are long but hither its pretty hard good way. ... ..Here you see very large fine sheep* [10] *and very good land, but some very deep bad roads."* [11]
It may be useful at this point, in the light of the above passage, to note the common practice in seventeenth century England of referring to a county as a country and to every settlement above the size of the smallest hamlet as a town.
She adds later, following her stay in Leicester, *"This Country as I said was all Rich deep land, and they plough their land all with ploughs without wheeles as they do in Oxfordshire and other deep lands."* [12]

Leicestershire at this time was still essentially an agricultural and rural community with marked social stratification amongst its inhabitants. Authority in such a society was a function of social position, which in turn was traditionally linked to landowning. Grazing and farming were the main economic activities. Although coal was mined in the north west of the county at Coleorton and Swannington it was on a very small scale and coal was brought from Derbyshire and Warwickshire as well as from these local workings along trackways through the Leicester Forest. The hosiery industry was not established in the county until the second half of the century and it was only in the eighteenth century that improvements in communications brought Leicestershire into relatively easy contact with other parts of England, especially London.

Radiating out in an approximate circle of satellites around Leicester, and acting as the focal points of the hinterlands of the county hundreds, were the market towns of which the largest were Ashby-de-la-Zouch and Loughborough (in West Goscote Hundred), Queniborough (in East Goscote Hundred), Melton Mowbray (in Framland Hundred), Lutterworth (in Guthlaxton Hundred), Market Harborough (in Gartree Hundred), Market Bosworth and Hinckley (in Sparkenhoe Hundred).

The poor harvests and diseases which appear to have dominated the period 1625 to 1640 had deep repercussions on the politics of the town and county. These found their expression in Leicester partly in attempts to secure extra privileges for the corporation of the borough, as against the county generally and the leading families, and partly in general opposition to aspects of the economic, social and religious policies of the royal government. At various stages before actual civil way broke out the borough and its magistrates found themselves in opposition to the royal authority. One of the outstanding causes of discontent was the move by Charles I in 1628 to enclose Leicester Forest. This proposal was strenuously resisted by the people of Leicester and the surrounding countryside. The townsfolk had enjoyed the right to cut firewood in the forest since the time of the Beaumont Earls, and the main route by which coal was brought in from the workings in the western part of the county ran through it. The Corporation offered a payment of £500 for the abandonment of the scheme. Unruly persons damaged the ditches that were cut as boundaries. An appeal was addressed to Parliament in the form of *"A petition from divers glaziers* (sic) *of Leicester."* It was presented to the House of Commons on 17th February 1629, and referred to the Committee of Grievances. [13] The contents are not recorded in detail but the Journal of the House of Lords contains a reference to grievances including *"the disafforestation of Leicester Forest."* [14] It is almost certain that the `divers glaziers' mentioned as the authors of the petition were in fact graziers. The king was forced to make a compromise and conceded an allocation of forty acres to the townspeople as a whole and other grants were made to those with special claims. The forty acres were let and the income from the rent applied to poor relief. In spite of these concessions the royal action was very unpopular in Leicester. The cash gained by the Crown from the enclosure of the Leicester Forest was outweighed by the ill-will that it created locally. This may have contributed towards the antagonism which the Royal interest encountered later in Leicester.

The general quarrel, however, between the king and his opponents was a long-standing one; it predated both Charles I and the Long Parliament which he reluctantly called to assemble in November 1640. The issues were both deeply rooted and considerably interwoven, making it difficult to set out and separate them briefly.

The story of the gradually deteriorating relations between king and parliament after 1603, the year of James I's accession, was highlighted by a series of major issues and crises. The new dynasty, the Stuarts, were firm believers in the idea of the 'Divine Right of Kings' (i.e. they saw themselves as God's representatives on earth). Their word was law and therefore there was little necessity for a parliament to do anything other than to assist the ruler when he thought fit. Parliament, however, thought differently. For the first time in its history the balance of wealth was shifting from the Lords to the Commons and the latter appears to have been keen to exercise the power which they thought their wealth entitled them to. Conflicts, therefore, arose between Crown and Parliament. Parliament in the late 1620s attempted to invest itself not only with the rights to assess and levy taxes, but also with the right of deciding where the money was spent. James I had ruled for seven years without a parliament in England. Charles I, free, after the death of his father's favourite, the Duke of Buckingham, from costly foreign ventures, dispensed with his parliament for eleven years. He dissolved the parliament in 1629 and provoked the first real crisis by imprisoning its popular leaders in the Tower of London (where one, Sir John Eliot, died three years later) and ruled himself through strong ministers, with unpopular policies in Church and State, Archbishop William Laud and Thomas Wentworth, Earl of Strafford.

To increase his slender income Charles I re-introduced, or further developed, several ancient forms of taxation. Thus, for example, he exploited the Court of Wards by which the Crown took charge of the lands of anyone who, under the age of twenty one, had come into possession of estates. This became one of the most unpopular royal courts as the family of the minor were forced into attempting to buy the wardship from the king in order to prevent their estates from becoming an economic ruin or the ward married off by the Crown to the daughter of a spendthrift courtier. The unpopularity of this system was increased because of the rake-offs taken by the officials who controlled the procedures. Henry Grey, the first Earl of Stamford at Bradgate in Leicestershire, was aged only fifteen when he became Lord Grey of Groby. When he married at the age of twenty he was referred to as being the ward of his mother, so clearly the family had purchased the wardship back from the Crown by then. The king also extracted loans from nobles and fined people who had extended their estates at the expense of the royal forests.

In addition, Charles instituted committees in each shire to investigate the non-payment of distraint of knighthood, the fine paid by those eligible because of their wealth and status to become knights at the coronation of a new monarch but who failed so to do. In Leicestershire the Earl of Huntingdon, the head of the Hastings

7

family of Ashby-de-la-Zouch and Castle Donington, had been appointed to head the committee. Resistance to such payment was high and the Earl had many occasions to complain to the Mayor of Leicester about the laxity of payment by those eligible.

The most notorious cause of unrest, however, in the 1630s was the collection of Ship Money. This was an old tax levied in coastal counties in order to pay for the building of naval vessels. In 1635 Charles extended this collection to the inland counties in order to build up his navy which had suffered under the Duke of Buckingham's unsuccessful foreign enterprises. Resistance to the payment was widespread, the stand of John Hampden in Buckinghamshire becoming of particular importance nationally. In Leicestershire the heavy-handedness of the Earl of Huntingdon's associate, Henry Skipwith of Cotes, resulted in a great deal of reluctance to pay the assessed contribution to the building of a 450 ton ship. The writ sent to the High Sheriff of Leicestershire and the Mayor of Leicester demanded payment of £200 towards the provision of the ship, which was to be provided with ammunition and crewed by 180 sailors. This expenditure, which was equivalent to a quarter of the town's normal annual expenditure, was regarded as unreasonable and, though quickly raised, met with an understandably hostile reception. Similar writs were issued for the same sums in 1637 and 1639, although the amount required in 1638 was only £72. By 1638, however, thirty people in Leicestershire had had their goods confiscated to pay their part of the assessment. A king making such demands was unlikely to enhance his reputation with his Leicester subjects. It was the sort of action that would be remembered.

The Earl of Huntingdon's involvement in these unpopular activities of the king further alienated him from many of the people of Leicester as well as a concerted body of the county gentry who allied themselves to the Earl of Stamford. The traditional Hastings' domination of the county and the borough had already begun to weaken after the 1621 parliamentary elections. They had gained representation in the 1628 elections but it was no longer the monopoly which it had been hitherto. Between 1547 and 1625 seven members of the Hastings family had represented Leicestershire in Parliament and either they or their nominees had held the borough seats. Now the animosities and jealousies of the county gentry towards the resented Hastings hegemony found focus at Bradgate. Here in 1628 Henry Grey had become Earl of Stamford through his wife's inheritance. It was also the year which had seen the assassination of the previous king's favourite and Chief Minister George Villiers, Duke of Buckingham, a scion of the Leicestershire Villiers family of Brooksby. The times had proved propitious during the 1630s for the marked revival of the influence of the Greys who had been eclipsed since the tragic time of Lady Jane Grey, the Nine Days Queen. The Earl of Stamford took advantage of the growing discord between members of the Leicester Corporation and the other county magnates, notably the Hastings clan. As the decade had progressed the Hastingses were increasingly seen as *"a decaying family"* [15] on the defensive everywhere against the reviving power of the Greys of Groby and Bradgate. By 1640 the heart-shaped shire lying in the centre of England found itself riven by faction and dissent on both national and local issues.

As the dispute between King and Parliament began to gain momentum the Earl of Stamford had become a zealous Parliamentarian at the national level and the leading figure amongst their number in Leicestershire. In the elections to the so-called 'Long Parliament' held in 1640, a considerable victory was achieved locally over the pro-court party as represented by the Earl of Huntingdon, Lord Lieutenant of the county and leader of the Hastings family, and his nominees. Returned as members for the shire were Sir Arthur Hesilrige of Noseley who was to prove a firm republican, and Lord Grey of Ruthin, a committed Parliamentarian and a member of the Burbage branch of the Grey family, who was to become Earl of Kent in 1643. [16] Returned as members for the Borough of Leicester were a Mr. Thomas Cooke, subsequently expelled from the Commons in 1645 for having royalist sympathies, and Thomas, Lord Grey of Groby, son and heir of the Earl of Stamford, at the ripe young age of seventeen.

On the position of the town of Leicester itself in 1640 we read that **"the party that dominated the town's affairs clearly tended to sympathise with the opposition** (to the king)**; but did not declare itself imprudently."** ⁽¹⁷⁾ When the Civil War eventually broke out in 1642 the desire of the Mayor and Burgesses appears to have been to choose a safe course, but on the whole they clearly inclined towards the Parliamentarian side.

That the Puritan element was strong in Leicester is clear. In James I's reign there had been a movement for closing shops on Sundays, and there still exists a list of prominent townsmen who were willing to pledge themselves to do this. In Charles I's reign the Aldermen were instructed by a Common Hall to insist on house-holders attending the weekly sermon given by the Town Lecturer on Wednesdays; although this was an enforcement of an earlier order. The Mayor and the Burgesses were a good deal concerned with ecclesiastical affairs, but the question which appears to have occupied them most was the organisation and appointment of those who undertook such work for the town. The relative duties and salaries of the Schoolmaster, the Vicar of St. Mary's and Master of the Newarke Hospital, and the Town Preacher or Lecturer were frequently debated and various resolutions were passed about them.

In May 1641 the Earl of Stamford was proposed by the House of Commons for the Governorship of the Isle of Jersey but the appointment was refused by Charles I who recognised him now as an opponent. In November 1641 the Grand Remonstrance and Petition were drawn up by Parliament to protest to the king about 'Oppressions in Religion, Church Government and Discipline'. Not only did Stamford and Grey append their names and seals but Grey of Groby was one of the twelve members of the Committee selected to present it to the monarch.

In 1642 in a debate about the troubles in Ulster, following the rising of the native Irish against the Protestant settlers, which touched upon the losses suffered by his grandmother Elizabeth in that province, Lord Grey of Groby was referred to as *"a young lord dear to the*

House of Commons. "[18] Father and son were clearly both active in the cause of the Parliament.

The Journal of the House of Commons records that on 15th February 1642 'divers gentlemen of Leicestershire' attending at the door of the House were called in to present a petition to that House, and the copy of a similar petition they were also presenting to the House of Lords, on behalf of the Knights, Gentlemen, and Freeholders of the county. Both petitions supported the Grand Remonstrance, criticised the king's wicked counsellors, registered revulsion and fear at events in Ireland, and pledged support for Parliament. Despite the remoteness of their dwellings from London the petitioners were resolved to *"boldly affirm, that the last drop of our bloods had been freely and speedily hazarded in the defence of your persons, and maintenance of your privileges"* [19] and to *"serve you with our lives as freely as they were given us, and with our estates to the utmost values"* [20]. They were warmly thanked by both Houses of Parliament for the great care and affection they had shown for the public interest.

Many messages and responses then passed between the king and parliament but the gulf between them widened rather than narrowed. In particular the question of who should control the local militias or any army raised to quell the Irish rebellion came more and more clearly into focus. Both sides began to seek means of securing weapons, provisions and men for their cause.

Charles' queen, the French Catholic Henrietta Maria, left England for the continent towards the end of February to raise support and arms for her husband's cause abroad. By March 1642 the king had established himself in York with the nucleus of what was to be the Cavalier party. Noblemen and gentlemen came in to join him with horses and servants; amongst them was Henry Hastings, son of the Earl of Huntingdon. On 12th February Parliament had voted to replace his father as Lord Lieutenant of Leicestershire with the Earl of Stamford. By issuing laws without the royal signature (ordinances) they sought to take control of the local Trained Bands

11

with a Militia Ordinance. Through this device they had by March replaced all the Lords Lieutenants of the counties with men of their own choice. The Earl of Huntingdon considered himself too old to take part in the crisis and sought peace and quiet in his residence at Castle Donington. His heir, Ferdinando Lord Hastings, was content for the time to stay with the Parliament; only Henry Hastings, his younger son, openly upheld the King's cause and was to become its most active representative in the county during the civil war.

Until the queen could return from abroad with arms and money the king, having given up London, had to secure the munitions in the magazine at Hull, a well fortified port convenient for the supply of the army with which Charles and Strafford had intended to teach the rebellious Scots a lesson a year earlier in the so-called 'Bishops War'. The time for propaganda and psychological warfare was running out. The Parliament began to raise troops to defend itself against the king. Charles prepared to occupy Hull where he would find not only the magazine for last year's army but also a port ideally suited to receive the arms being bought by the queen in the Netherlands. Hull was commanded by Sir John Hotham, a local East Riding landowner, whose sympathies inclined, though not particularly strongly, to the Parliament. During April the Earl of Stamford and Lord Willoughby of Parham, together with a committee of the Commons, were dispatched by Parliament to confer with Hotham at Hull, to stiffen his resolve, and to draw up a report of the proceedings. Moving on afterwards from Hull to York the Earl presented to the king on the 18th April a petition in the name of both Houses of Parliament in response to an earlier royal message informing them of his intention of going to Ireland. The petition called for him to seek a reconciliation with Parliament and to dismiss his evil counsellors. There was no such reconciliation between the parties.

Towards the end of April, King Charles appeared before the gates of Hull but Hotham respectfully denied him admittance. The king furiously declared him a traitor and returned to York. (Hotham was to attempt secretly to hedge his bets by keeping in clandestine contact with the king and his advisers. His promise to deliver up Hull to the king in July when the latter made a second appearance at the head of two thousand troops had to be broken, however, because of the loyalty to the Parliament's cause of his subordinate commanders such as Captain Robert Overton of Easington, and because of parliamentary suspicions of his own, and his son's, unreliability. The result was that the king suffered a second humiliation at his second attempt to summon Hull). For the moment though the pressure mounted on those who wished to take no side or who preferred not to declare their support prematurely. Parliament in London had issued its Militia Ordinances and entrusted their newly appointed Lords Lieutenants and the local MPs with their enforcement. In response, from York, the king on 27th May issued a proclamation forbidding the raising of any troops whatsoever without his own express command or of those acting under his immediate authority.

NOTES:

1. The five parishes of the Borough of Leicester were St.Mark's, All Hallows or All Saints, St. Mary's, St. Nicholas', & St. Margaret's. A former sixth parish, St. Leonard's, had become defunct since plague and famine in the medieval period.
2. John Evelyn, *Diary of John Evelyn*, (1654) ed. H B Wheatley (Bickers & Son, London,1906).
3. Celia Fiennes, *Diary of Celia Fiennes*, (c.1700) (Field & Tuer, the Leadenhall Press).
4. Jack Simmons, *'Leicester - The Ancient Borough to 1860'* (Alan Sutton, Gloucester, 1983) p.73.
5. Ibid. pp.68 & 69.
6. Richard Symonds, *Diary of the Marches of the Royal Army During the Great Civil War,* ed. C E Long (Camden Society, Vol. LXXXIV, 1859).
7. John Evelyn, op. cit.
8. Ibid.
9. Ibid.
10. The sheep bred in Leicestershire were apparently "without comparison, the largest, and bear ... The greatest fleeces of wool on their backs of any sheep in England." (Daniel Defoe, *Tour of the Whole Island of Great Britain,* first published in 1724. Everyman Edition, Vol.ii p. 89). Sheep were so important to the local economy during the seventeenth and eighteenth centuries that Leicestershire people were known to their neighbours as 'woollybacks'. In the modern era one of the supporters chosen for the shield on the coat of arms of Leicestershire County Council was, and remains, a sheep. (The other supporter is a black bull and the crest is that of the more familiar running fox).
11. Celia Fiennes, op. cit.
12. Ibid.
13. Journal of the House of Commons (C. J.) Vol. I., p.930.
14. Journal of the House of Lords (L. J.) Vol. III, pp.872, 875, 878.
15. Edward Hyde, Earl of Clarendon, *'History of the Great Rebellion'*, ed. W D Macray (1888) Vol. III., p.473.

16. It is difficult to agree with the following point made by John Morrill, as far as Leicestershire is concerned, when he states that, "No English county except Middlesex returned men to Parliament in 1640 who spoke with one voice in 1642 or later." It rather depends just how much later! The knights of the shire returned for Leicestershire in 1642, Sir Arthur Hesilrige and Lord Grey of Ruthin, were both firm Parliamentarians. See John Morrill *The Revolt of the Provinces - Conservatives and Radicals in the English Civil War, 1630-1650* (Longman 1980) p. 18.
17. Jack Simmons, Ibid. p. 86.
18. Calendar of State Papers (Domestic Series), 1641-3, p.359.
19. Journal of the House of Commons (C.J.), Vol. II, p. 433.
20. Journal of the House of Lords (L.J.), Vol. IV, p. 590.

Early C18th aspect of Leicester from the North

16

Queen Elizabeth I with Coat of Arms and Motto

17

Meliora Retinete

John Evelyn

18

FAC-SIMILE OF A BIRD'S-EYE VIEW OF LEICESTER,

PUBLISHED IN THE YEAR 1610.

Cheife places of ỹ Citie by figures noted.

1 S. Leonards
2 Leicester Abbay
3 Abbay gate
4 Sunlaue Bridge
5 North gate
6 North gate street
7 Senius gate
8 The Spittle
9 S. Mary들

10 Churche gate
11 Belgrase gate
12 Humberston gate
13 East Gate
14 Swinesmarket
15 Satterdaies market
16 Cankwell Lane
17 S. Martines

18 Martins street
19 Alhallowes
20 High street
21 Huntingdon place
22 Woole Hall
23 Graye fryers
24 Gray fryers gate
25 S. Nicholas
26 S. Nicholas shambles

27 Redd crose street
28 S. Maryes
29 The Castell
30 Castell street
31 Black fryers lane
32 Child Hospitall
33 The newe marke
34 The Grange

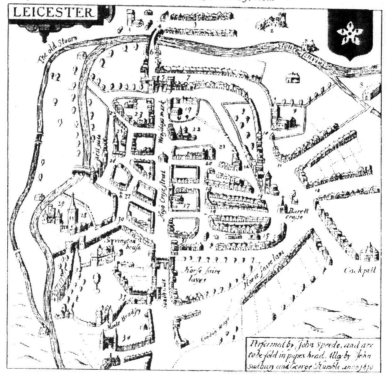

Leicester 1610 - Speed

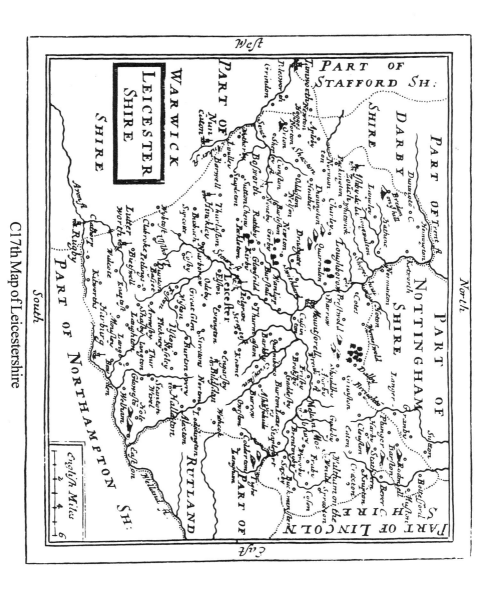

C17th Map of Leicestershire

20

CHAPTER TWO

FOR KING *AND* PARLIAMENT?
- from first skirmishes to Civil War (1642-1644)

"... ... The Lord Stanford's Warrant is to be obaied yf the Kings Proclamacion be not Proclaymed and yf yt be the Proclamacion to be obaied."

Record of the Borough of Leicester, 1642

Lucy Hutchinson, the wife of the parliamentarian governor of Nottingham, Colonel John Hutchinson, recalls in her *Memoirs of the Life of Colonel Hutchinson*:-

"Before the flame of the war broke out in the top of the chimneys, the smoke ascended in every country; the king had sent forth commissions of array, and the parliament had given out commissions for their militia, and sent off their members into all counties to put them into execution. Between these, in many places, there were fierce contests and disputes, almost to blood, even at the first; for in the process every county had the civil war, more or less, within itself." [1]

Empowered by Parliament to raise the trained bands of the borough and county in Leicestershire in order to assist in *'delivering the king from his evil counsellors'* (for so ran the parliamentarian line) the Earl of Stamford began to encourage popular feeling locally and made preparations to mobilise them in early June. He wrote from Bradgate to the Mayor and the Corporation of the Borough of Leicester informing them of his intention to raise the trained bands of the borough on 8th June. Similar arrangements were to be made to muster the trained bands of the shire in their respective hundreds.

We may well imagine the dilemma that now faced Mayor Thomas Rudyard and the other honest and sober representatives of the burghers of Leicester. As they met in Common Hall in the medieval

Guildhall with its neat enclosed courtyard, seated at the long dark oak tables behind the mullion windows, this collection of mercers, linen drapers, goldsmiths, chandlers, slaters, cordwainers, graziers and the like had a most difficult decision to make. Should they obey the militia ordinance and thus defy the king and be pronounced rebels, perhaps losing life and/or earthly possessions? Or should they have regard to the royal proclamation and incur the displeasure of the Earl of Stamford, the majority of the House of Commons, and their own consciences for the many of them who were puritans? The ambiguous slogan of 'King **and** Parliament' would not always serve as sufficient cover. After much deliberation they settled on the following compromise resolution:-

"That the Lord Stanford's Warrant is to be obaied yf the Kings Proclamacion be not Proclaymed and yf yt be the Proclamacion to be obaied." [2]

Just what was the nature of this militia which both sides were so eager to secure for their cause? The Trained Bands had evolved from the shire levies of the medieval period. Briefly, this part-time 'home guard' was raised, in both recruits and arms, from people of sufficient affluence graded according to their possessions. The old system which Charles I had tried to improve specified that (in 1621) a man with land worth £10 per annum was to provide a whole 'foot armour' (i.e. breast plate, back plate, tassets or thigh guards, and helmet) and half the cost of him that wore it; if £40 per annum, two foot armours; if £80 per annum, a light horse and foot armour, etc. The assessment of such 'taxes' was a contributory grievance to the civil war. In the general view of the times, however, the trained bands were seen as neither trained nor disciplined. Dryden described them cynically in rhyme as follows:-

> *"The country rings around with loud alarms,*
> *And raw in fields the rude militia swarms;*
> *Mouths without hands, maintain'd at vast expense,*
> *In peace a charge, in war a weak defence;*
> *Stout once a month they march, a blustering band,*
> *And ever, but in times of need, at hand."* [3]

Some of these criticisms were well justified. In some counties the so-called 'trained' bands were in such a poor state of readiness that they need not have existed. Some took several days to be mustered, mobilised, and made operational. One critic claimed that even the monthly training and drilling sessions were not taken seriously,

"by the time the arms be all viewed ... it draws towards dinner time, and indeed the officers love their bellies so well that they are loath to take too much pains ..." [4]

Venn claimed that they worshipped not Mars the god of war but Bacchus the god of wine and strong drink. Another critic wrote that they were *"effeminate in courage and incapable of discipline, because their whole course of life alienated from warlike employment."* [5]

A marked exception to this state of decay were the trained bands of London which in 1642 had been expanded by the Common Council of the City to six regiments containing 40 companies of 200 men each. These were well organised, well drilled and well led and were to prove very useful in the service of Parliament in the early years of the civil war. They were to perform good work in the field at Turnham Green where they halted a royalist advance on the capital and they played a major role in the relief of Gloucester. It was unusual, however, for trained bands to move far from their own locality and when they did they were not at all happy about it. Both sides came to realise very quickly the need to raise new, more mobile, regiments to constitute field armies.

There was another factor at stake in the race to secure control of the local militia. The trained bands were equipped with muskets, pikes, halberds, and other weapons which were often stored centrally along with the slow-match and gunpowder for use with both muskets and cannon - usually at the county magazine or powder store. In county towns all over the land the struggle was on to seize control of the local magazine and its contents on behalf of either 'the King' or 'the King and Parliament'. At Hull, for example, Robert Overton had moved swiftly to secure the important arsenal there for Parliament, thus enabling it to send Sir John Hotham to take command with the results that have been noted. In Nottingham, John Hutchinson, MP for the town and later parliamentarian Governor, managed temporarily to frustrate the designs of his cousin, Lord Newark, Lord Lieutenant of the county, and Sir John Digby, High Sheriff of the county, who with some 'cavalier' captains tried to seize the weapons and powder stored at the town-hall for the king and carry it off to York. He was supported in this by a crowd of 'honest countryfolk' or yeomen, cursed as a 'roundhead' by those with royalist views, and managed to have the contents of the magazine locked up with two locks - the Mayor of Nottingham having the key to one and the Sheriff of the county the key to the other. [6]

The accounts of the struggle to secure the contents of the Leicester magazine and control of the trained bands of the town and county would seem more appropriate to a Ruritanian comic opera in retrospect were not the issues and consequences of the actions so serious for those concerned. They will be related here in some detail.

On 4th June 1642, the day that the House of Commons enjoined Lord Grey, Lord Ruthin, and Sir Arthur Hesilrige to return home to assist in the enforcement of the Militia Ordinance, the Earl of Stamford travelled into Leicester from Bradgate. He had earlier instructed the Mayor and Corporation of the borough of Leicester to muster the trained bands of the town on the Horsefair Leas, an open grassy area just outside the town walls near the South Gate, on Wednesday 8th June. Since then he had, as Lord Lieutenant appointed by Parliament, granted warrants to the deputy lieutenants, the deputies to the Sheriff, and to the Under-Sheriff in the absence of the High-Sheriff, to command the county trained bands from the various hundreds to join in this general rendezvous at Leicester. Upon arriving at the *Angel* Inn, however, where he intended to stay until the mustering took place, he was met by a nobleman sent down by the king from York with a commission under a broad seal to

The altercation at the *Angel Inn,* Leicester

carry out a similar mission. Both noblemen had a number of servants with them, most being armed with swords in the fashion of the time. The Earl of Stamford was accused by the other of seducing the people from their allegiance to the king and ordered to depart at once in the king's name. The Earl became so incensed that he drew his sword, telling the other that he was the one who should leave immediately or else he would make the place *"too hot for him."* An ugly situation developed when the king's men drew their swords. The Earl of Stamford's men did likewise and a sword fight started which spilled out of the *Angel* into the street and became *"a desperate combat."* It was market day, the town was crowded, and the noise of the melee attracted people to the scene. These were in the main quick to take Stamford's side. The king's representatives, outnumbered and fearing for their lives, were obliged to withdraw and hastily left the town to hisses, cries of *'Popish Lord'*, and other insulting terms ringing in their ears. The Mayor and the Aldermen subsequently came to the Earl of Stamford at the *Angel* to make an expression of their regret for the unfortunate incident. They presented to him a paper containing a resolution of themselves and the borough to submit to the High Court of Parliament, knowing it to be most expedient both for the king's safety and the kingdom's future security. The Earl duly thanked them, saying he would inform Parliament of their good service; at which the assembled people gave a general shout, crying, *"A Stamford! A Stamford!"* with such joy that apparently *"the good Earl was forced to withdraw, tears of joy standing in his eyes to see his Country's love and obedience."* [7]

The Parliamentarians in Leicester were greatly heartened by these events and looked forward to a good turnout for the general muster set for 8th June. Royalist partisans were active in the county, however, particularly in the north west of the shire where the Hastings territory and influence were concentrated. Constables, petty constables, and some clergymen loyal to that interest issued instructions to trained band men in some of these villages, under the authority of the king's proclamation against Stamford and the Militia Ordinance, to ignore the muster call or suffer consequences to life, liberty, and property. Evidence of such activity and intimidation was later reported to Parliament by men from the villages of Ibstock, Belton, Whitwick, Ravenstone, Donington-on-the-Heath, and Hugglescote. As a consequence it was resolved that *"Captain Wolseley, Ensign Dudley, and John Loveton, parson of Ibstock, be forthwith sent for as delinquents for opposing and giving obstruction to the execution of the Ordinance of the Militia in the county of Leicester."* [8]

According to Parliamentarian reports the muster on the Horsefair Leas on 8th June was a great success despite the circulation of warrants prohibiting it under the king's proclamation. We are told that *"the country came in, both trained soldiers, private men, and volunteers, far beyond expectation, who generally declared themselves for the King and Parliament."* The Earl of Stamford decided, however, to call for musters in the following week in various parts of the county for the five companies of the shire trained bands, probably to 'show the flag' in the localities and to reduce the threat to men having to travel some distance in to Leicester. The companies were to *"appear severally in such convenient places as might be most for their ease, and least chargeable."* [9] The venues chosen, for different days, were Broughton Astley, Kibworth, Melton Mowbray, Queniborough, and Copt Oak.

Meanwhile at York, as June progressed, the King realised there was an imminent danger of Parliament raising troops in Leicestershire and other counties despite his prohibitions to the contrary. A more positive and active approach was clearly called for. He therefore issued on 12th June the first Commission of Array, the traditional manner by which an English sovereign mobilised the part-time soldiers, to Henry Hastings. Hastings was sent back to Leicestershire with the Commission and a letter from the king which jointly authorised him, along with his father Huntingdon, the Earl of Devonshire, Sir Richard Halford, Sir Henry Skipwith, and others deemed loyal to the Crown, to raise the local trained bands in the king's name.

The first parliamentarian county muster was held on 14th June in Guthlaxton Hundred at Broughton Astley, a Grey manor, and saw a good turnout of over a hundred men. The second took place the following day at Kibworth in Gartree Hundred where it is reported that there was a very good appearance, with the exception of some clergymen, of over a hundred men again. On the Earl of Stamford's return to Leicester after this muster he was informed that Henry Hastings had arrived in the county with the Commission of Array. Hastings had issued instructions under it to the Head Constables, endorsed on the back of these documents in his own name, through Under Sheriff Gregory (in the absence of the pro-Parliament High Sheriff Archdale Palmer), for the trained bands of the town and county to muster at the Raw Dykes on the south side of Leicester at 8 am on Wednesday 22nd June. Upon hearing this news Stamford sent Lord Grey of Groby with a copy of one such summons and a message post haste to the Parliament in London asking for advice. He also removed the major part of the arms and powder from the county magazine in Leicester to his home at Bradgate the following morning. Having effected this important transfer he rode eastwards with a group of supporters into Framland Hundred to review the muster at Melton Mowbray where there was *'a general appearance'* of the militia. Staying on the northern and eastern side of the county, but coming rather nearer to Leicester, the Earl and his colleagues then presided over the mustering of the trained band of East Goscote Hundred at Queniborough. It was recorded that the turnout here was very good *"considering how many great Papist and ill-affected people live thereabouts."* This association of the Queniborough gentry with the royalist cause will be noted again later.

Whilst the local Parliamentarian leaders were out in the county at these musters Henry Hastings and other active Commissioners of Array, that is some of the knights but none of the nobles named in it, rode into Leicester. Hastings informed the Mayor, Thomas Rudyard, of the king's displeasure with the recent behaviour of the town and his own dislike of Stamford's taking away to Bradgate of part of the magazine. He desired that the borough would place a strong guard on the remainder of the magazine day and night and was sure that the town would swiftly return to its true allegiance to His Majesty. The Mayor agreed to mount such a guard. These proceedings were duly reported back to Parliament by Lord Ruthin and Sir Arthur

Hesilrige. On 18th June Parliament debated the Commission of Array for Leicestershire and declared it illegal, also declaring Henry Hastings a delinquent and summoning him to attend the High Court of Parliament. Hastings ignored this.

In the meantime the Earl of Stamford had heard of many threats uttered against him in the locality, hazarding his life and the destruction of his home at Bradgate. Accordingly, on 20th June he raised a guard of 150 men for Bradgate, recruited from servants, tenants, and neighbours, and maintained - or so he claimed - at his own cost. The same day Stamford, Ruthin and Hesilrige rode out to the mustering point for the fifth and final rendezvous of the county trained bands. This was at a traditional meeting point in the northwest of the county, the Copt Oak, at a junction of trackways three miles or so from the edge of Bradgate. It was on the joint border of the hundreds of West Goscote and Sparkenhoe and, perhaps as significantly, in an area of mixed Grey and Hastings holdings in the Charnwood Forest. It was doubly important to ensure a good turnout here and the Parliamentary record shows *"a general appearance of the trained and private men, with 200 volunteers at least; and in every one of these places very many of the countrymen came to the said Earl, and desired him to help them to arms for their own defence and the public safety."* [10]

Also that day, whilst Stamford was at the muster at Copt Oak, two Parliamentary messengers, a John Chambers and a James Stanforth, arrived at Bradgate about midmorning. When the Earl and the MPs returned from Copt Oak that evening they accompanied the messengers into Leicester. Here they sent for the mayor and the town magistrates and persuaded them to remove the remainder of the magazine from its store at the South Gate into a strong tower called Newarke Gate, which has since then been known in Leicester as the Magazine Gateway. On the Tuesday news came in that Henry Hastings was collecting together a large force of men at Ashby-de-la-Zouch and Loughborough with the intention of marching into Leicester on the following day to enforce the Commission of Array and to muster the trained bands at the Raw Dykes as he had previously announced. The Earl and the MPs fixed notices of the votes of both

Mustering the Trained Bands for Parliament at Copt Oak

Houses of Parliament declaring the Commission of Array illegal on the entrance gates to the town and then departed for Bradgate at about 9 o'clock in the morning. They left behind them Chambers and Stanforth, together with one of Sir Arthur Hesilrige's servants, to assist High Sheriff Palmer in resisting Henry Hastings and his forces on the morrow. Whilst the parliamentarian representatives of law and order were awaiting, one would imagine with some trepidation, the arrival of 'Master Hastings' and others of the royalist version of the same, they arrested Under Sheriff Gregory for issuing warrants under the Commission of Array and sent him off to London under guard to answer to Parliament.

Leicester must have held its breath in anticipation and apprehension on the morning of Wednesday 22nd June 1642.

Since his return to Leicestershire from York Henry Hastings had gathered at Ashby Castle his friends, retainers, tenants, and about 100 colliers brought from his father's coalmines in south Derbyshire. From the castle armoury he equipped this force with muskets and pikes. The warrants being sent out under the Commission of Array for the assembling of the trained bands at Raw Dykes in Leicester on the 22nd June, he called for those parts of the county near to Ashby and Loughborough to join him on the march south into Leicester on that day. On Tuesday 21st June he left Ashby with his followers, taking with him all the horses, saddles, powder and weapons that could be found and marched to Loughborough. Here they assembled in the market place at 10 am : Hastings himself doubtless striking an imposing martial figure on horseback, armed, and wearing the scarlet sash of an officer in the King's Army. He had, of course, previously raised the local contingents for service in the 'Bishops Wars' against the Scots. A proclamation was read out at the Market Cross to the effect that weapons were available to volunteers at Garendon Abbey at the end of town. The Commission of Array was also read out. According to contemporary reports very few trained bandsmen joined Hastings at Loughborough, thanks to High Sheriff Palmer having arrested Under Sheriff Gregory just as he was dispatching the warrants. Nevertheless, Hastings was joined by *"his friends (many of them Papists, and such others as were ill-affected towards the proceedings of the Parliament)."* [11] According to another account, having read out the proclamation and the Commission, Hastings then had his musketeers charge their muskets and light their matches as if in preparation for action. He then made threats against the Earl of Stamford's life, and finally *"caused the drums to be beaten and colours displayed; and marched, to the great terror of the people."* [12]

The force that left Loughborough numbered around three hundred men and included a party of horse in addition to pikemen and musketeers, all armed with an assortment of weapons. They marched for eight miles in the direction of Leicester with colours flying and drums beating. Each time they entered or passed near to a village Hastings would take his place at the front of the body for the local inhabitants to see. The force stopped some three miles short of Leicester and, whatever the show for effect earlier at Loughborough, this time the sergeants of the musket checked that all musketeers were loaded and had lighted slowmatches. Orders were given to fire if so commanded by Henry Hastings. The Royalists were very near to Bradgate and clearly feared an attack by the Earl of Stamford during their march to Leicester. The latter had ample opportunity to stage an ambush and was kept well informed of Hastings' progress by his scouts. He had a force at Bradgate of about one hundred and fifty musketeers and twenty horse armed with carbines and pistols, added to which were neighbours and volunteers who had come to him in case of an armed confrontation. Yet he decided to stand guard at Bradgate rather than sally out and engage Hastings at this stage; either not wishing to precipitate the first bloodshed locally of the imminent civil war or simply deciding that discretion (and the defence of his patrimony) was the better part of valour. According to the reports brought in by his scouts from the villages along the route of the march, such as Quorn, Mountsorrel, and Rothley, Hastings' men threatened *"that they would fetch away the magazine from him, fire his house*

(Bradgate), *have his heart's blood, and never leave him*
(Stamford) *till they had made him turn up the whites of his eyes."*
(13)

Finding themselves thus far unopposed the royalists marched on into Leicester. They did not, however, head for the assembly point formerly specified in the warrants issued under the Commission of Array - the Raw Dykes. Instead they marched through the town with much shouting, flourishing of colours, and beating of drums. Word had reached Hastings as he had entered the town and seen the notices carrying the votes of Parliament fixed by the local MPs on the town gates that his planned muster had been frustrated and that opposition might be expected at the Horse Fair Leas.

Earlier that morning at about eight o'clock High Sheriff Archdale Palmer, accompanied by a body of armed men, had entered Leicester and joined the Parliamentary messengers, Chambers and Stanforth. Whilst Chambers was in the *Heron* Inn he noticed a barrel of gunpowder being brought in by a porter. Upon investigation it was found that it had been sent by Andrew Halford, brother to the royalist Sir Richard Halford. It seemed that the *Heron* was to be used as a meeting place for royalists coming into Leicester from other parts of the county to join Henry Hastings and his force for the muster. The barrel of gunpowder was seized by the High Sheriff under the authority of an enabling order issued by the Parliament eleven days previously. At about ten o'clock, whilst Henry Hastings' force was assembled in the market place at Loughborough, three horsemen equipped in *'a warlike manner'* rode into the yard of the *Heron*. These were Walter Hastings, a cousin of Henry's, a Lord Lovelace and a Master Killegrew. Their leader, Walter Hastings, then proceeded to ride up and down the inn yard and is reputed to have shouted out loudly that he would *'eat up'* the Earl of Stamford. One of his companions asked that one bit be left for him to devour, or words to that effect. Having drawn a crowd in this manner Walter Hastings, seated on his large bay charger, then addressed them saying, *"What, my friends and countrymen, ye stand for the King and the Hastings, who have ever been true to the Crown?"* According to the report that reached Parliament later the people answered, *"We are all for the King and Parliament."* Then Walter Hastings required Archdale Palmer, who was now present, as High Sheriff to read out the royal proclamation which he had received concerning the control of the militia. Palmer denied that he had ever received the proclamation. At this *"the said Hastings departed, and the rest of his company, in an outrageous and uncivil manner, swearing and cursing as they rode out of the said inn."* [14]

It was at about two o'clock in the afternoon that the three hundred strong force of Henry Hastings and his supporters assembled on the common known as the Horse Fair Leas. Waiting for them were the Parliamentary Messengers (Chambers and Stanforth), the High Sheriff and his body of armed footmen. According to the several (mostly parliamentarian) accounts of the event the following ensued. Hastings alighted from his horse and addressed the High Sheriff and the rest of the assembled host to the effect that *"he was come hither to execute His Majesty's Commission of Array, to himself and others then granted, for that county."* He then attempted to present to Archdale Palmer two bundles, the first consisting of the royal proclamations concerning the militia, the second of books, with an instruction to the High Sheriff to read and publish the same. (It should be remembered that the Corporation of the borough had earlier voted only to obey Stamford's warrant concerning the matter of the militia if the king's proclamation had not been proclaimed first). Hastings several times repeated his request to the Sheriff that he read out the proclamation and declared that he himself was *"the King's; body and soul."* At last Palmer replied by stating *"I cannot perform His Majesty's single commands till I have acquainted the Parliament therewith, nor do anything contrary to their votes: I am for the King and for the Parliament; and if I perish, I perish."* At this point John Chambers produced the recorded votes of both Houses of Parliament concerning the illegality of the commissions of array and read them out for all to hear. He did likewise with the last declaration of both Houses concerning the control of the militia and concluded with the words *"God save the King and Parliament."* This slogan was echoed by some others present and drew from Henry Hastings a reiteration that he was *"the King's, body and soul."* Chambers then produced the warrants of both Houses voted on the 18th June and called for silence whilst he read them out. This he then proceeded to do, listing as delinquents Henry Hastings, Sir Richard Halford, Sir John Bale, and Master John Pate - all present, and requiring them at their utmost peril to obey the said warrants. He then called upon the Sheriff to assist in the execution of these warrants. To counter this and to assert his own position Henry Hastings then began to read out loudly the Commission of Array from the king, which was in Latin, pausing every now and then to comment upon its meaning in English. This was not too successful and a Master Edward Palmer, the town clerk of Leicester, taking the Commission from him read it out in full in the Latin text. This was listened to in silence. It would have meant nothing to most of the listeners. Chambers then attempted again to have the Sheriff arrest the `delinquents'. At this Sir Richard Halford, being near to Chambers, informed the Sheriff that when His Majesty's `**great business'** was over he would come to him and give such security for his attendance on the Parliament as might be fitting. Henry Hastings invited Chambers to repair to the *Angel* Inn in Leicester where they were all intending to stay for the night and *"where he should have civil deportment from them."* Chambers was none too impressed by the friendly intention of this invitation which he promptly declined. He repeated instead his instruction to the Sheriff to take the leading `delinquents' into custody. Henry Hastings then gave orders for his force to divide into its four companies and, having created both a tactical advantage and some confusion amongst his opponents by this device, he sought to remount his charger. He was assisted in this by two butchers (one named as Henry Cotes) who lifted him up into his great saddle and thrust a loaded and cocked pistol into his hand.

"Then the cavaliers and the rest of the soldiers, joining with the rude multitude, and about 24 parsons in canonical coats, well horsed, rode all towards the town, with load exclamations of `A King! A King!' and others, `For a King! A King!' in a strange and unheard of manner : Captain Worseley giving the word of command to the soldiers, `Make ready! make ready!'" [15]

Henry Hastings reading out the King's Commission of Array in
Leicester

The mounted Royalists thus rode at the Parliamentarians, who were mostly on foot, whilst the musketeers on both sides made ready to fire. Walter Hastings discharged his pistol at John Chambers but missed him. Other cavaliers drew out their pistols and both sets of musketeers presented their muskets only awaiting the order to 'give fire'. There was at that point, however, a sudden and most extraordinarily heavy downpour of rain which extinguished the slowmatches and thus prevented the musketeers from firing. Walter Hastings then attempted to ride over Chambers who, in order to prevent this, got up on a high bank only to be knocked down by a Hastings supporter who struck him with a club on the chest with such force that he fell backwards into a ditch. Recovering his strength and fearing for his life he began to run back towards the town as fast as he could, along with Stanforth and Palmer, pursued by the Royalists all the way. The latter harried them, crying out, *"At the cap! at the cap!"*; this being a reference to the official cap of a Parliamentary Messenger which was being worn by Chambers at the time. One of the mounted Royalists attempted to ride down Palmer and another tried to do the same to Stanforth. Walter Hastings would have fired a second pistol at Chambers but this time it failed to discharge. The fleeing Parliamentarians eventually reached the safety of the *Heron* Inn where they barricaded themselves in and stood guard, exhausted and much alarmed by the afternoon's events. Chambers wrote a letter, which was smuggled out of town to the Earl of Stamford and the others at Bradgate, informing them of what had transpired and requesting further instructions. They probably also hoped for rescue and reinforcements. The Royalists in the meantime had entered the town in some jubilation and proceeded to live up to what was to become the simple caricature of their party by getting drunk in the taverns, inns and ale-houses of Leicester.

At about one o'clock the following morning a messenger from Bradgate returned to the Parliamentarians at the *Heron* with instructions from the Earl of Stamford that Stanforth and Chambers, with the help of the Sheriff, Mayor, and the justices of Leicester, should use their best power and endeavour to surprise the delinquents. A force of about fifty men was gathered at the *Heron* and at two o'clock a co-ordinated search of the town's ale-houses and taverns began. The royalist 'soldiers' were taken unawares, being either drunken or asleep. When the *Angel* was raided, however, it was found that Henry Hastings and his leading confederates had left earlier in the night to rejoin the King at York. Upon his arrival there on 25th June Hastings was appointed by Charles as High Sheriff of Leicestershire, thereby replacing Archdale Palmer. In addition the Earl of Stamford was proclaimed a traitor by the king and orders were issued for his arrest. Meanwhile, back in Leicester, in the early hours of 23rd June the slumbering Derbyshire colliers were disarmed and, having pleaded duress, were allowed to return home. The following items were taken back to Archdale Palmer at the *Heron*:- a great saddle, three pistols, about a hundred pikes, a lance, over sixty muskets and calivers, about twenty swords, and four long firing pieces about seven feet in length. Some of the pieces, muskets, and pistols were found to be charged, some with ball or bullet, some with half shot, and others with dangerous goose shot. All the ammunition found was given to the Sheriff, who delivered some to the trained bands, and the rest was presented by Chambers to the Earl of Stamford. Thus, after an initial set-back, Leicester had been secured for the Parliament.

In their report to the two Houses of Parliament Chambers and Stanforth commented that the mayor of Leicester, Thomas Rudyard, had seemed more keen to further the activity of Henry Hastings than of themselves. Rudyard was summoned to London and detained for some months. Archdale Palmer was appointed by Parliament as a deputy-lieutenant for Leicestershire. People were now having to show their allegiance to one side or the other. Yet there was still some considerable confusion. For example, Sir Wolstan Dixie of Market Bosworth was named as one of the Commissioners of Array by the King and as one of those responsible for implementing the Militia Ordinance by the Parliament. Those who could still do so attempted to hedge their bets.

At the beginning of July, Henry Hastings returned to Leicestershire. He was accompanied by the cavalier captains Lunsford and Digby with other soldiers, match, powder, ammunition, and four field pieces of artillery. Hastings proceeded to issue warrants under his new authority as High Sheriff of the county to the high constables of the county hundreds seeking to raise sufficient forces to seize the magazine at Bradgate by force. He also declared William Reymer, the guardian of the Leicester magazine, a traitor for not delivering it up to him. Reports of his actions were sent to Parliament who resolved that more support be given to the Earl of Stamford for the preservation of the peace of Leicestershire, the suppression of insurrections and the safe keeping of the magazine.

During the next few weeks both the King and the Parliament experienced difficulties in establishing regular and reliable control of trained bands in counties all over the kingdom. Increasingly both sides turned instead to issuing individual major supporters with commissions to raise regiments which could be used as part of national field armies if need be.

Towards the late middle of July the King, having been denied access to Hull by Hotham for a second time, decided both to ascertain and to rally support for his cause by moving around Yorkshire and the Midlands. From Beverley he went to Nottingham on 21st July. The following day, anxious to obtain first-hand knowledge of local feelings, he moved on to Leicester accompanied by his eldest son, Prince Charles, and his nephew, Prince Rupert of the Rhineland Palatinate. The royal party received a cool but polite welcome from the new Mayor, Richard Ludlam, and the Corporation at Frog Island, outside the North Gate of the town. They then proceeded to Lord's Place in High Street, the town residence of the Earls of Huntingdon, the route lined by a crowd estimated at ten thousand people. The Assizes were in progress and the King personally addressed a large assembly at the Castle, desiring that all should assist the royal cause *"with vigour"* and furnish support for his army. If the occasion was to arise he said, *"I know you will bring horses, men, money and hearts worthy of such a cause."* He was offered one hundred and twenty horses and men. The sum of fifty pounds was presented to Prince Rupert on behalf of the town. The king said that he came *"rather to prevent crimes than to punish them"* but he was asked to receive a petition which regretted his long estrangement from the *"highest and safest council of Parliament."* The Grand Jury for the Assize complained that while the king protected such delinquents as Henry Hastings there could never be peace and they prayed that the Commission of Array be left in the hands of the good Earl of Stamford. (The King had already declared the Earl a traitor. Stamford had left Leicester that very day by a different Gate just as the king had entered the town. He was granted an indemnity by Parliament the following day.) Three later demands for the distribution of the remainder of the magazine among the hundreds of the county were finally met after the king's departure by the mayor and the corporation adopting a compromise approach once more.

As on his previous visit in 1634 the King attended a civic service at St. Martin's Church (now Leicester Cathedral) on the Sunday accompanied by the robed Mayor and Corporation in walking procession. The route took them from Lord's Place (the Hastings family town residence) up High Street to the High Cross and then left and left again into St. Martin's Lane (now Guildhall Lane), probably entering the church by the west door. A throne had been set up at the instigation of Christiana, the widowed Countess of Devonshire, whose home was at Leicester Abbey. The bill for decorating the church and strewing its floor with flowers, herbs, and six bundles of rushes was met by the Corporation. Prince Charles graciously accepted *"a fair wrought purse with fifty pieces of gold"* from the Corporation too. The royal party could derive little comfort from their visit to Leicester, however, and they departed quietly early the following morning without taking their leave of the mayor and corporation.

Whilst the king was at Leicester he sent for the mayor and sheriffs of Coventry to attend upon him. The message reached them as intended whilst they were out riding on the Sunday morning. They were, however, being closely watched by others from the staunchly pro-Parliamentarian town and were compelled to return to Coventry without meeting the king.

King Charles I in procession at St. Martin's Church, Leicester

Shortly after the departure of the king from Leicester Henry Hastings made his first and long anticipated attack upon Bradgate.

"Information came out of Leicestershire to the Parliament that many of the well-affected in that county, having vigilantly taken care to make the Lord of Stamford's house their magazine, and had conveyed their arms, powder, and ammunition thither, did most valiantly and courageously oppose and withstand Mr. Hastings, the new-made High Sheriff, and a most notorious malignant; and how glad he was to retreat from thence, and fly to York for more aid, which afterwards occassioned much mischief and molestation among them in the county of Leicester, he being a most desperate malignant." [16]

On 4th August the king empowered Hastings to raise a regiment of dragoons (essentially mounted infantry armed with carbines) and commissioned him as Colonel Hastings. [17] The House of Commons responded on 13th August with a resolution, *"that Henry Hastings, esq. shall be accused of high treason, for actual levying of war against the King and kingdom.* [18]

Both sides were mobilising. The King had by now received supplies purchased by the Queen in Holland and had granted many commissions to his supporters to raise regiments. He made the veteran Earl of Lindsey his General, with Sir Jacob Astley as Major-General of Foot and Prince Rupert in command of the Horse. These generals set about the task of creating an army of cavalry and dragoons, foot regiments and artillery sufficient to defeat any forces that the Parliament could put into the field against them. In mid-July Parliament had voted that an army of ten thousand men should be raised in London and its neighbourhood. By an order of the Committee of Safety set up by both Houses of Parliament dated 6th August 1642 a grant of 17 shillings was made for equipping each man recruited with a coat, shoes, shirt, and cap. Breeches were obviously to be supplied by the individual or by the more affluent and fastidious colonel in chief who favoured a uniform appearance for his regiment! Within a few weeks regiments for the army of the

Parliament's Lord General, the Earl of Essex, were being formed and began marching to the appointed rendezvous at Northampton.

On Friday 18th August King Charles with the Prince of Wales and a cavalry escort passed through Leicester again on the road from Nottingham to Stoneleigh Abbey in Warwickshire. From Stoneleigh, where he spent the night, he went to Coventry which refused him entry knowing that he was interested in gaining their supplies of ammunition and that they were notoriously pro-Parliamentarian. Leaving most of his forces outside Coventry to besiege it and for his artillery to bombard the town's walls to no great effect, the king rode with some lords and others from his camp back to Leicester. Here he dined and stayed overnight with the Countess of Devonshire at her Leicester Abbey mansion. He returned again to Leicester a couple of days later when Coventry remained obstinate. On his journey back through Leicester he did not wait to be pressed with politely worded demands for Hastings' arrest and for a reconciliation between himself and his 'loyal' Parliament on the latter's terms. After another dinner and overnight stay at Leicester Abbey he left early the next day for Nottingham.

That same afternoon, 22nd August 1642, the King raised his royal standard, amidst strong winds and lightning, on what has since been known as Standard Hill. This was the time-honoured signal used to raise royal armies and to declare war. The raising of the standard at Nottingham has often been held to be the act which symbolised the beginning of the English Civil War. In fact, as we have seen, hostilities had already started. It was to become increasingly difficult for people to avoid involvement or commitment to one side or the other from now on.

The patterns and causes of partisan allegiance locally could be quite complicated. Leicestershire, from its central situation, was subject to the ebb and flow of warfare throughout the period of the first civil war, both from the incursions of field armies on either side but also from skirmishes and forays between groups of local 'Cavaliers' and 'Roundheads'. In 1642 Leicester and the surrounding county, as we have seen, aimed initially at neutrality whilst inclining mainly to Parliament in their sympathies. There was, however, as noted earlier, *"a notable animosity"* [19] between the Grey and the Hastings families. Their deep-rooted and centuries old jealousy and rivalry made Leicestershire *"like a cockpit, one spurring against another."* [20] Some commentators, following Clarendon, have maintained that the civil war allegiances of the other major county families who traditionally supported their interests effectively constituted the local Parliamentarian and Royalist causes respectively. This is, however, very much an oversimplification.

It seems that the division of support between the two sides in the county was relatively evenly balanced. This was to have some far reaching consequences. The division in the county tended to be geographical as well as political. Royalist support was strongest north and west of the old Fosse Way and in the protrusion towards the Vale of Belvoir in the far north east. Parliamentarian support was found mainly in the central area, the south, and the east of Leicestershire. The reasons for this were partly personal and partly economic - with social, political and security implications. Hastings property and influence was concentrated in the north of the county. The Greys were stronger in the centre, supported by the majority of the Borough Corporation; other parliamentarian notables such as Sir Arthur Heselrige bulked large in the south. After Belvoir Castle was secured for the Crown on the night of 28th January 1643 by Colonel Gervase Lucas, formerly gentleman of the horse to the absent Earl of Rutland, the Leicestershire parliamentarians continued to be pestered by recurrent raids from Belvoir Castle in the north east and from Ashby Castle in the north west of the county.

Within four days of the raising of the royal standard at Nottingham, Bradgate House was attacked by a force of royalist horse. Fortunately for the Parliamentarian cause most of the magazine had by this time been returned to Leicester. The attack was recorded by a Parliamentarian chronicler in the following terms:-

"Upon 26th August Prince Rupert, together with Master Hastings and many cavaliers, went to my Lord Grey, the Earl of Stamford's house, from whence they took all his arms, and

took away and spoiled all his goods, and also the clothes of his chaplain who was fain to flee for his life: And some chief ones asked, 'Where are the brats, the young children?' Swearing, 'God damn them! They would kill them, that there might be no more of the breed of them'. But God stirred up some friends to succour them. They have also disarmed many of the inhabitants thereabouts ; and taken away many of their goods ; but no doubt their account is at hand. Amen, Lord!" [21]

The 'brats' referred to here would be Stamford's younger children; his other sons, Anchitel, John, Leonard, and his five daughters, Elizabeth, Diana, Anne, Jane and Mary. The raid had encountered so little resistance this time because the Earl of Stamford had left Bradgate earlier in August and raised a troop of horse and a regiment of foot. The knowledge, however, that their home and property were so vulnerable to enemy attack was to be a major consideration for both Stamford and his heir, Thomas, Lord Grey of Groby during the first civil war.

The Earl of Stamford's newly raised regiment of foot had marched during the latter part of August down to the rendezvous set by the army raised by the Parliament at Northampton. The men in the regiment were issued with blue coats, this being the colour of the Grey family's livery as worn by their servants and household retainers. As with most foot regiments of the time there was a double strength Colonel's company of around two hundred men, a Lieutenant Colonel's company of one hundred and sixty men, a Sergeant-Major's (or Major's) company of one hundred and forty men, and seven Captain's companies of a hundred men each. Every company was made up of pikemen and musketeers with two sergeants, three corporals, two drummers, and the junior officers - a lieutenant and an ensign. Whilst Stamford himself was the Colonel he had as his second-in-command and Lieutenant Colonel a certain Edward Massey. His (Sergeant) Major was Constantine Ferrar. Massey, like Stamford, was a Presbyterian and was to become famous later as the heroic Parliamentarian defender of Gloucester during its siege in the first civil war. Later still he was to become a royalist, like other Presbyterians, in the Worcester campaign of 1651.

45

The colours carried by the ensigns of each company in the regiment were blue. The Colonel's colour consisted of three lines of writing upon blue bands - *'For religion'*, *'King and Country'*, *'A MA PUISSANCE'* - on a blue field. The other companies bore versions of this in accordance with the style laid down by prevailing military custom. *"The Colonel's colour in the first place is of a pure and clean colour, without any mixture,"* wrote Captain Venn, a veteran of the English Civil War later. *"The Lieutenant Colonel's only with Saint George's arms in the upper corner next the staff, the Major's the same, but in the lower and outmost corner with a little stream blazant. And every captain with Saint George's arms alone, but with so many spots or several devices as pertain to the dignity of their several places."* These flags or 'colours' on painted taffeta measured six feet square, and served as rallying points for the soldiers either when in quarters or on the field of battle amongst the confusion of noise and smoke. They also symbolised and enshrined the honour and integrity of the unit. It was a major triumph to capture an enemy colour and a disgrace to lose one. According to the code of the time a unit which had lost its colour in battle could not have another until it had in turn taken one from the enemy.

Most regiments had, in addition to their constituent companies, a regimental staff consisting of a quarter-master, a chaplain, a provost-marshal, a 'chirurgion' or surgeon and his mate, a carriage-master and a drum-major. Each company included both pikemen and musketeers, varying in proportion early in the war from two to one respectively to a later ratio on the parliamentarian side of almost one to one in the New Model Army.

The officers were to be distinguished from the rank and file by the quality of their clothing which they provided themselves as gentlemen and by their personal weapons such as halberds, partisans, expensive swords, etc. This being the time before uniform clothing was adopted for armies it was difficult to tell which side a man was on by his clothing alone. The rank and file of each regiment of foot would wear a coat of the same colour but even this could be confusing on the battlefield. Even the flags of opposing regiments could be very similar. For example, both Stamford's and Henry Hastings's regiments of foot wore blue coats and carried blue colours. Blue was the livery colour of both the Grey household at Bradgate and the Hastings household at Ashby-de-la-Zouch and was a popular colour for servants' coats nationally. This confusion was increased in the case of officers wearing their civilian clothing with military additions such as the gorget (metal throat guard and badge of rank), the buffcoat, the sash, and 'bucket top' riding boots. In short, clothing reflected social class and status rather than allegiance. The usual way to indicate which cause a regiment served was the colour of the sashes or 'scarves' worn by its officers over their shoulders or around their waists. Even this was not without its complications however. Field-signs such as a piece of paper or coloured ribbons were also worn and field-words, like passwords, were used for particular battles or campaigns.

Following the attack upon Bradgate Prince Rupert set up his advance cavalry headquarters at Queniborough, to the north of Leicester, where there was local royalist support. From here he sent, on 6th September, a letter to the now reinstated mayor of Leicester, Thomas Rudyard, stating that *"His Majesty, being confident of your fidelitie and desire to doo him all possible service ... doth earnestly desire and require you and his good subjects of the Citty of Leicester forthwith to furnish him with Two Thousand pounds sterling, which he with much care will take order to see repaid in convenient time ... "* The letter demanded the money be delivered *" by ten of the clock in the forenoon"* of the next day, adding that if the mayor refused, he would *" appear before your town in such a posture with horse, foot and cannon, as shall make you know 'tis more safe to obey than 'tis resist His Majesty's command."* The letter was signed *"Your Friend, Rupert."* [22]

The town appealed to the king, whose reply, written at Nottingham on 8th September, expressing surprise at Rupert's conduct, discharged the Corporation from its fulfilment. The king's letter was from *"Charles R"* and was addressed *"To Our Trusty & Welbeloved ye Mayor & Aldermen of our Towne of Leicester."*

"Trusty and welbeloved Wee greete you well; Wee have seene a warrant under our Nephew Rupert's hand, dated ye 6th of this month, requiring from you & other ye Inhabitants of our Towne of Leicester ye loan of 2000 li., which as wee doe utterly disavowe & dislike, as being written without our privity or consent, soe wee doe hereby absolutely free & discharge you & that our Towne from yielding any obedience to ye same, & by our owne letters to our said Nephew wee have written to him presently to revoke ye same as being an Act very displeasing to us.

"Wee indeede gave him direccons to disarme such persons there as appeared to be disaffected to our person & Government, or ye peace of this our Kingdome, & should have taken it well from any of our subjects, that would voluntarily assist us with ye loane of Armes or money, But it is soe farre from our hart or intencon by menaces to compell any to it, as Wee abhore ye thought of it, & of this truth Our Accons [Actions] *shall beare us testemony. Given att our court att Nottingham, 8 Sep'bris, 1642."* [23]

Six dragoons had, however, already been sent from Leicester with £500, in the form of a deposit, to Rupert. He issued them with the following receipt dated September 9, 1642.

"Receyved by me Prince Rupert, Prince Palatine of the Rhine, & Generall of all His Majesty's Cavallerye in this present expedition, the full summe of Five Hundred pounds for His Majesty's use, of the Mayor, Bayliffs, & Burgesses of the Borough of Leicester : to be repayed agayne by His Majesty of sayd receyved Five Hundred pounds.
Rupert." [24]

In the event this money was never repaid and Prince Rupert was to return in the summer of 1645 at the head of a field army to teach Leicester the very lesson he had threatened.

The battle of Edgehill, the first major battle of the civil war, was fought on Sunday, 23rd October 1642. The two armies were about equal in size. The royalist cavalry of some 2,800 and 1,000 dragoons slightly outnumbered the estimated 2,150 horse and 720 dragoons of Parliament. On the other hand, the twelve parliamentarian regiments of foot who took part in the battle comprised about 12,000 men compared to the king's infantry forces of some 10,500 pikemen and musketeers. The royalist forces were arranged along the foot of the steep north slopes of Edgehill with their left wing against Radway village. The Earl of Essex drew out the army raised by the Parliament from the village of Kineton into a great broad field about half a mile away from the enemy and facing them in a broad line. On both sides regiments had been grouped together to form main divisions or brigades. Both generals positioned their foot brigades in the centre of the battle line with clumps of horse on both wings. In order to assist identification in the forthcoming battle officers of horse and foot on both sides, together with cavalry troopers, wore 'scarves' or sashes. The colours of these were mostly red for the Royalists and tawney orange (the livery colour of the Earl of Essex) for the Parliamentarians.

Although the Earl of Stamford's Bluecoat Regiment of Foot was absent, owing to its duties in Hereford, leading Leicestershire families were still represented at Edgehill. Colonel Henry Hastings had command of a foot regiment in the Royalist Army List of 1642; its men wore blue coats and its colours seem to have been blue. At Edgehill, however, Hastings was commanding his cavalry troop who also wore blue coats but whose colour, or cornet, was red and bore the device of a fiery furnace or burning oven within an archway, with the ferocious and intimidating Latin motto, *'Quasi Ignis Conflatoris'* ('That which I light is consumed'). It is likely that he was stationed in the cavalry division of his friend Prince Rupert, on the right flank of the royal army. His elder brother, Ferdinando, Lord Hastings, was on the opposing side at the head of the seventh troop of horse in Essex's army, under the command of Sir William Balfour, the lieutenant-general of the horse. Balfour's division was positioned on the centre left of the parliamentarian front line between Sir Philip Stapleton's Horse on their right and Sir John Meldrum's large brigade of foot on their left.

Cavalry charge at the Battle of Edgehill

Also in Balfour's division and in charge of the third troop of cavalry in the Parliamentarian Army List of 1642, after only those of the Lord General's troop and that of Balfour himself, was Thomas, Lord Grey of Groby. This troop had been raised locally in Leicestershire from amongst friends, neighbours, tenants and servants. It was to see service with Lord Grey in the Midlands in the following years and also to distinguish itself further afield during the civil war. The lieutenant of the troop, under Grey's captaincy, was a Simon Matthews. The cornet, the junior officer who carried the colour of the same title, was listed as a Thomas Barington. This may well have been Thomas Babington of the local Rothley family. The troop's quarter-master was a Daniel Maddox and, to complete the complement in addition to the sixty or so troopers, there were two corporals and a farrier. The members of the troop would have been equipped, like most cavalrymen of the period, with long leather thighboots and buffcoats, back and breastplates, helmet and/or broad brimmed felt hats, a brace of pistols and a basket hilted cavalry sword. The tawney-orange sashes worn in their case would have been either made up by the ladies of the Bradgate estate or, as was quite common, derived from some appropriately coloured drapery 'borrowed' from a local Laudian church. Initially, at least, most troopers would have provided their own horse. The cornet, or flag, of the troop was a half blue and half red field fringed in silver and red upon which was set an ermine unicorn on a sun in splendour with the Latin motto *'Per Bellum Ad Pacem'* ('Through War To Peace').

Sir Arthur Hesilrigg's troop was also on the field amongst the parliamentarian horse, but this time with the main body on the left flank under Commissary-General Sir James Ramsey and facing Prince Rupert. This was the forty-third troop in the Parliamentarian Army List and was to be expanded after Edgehill to a whole regiment and to serve in Sir William Waller's campaigns in the south and the west of England. This troop, and the later regiment, was to become famous as the 'lobsters' because of their complete suits of three-quarter armour. At a time when most cavalry units wore only buffcoats with helmets, back and breast plates Hesilrigg's troopers alone, other than the King's Life Guard of Horse and the Earl of

Essex's Life Guard of Horse at Edgehill, wore full armour. Clarendon was to say of them, *"the soldiers of this troop were so prodigiously armed that they were called by the other side the regiment of lobsters because of their bright iron shells."*

The king was to observe of Sir Arthur himself during the action at Roundway Down later where he was surrounded by cavaliers, *"if only he had been supplied with food and water he could have withstood a siege."*

The colonel's colour of the 'lobsters' was a famous green cornet fringed white and green with a golden anchor (for hope) fixed at the top in silver clouds and in golden letters the motto *'Only In Heaven'*.

After a preliminary exchange of cannon fire lasting about one hour, the confident cavaliers charged and easily chased away most of the parliamentarian horse on the wings. On the parliamentarian left Prince Rupert swept away twenty-four troops of horse under Ramsey, including the reserve which had been placed on a little hill. On the parliamentarian right wing Lord Wilmot with ten royalist troops of horse scattered both Stapleton's Horse and Lord Fielding's Horse which had been its reserve. The troops in the two regiments commanded by Sir William Balfour mostly stood their ground, however, being partly shielded from Wilmot's charge by the embattled phalanxes of foot regiments in the centre of the field. Some troops, such as that led by Ferdinando Hastings, broke and fled. He is said to have ridden back to London to report that all was lost. This led to his temporary imprisonment and his practical disengagement from the parliamentarian cause which, despite his protestations, he had never supported very zealously.

Lord Grey of Groby's troop under Balfour stood firm and distinguished itself in the action that followed. Whilst the cavaliers on both wings wildly pursued their broken opponents into Kineton and beyond, the royalist infantry in five brigades advanced and engaged the parliamentarian foot, now reduced to two large brigades commanded by Sir John Meldrum and Colonel Thomas Ballard since the breaking and running away of Colonel Essex's brigade. The

52

Henry Hastings with standard (upper) and Thomas, Lord Grey
of Groby, with standard (lower)

terrible fight ebbed and flowed with the fury of charge and counter-charge and brief moments of respite. Noise, confusion, and smoke from cannon and massed musketry were everywhere. Balfour's Horse took the royalist left wing foot brigades in front and rear. The battle which had first seemed won for the King seemed now to swing to Parliament, largely because the victorious cavaliers had failed to rally and to return to the field to assist their Foot; a failing which was to prove so common and so costly to their cause. The royal standard was taken and presented to the Earl of Essex but was recaptured by a clever subterfuge involving a change of sashes. As the battle raged on some of the cavalier units did drift back and the struggle became more evenly balanced again.

The arrival of Colonel John Hampden with another parliamentarian brigade just as daylight began to fade led to an acknowledgement of a stalemate on both sides. The battle was indecisive with neither side able to gain an outright victory. During the night, however, the Earl of Essex did withdraw to Kineton leaving the King in possession of the field and preparing to fight the next day. In propaganda terms this draw favoured the royalists, yet on neither side did the leadership attempt to seize the initiative. Essex moved his army back to London whilst the King moved to Oxford and made it his headquarters for the rest of the war.

Following Edgehill some parliamentarians wavered so much in their resolve as to cease their military involvement against the King altogether. One such, not surprisingly perhaps, was Ferdinando Hastings. He expressed himself as follows in a letter written to the Earl of Essex on 3rd November 1642, excusing his leaving the Army without permission or leave:-

"... And only profess that my affection to the Parliament cause is still firm, though there are some reasons to withdraw me from continuing my service in the war, but in any particular service to your Lordship I shall be most ready to appear, my Lord, your Excellency's very humble servant." [25]

Ferdinando, Lord Hastings never again appeared in arms for the Parliament although his younger brother, Henry Hastings, was a most active partisan and promoter of the royalist cause. In fact, during the winter of 1642/43 the duplicitous Ferdinando was writing an equally sincere sounding letter to Sir Edward Nicholas, Principal Secretary of State to the King at Oxford from Tutbury Castle in Staffordshire.

"... Sir, I assure you my want of arms makes the service I ought to do the King very difficult, the Rebels lying upon me on every side and within walls that I can attempt nothing against them ... (they) *hath made Ashby often troubled with them ... The force of Graye and Gell ... Gray is marched with some troops but whether to Essex ... I am not certain. You shall hear daily from me that am Yr. Affectionate friend & servant -*
F. Hastings" "Haste, haste. Post haste."* [26]

Clarendon, then Sir Edward Hyde, includes the following passage in his description of the situation in the Midlands during the opening stages of the civil war.

"... The Lord Grey, son to the Earl of Stamford, had the command of Leicestershire, and had put a garrison into Leicester. Derbyshire, without any visible party in it for the king, was under the power of Sir John Gell, who had fortified Derby. And all those counties, with Staffordshire, were united in an association against the king under the command of Lord Brook (sic - Brooke); *who was, by the Earl of Essex, made General of that association; a man cordially disaffected to the government of the church, and upon whom that party had a great dependence. This association received no other interruption from, or for the king, than what Colonel Hastings gave; who being a younger son to the Earl of Huntingdon, had appeared eminently for the king from the beginning; having raised a good troop of horse with the first, and, in the head thereof, charged at Edgehill.*

After the king was settled at Oxford Colonel Hastings, with his own troop of horse only and some officers which he easily gathered together, went with a commission into Leicestershire as 'Colonel-General of that county', and fixed himself at Ashby-de-la-Zouch, the house of the Earl of Huntingdon, his father, who was then living; which he presently fortified; and, in a very short time, by his interest there, raised so good a party of horse and foot, that he maintained many skirmishes with the Lord Grey: the king's service being the more advanced there, by the notable animosities between the two families of Huntingdon and Stamford; between whom the county was divided passionately enough, without any other quarrel. And now the sons fought the public quarrel, with their private spirit and indignation. But the king had the advantage in his champion, the Lord Grey being a young man of no eminent parts, and only backed with the credit and authority of the parliament: whereas Colonel Hastings, though a younger brother, by his personal reputation, had supported his decaying family; and, by the interest of his family, and the affection that people bore to him, brought no doubt an addition of power to the very cause. Insomuch as he not only defended himself against the forces of the parliament in Leicestershire, but disquieted Sir John Gell in Derbyshire, and fixed some convenient garrisons in Staffordshire." [27]

Here, then, we have Clarendon's famous description of Lord Grey of Groby as *"a young man of no eminent parts"* and unfavourably compared to his older adversary Henry Hastings. (This assessment is considered fully and critically in my biography of Thomas, Lord Grey of Groby entitled *Aristocrat and Regicide*). At this point, however, an inaccuracy which occurs a little earlier in the above passage should be noted. Lord Brooke is referred to by Clarendon as being in command of a Midland Association of the counties of Northamptonshire, Warwickshire, Leicestershire, Derbyshire, and Staffordshire. In fact Lord Brooke was in command of the parliamentarian forces of Warwickshire and Staffordshire only. He was killed by a royalist sniper stationed in a tower of Lichfield Cathedral on 2nd March 1643 when, having taken the town, he was besieging an enemy force in the Cathedral Close. Indeed, it was the young Lord Grey of Groby who, at the age of nineteen or twenty, became one of the first commanders of the forces created by Parliament through its Ordinances of Association. These stipulated that the local parliamentary forces in specified counties, *"... . should associate themselves to protect the counties, raise horse and foot, money and plate, give battle, fight and levy war, put to execution of death, and destroy all who should levy war against the Parliament."* [28]

According to Vicars, on 13th December 1642:- *"... The two Houses of Parliament appointed the noble and pious Earl of Stamford to be Lord General of all South Wales, and the four next adjacent counties, viz. Gloucester, Worcester, Hereford, and Cheshire; and gave him power to raise forces in all the said counties, and to appoint officers and commanders over them, to train and exercise them, and to fight with, kill, and slay, all that came against them.*

"And upon the confidence and trust which the Parliament had in the fidelity of the noble Lord Grey, son and heir of the said Earl of Stamford, they appointed him also Lord General of the five northern (sic) *counties, Leicester, Nottingham, Derby, Rutland, and Lincoln, giving him the like power as his father ..."*
[29]

These commissions were issued by the Earl of Essex as the Lord General of all the forces raised by the Parliament. Essex seems to have been a particular patron of Lord Grey. Denzil Holles later referred to the Lord Grey of Groby *"who had before been zealous for my Lord Essex, as he had good reason for the respects he had received from him."* [30] Mark Noble also mentions *"the many obligations"* and *"a peculiar devoir"* [31] for which Grey owed Essex. It is not clear just what these were exactly, but the two families of Grey and Devereux were related through the Ferrers connection and the Earls of Stamford and Essex were friends and former comrades in arms in the Thirty Years War in Germany. Essex's family life was unhappy. Two failed marriages had left him childless and Lord Grey seems to have been a surrogate son for him in some way. Even though aged only nineteen or twenty at this stage Thomas Grey was well enough known to protagonists on both sides through his activities in Parliament. On 15th October 1642 he had chaired a Joint Committee of the two Houses of Parliament.

On 15th December 1642 the Journal of the House of Lords records a declaration that an Association of the Counties of Leicester, Derby, Nottingham, Rutland, Northampton, Buckingham, Bedford, and Huntingdon, had been formed for the mutual defence and safety of each other - with Lord Grey of Groby as Major-General. Huntingdonshire was shortly to become, along with Lincolnshire, Cambridgeshire and East Anglia, part of the rather more famous Eastern Association.

Throughout the first civil war, from 1642 to 1645, neither side exercised full control in Leicestershire. On 30th October 1643 the Earl of Stamford made a plea to the House of Lords that whilst he had been away commanding in the West Country for eleven months (mostly without any pay for his men) his house at Bradgate had been plundered, his horse and cattle driven away, and his tenants robbed; and that he humbly entreated their lordships that *"some malignant's house that was ready furnished might be allotted unto him for his family."* [32] In 1644 he was awarded the estates of the sequestrated Lord Stanhope of Harrington in Leicestershire and Rutland, his own estate (he claimed) *"being under the enemy's power."* [33] He played no further active military role in the first civil war. The Earl of Stamford appears to have been a monarchist at heart; of the same type as those other early Parliamentarian generals, the Earls of Essex and Manchester. He was, as his Colonel's colour proclaimed, a 'King and Country' man. In religion he favoured a state church formed on the model of the Scottish kirk system and he was also a political Presbyterian, allying himself with that group of men very much like himself in terms of status and background who dominated the rebel Parliament in the early period of the Great Rebellion. It seems that, like them, he had entered the war in the hope of limiting rather than abolishing the royal power.

By comparison with his father Thomas, Lord Grey of Groby, was militarily active and successful during the civil war. Clarendon, as has been noted, referred to him as being in 1642 at the outbreak of the war *"a young man of no eminent parts, and only backed by the credit and the authority of Parliament."* Whether Grey was indeed 'of no eminent parts' has been considered more fully elsewhere. [34] Certainly though he was backed by the authority of Parliament and he was a young man; in 1642 he would have been aged nineteen or twenty. We may compare this with the King's nephew, Prince Rupert, who at the same time had been given command of the Royalist Horse and was aged twenty-three. Due to the high mortality rate of the period young men often obtained positions of considerable responsibility very much earlier in their careers than is common today. This was all the more so if they occupied high social position by birth; authority being a function of social position. His main local adversary, Henry Hastings, so praised by Clarendon, was a mature man of around thirty-five at this time. After Edgehill Lord Grey expanded his troop of horse to a full regiment. He also had a Foot Regiment which was based on Leicester. This had five companies ; the first being commanded in Lord Grey's absence by a Colonel Henry Grey. Colonel Grey also acted often as the Governor of Leicester, again in Lord Grey's stead.

Throughout the county of Leicestershire during this early period of the first civil war conditions were anarchic and Colonel Henry Hastings appears to have attempted to secure some sort of order by declaring that he would use his utmost endeavour to prevent the plundering of those who had obeyed the ordinance of Parliament for the militia, upon a similar promise from Lord Grey to do likewise for those who had appeared for the king under his commission of array. [35] It is not known whether Lord Grey responded in writing to this suggestion but he must have remembered the attacks upon Bradgate that had already taken place and his subsequent actions indicate that he rejected it.

He had acted swiftly after the battle of Edgehill to secure Leicester for the Parliament. Prudence had led the Borough Corporation, which inclined towards the Parliamentarian cause, to steer a neutral course as far as possible in order to avoid military retribution from either side. Henry Hastings, strongly and menacingly based at Ashby-de-la-Zouch Castle, was not to be lightly ignored. The Corporation's dilemma is well illustrated by this reply dated January 1643 from the Mayor to Henry Hastings in the latter's capacity as (Royalist) High Sheriff of the county.

"Noble Sir,

Had I conceived your letter of the 6th of this instant in any way required an answer, I should have troubled you with the perusal of a few lines; but having nothing at that time worth committing to paper, I thought good to answer yr letter by word of mouth. As this day I imparted that letter to certain of the aldermen and those of the most ancient, whereupon having in our town neither arms nor power to resist, we resolved to send tomorrow to the right honourable the Lord Grey, by our town chamberlains, to desire his lordship to forbear bringing any forces to this town, lest otherwise he should be the means to cause our prejudice in this corporation. As for the admitting of forces into the town, I assure you, Sir, I shall be far from it; but if any happen to come I must confess I know not how to prevent them of possessing the towne. Worthy sir, I understand by some speeches given out by your last messenger (tending much to my prejudice, as I conceive) that you are informed that I should send for the Lord Grey the last Sabbath day, which I assure you is a false report, and so much troubleth me (knowing my innocency therein) that I earnestly entreat you would be pleased to vindicate me in that behalf ... . Thus in haste I take leave, and rest," & co.

Richard Ludlam (Mayor of Leicester)" [36]

Interestingly, in view of the reassurances and protestations made towards the end of this letter, Richard Ludlam was conspicuous shortly afterwards as an active partisan and captain of horse in the local parliamentarian militia under Lord Grey of Groby's command.

Having subsequently secured Leicester Lord Grey of Groby based his command of the Midland Association there and set up the local Parliamentary Committees. Garrisons were established throughout the county at Leicester itself, Leicester Abbey, Thurnby, Coleorton (near to Ashby-de-la-Zouch), Bagworth, Kirby Bellars, and Burleigh (at Loughborough). At an early stage he also entered Rutland, securing it, and neighbouring Rockingham Castle, for the parliamentarian cause.

In February 1643 the King created his own Association of the Counties of Leicester, Derby, Nottingham, Lincoln, and Rutland and made Henry Hastings the Colonel-General of all the royalist forces in them. [37]

There are records of many local skirmishes which took place in Leicestershire and around its borders between the rival forces of Lord Grey of Groby and Henry Hastings. [38] On 23rd October 1643 the latter was created Lord Loughborough by the King for his services to the crown. Despite a series of reported parliamentarian victories in local actions at such places as Melton Mowbray, Hinckley, Bosworth Field, Cotes Bridges, Belgrave, and Costock in south Nottinghamshire during 1643 and 1644 the royalist garrisons in the northwest and northeast of the county continued to pose problems. In May 1644 the 'Parliament Scoute' lamented:- *"... Poore Leicestershire! Not a county more right for the Parliament, and yet no county so tattered and torn as it hath been ... That a few men in a couple of noblemen's houses, [Ashby-de-la-Zouch Castle and Belvoir Castle], should waste a county as they have done."* [39]

On 25th May 1644 a letter was sent to the House of Commons from a Captain Edward Grey asking the House to settle some differences that had arisen between members of the local parliamentarian committee and the soldiers of the garrison at Leicester. Two days later the House of Commons read an Ordinance to create a Committee of the Militia for Leicestershire: a unification of the military co-ordinating and fund-raising functions. This new arrangement does not seem, however, to have solved the problem of disharmony between the leaders of Parliament's cause locally. On 16th August the House of Commons Journal records that:- *"Mr Carew presented from the Committee of Both Kingdoms certain informations given in by Lord Grey, containing certain passages betwixt him and the Committee for the Militia for the county of Leicester."* [(40)]

It seems from the evidence that Lord Grey had left the county sometime during the summer and was probably in London. On 4th September 1644 a petition *'of the inhabitants of Leicester'* [(41)] was presented to the Commons, asking that the differences that had arisen between Lord Grey's officers be resolved. It was referred to a committee of the House. A further petition was presented in November from the 'Gentlemen, Freeholders, and Best-Affected of Leicestershire' desiring that the Lord Grey of Groby, *('who first rescued us out of the hands of the malignants, gave the town of Leicester, then ready to be seized on by them, a garrison, and gave encouragement and life to the actions of the well-affected')* their commander-in-chief, be sent back to them to unify his officers and that the gentlemen of quality who should serve on the County Committee be enjoined so to do and not thus leave it to those of the *'mean middling sort'*. [(42)] The petition had 2,000 signatures appended.

The parliamentarian forces nationally had received a major boost with the victory at Marston Moor near York in July 1644. In spite of their territorial gains which followed from this, however, they were still unable to effect an outright victory. In short, the strife and uncertainty continued. *"Two summers past over"* lamented one parliamentarian commentator, *"and still we are not saved; our victories so gallently [sic] gotten, and (which was more pitty) so graciously bestowed, seem to be put into a bag with holes; what we wonne one time, we lost another; the treasure was exhausted, the countries wasted, a Summer victory proved but a Winters story; the game however set up at Winter, was to be new played again the next Spring, and men's hearts failed them with the observation of these things."* [(43)]

NOTES:

1. Lucy Hutchinson, *Memoirs of the Life of Colonel Hutchinson,* (Everyman's Library 317, Dent, London 1965) , p. 92.
2. Records of the Borough of Leicester, 1642. (BR./18/22)
3. John Dryden, *Cymon and Iphigenia.*
4. R. Ward, *Animadversions of Warre,* (London, 1639).
5. J. Corbet, *A true and impartiall History of the Militarie Government of the Citie of Gloucester,* (London, 1647) p. 11.
6. Lucy Hutchinson op. cit. pp. 81-87.
7. John Nichols, *The History and Antiquities of the County of Leicester,* Vol. III, Pt. II, App. iv. (1804) p. 19. (Source: *Horrible News from Leicester!* - a letter from Adam Jones in Leicester to his brother William Jones, Covent Garden, London, dated 6th June 1642)
8. L.J. Vol. V. p. 132.
9. C.J. Vol. II. p. 645.
10. John Nichols op. cit. p. 23.
11. Ibid. p. 23.
12. C.J. Vol II. p. 641. (Report to the House by Sir Arthur Hesilrige)
13. John Nichols op. cit. p. 23.
14. Ibid. p. 24. (A narration of the service performed by John Chambers and James Stanforth, to both Houses of Parliament, touching the Militia)
15. Ibid. p. 25.
16. John Vicars, *God in the Mount, Or, England's Remembrancer,* (London, 1642) p. 104.
17. Historical Manuscripts Commission : Hastings Collection. Vol. II. p. 86.
18. C. J. Vol. II. p.718.
19. Edward Hyde, Earl of Clarendon *The History of the Rebellion and Civil Wars in England,* ed. W. Dunn Macray, 6 Vols., (Oxford, 1888) p. 349.
20. J. H. Plumb, *Victoria County History of Leicestershire,* Vol. II, p. 109, quoting *Terrible News from Leicester,* (Thomason Tracts, E. 108.16)
21. John Nichols op. Cit. p.30. citing *Remarkable Passages from Leicester* 1642.

22. Letter to the Mayor of Leicester from Prince Rupert, 6th September 1642 - Leicester Museum Archives.

23. Letter to the Mayor of Leicester from King Charles I, 8th September 1642 - Leicester Museum Archives.

24. Receipt written by Prince Rupert, 9th September 1642 - Leicester Museum Archives.

25. Historical Manuscripts Commission : Hastings Collection, Vol. II p. 87.

26. Ibid. Vol. II letter No. 15. Pp. 14 - 15.

27. Edward Hyde, Earl of Clarendon, op. cit. pp. 348 -349.

28. John Rushworth, *Historical Collections - abridged and improved*, Vol. V. (London, 1703-08) p. 103.

29. John Vicars, op. cit. p. 31.

30. Denzil Holles *Memoirs of Denzil Holles* (London edition, 1815) p.270.

31. Mark Noble *Lives of the English Regicides,* (London, 1798) Vol. I pp.262-263.

32. Journal of the House of Lords (L.J.), Vol. VI, p. 346.

33. Journal of the House of Commons (C.J.), Vol. III, p. 601 & p. 605.

34. Jeff Richards, *Aristocrat and Regicide - The Life and Times of Thomas, Lord Grey of Groby (1623-1657)'*, (New Millennium, London), 2000.

35. Historical Manuscripts Commission : Hastings Collection, Vol. II. pp. 87 & 88.

36. Cited in James Thompson, *The History of Leicester* (1849), pp. 377 & 378.

37. Historical Manuscripts Commission : Hastings Collection, Vol. II. pp. 89-90.

38. These are dealt with more fully in *Aristocrat and Regicide'*, op. cit. (See 34 above).

39. *The Parliament Scoute,* No.61, 1644, cited by R E Sherwood in *Civil Strife in the Midlands, 1642-1651'*, (Phillimore, London and Chichester), 1974, p.154.

40. Journal of the House of Commons (C.J.), Vol. III, p.592.

41. Ibid, p.618.

42. Quarto Pamphlets, in the British Museum, 1644.

43. Joshua Sprigge, *Anglia Rediviva*, (London, 1647) p.6.

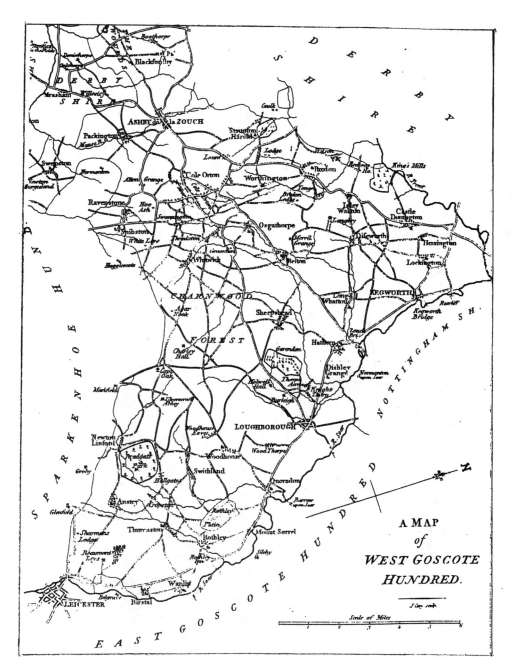

Map of West Goscote Hundred in Leicestershire

65

King Charles I

66

Henry Grey, Earl of Stamford (cica 1638) and signature

Henry Hastings, Lord Loughborough?

68

CHAPTER THREE

LEICESTER (1645)

"Of no considerable strength and full of wealth"
Henry Hastings, Lord Loughborough

Just as the parliamentarian victories nationally seemed to fail to deliver their promise, so locally, despite the bottling-up of the local royalist garrisons, there was still a feeling of insecurity at the beginning of 1645. There remained doubts about the ability of the Leicester garrison to defend the inhabitants of the county from the incursions of royalist forces from beyond Leicestershire's borders.

Even the security of Leicester itself was by no means guaranteed. Unlike either neighbouring Northampton or Nottingham it had never been the base of a large parliamentarian army. Indeed, the last large armed force Leicester had seen was the royal army when it left with the king to march to rebellious Coventry in the autumn of 1642. Clarendon had commented at the time that, *"If the King were loved* (in Leicester) *as he ought to be, the Parliament was more feared than he."* [1]

In fact the reverse was true. The king's cause only received a positive response from the people of Leicester when they were intimidated by armed force - and not even then in the summer of 1645. Yet Parliament had done little to make Leicester a military stronghold despite its clear adherence to their cause. As early as 1643 Henry Hastings had suggested to Prince Rupert that Leicester could easily be taken as it was *"of no considerable strength and full of wealth."* Indeed, he invited the Prince to join him in attacking both Leicester and Derby from Ashby-de-la-Zouch because:- *"the Woorkes at Lycester are two Myles about, and the West side of the Towne only defended by a narrow River w(i)thout Woorkes, for passing of w(hi)ch I will have Boates ready, and to make all these Woorkes good they have not five hundred men and boyes.*

69

The Workes at Derby are as large, and such another River as at Lycester, and not more men to defend them." [2]

The town had taken some precautions, but this was wartime and it had already become relatively impoverished. In 1640 reference had been made to *"the small trading we have had of late in our poor Corporation."* This was attributable in part to a plague epidemic of the previous year. In 1643 the Corporation had decided to sell as much of the town plate as the Mayor and Chamberlains thought necessary to discharge the civic debts. £86 was raised in this manner. As the civil war progressed more private wealth was concentrated in Leicester, however, as those gentry not strongly committed to the King's cause tended to move, with their valuables, into Leicester, which seemed more secure than their own undefended homes and had a garrison. Worse than the town's lack of corporate wealth though was its relatively defenceless condition. The river Soar protected it on the west side and toward the north; the low-lying ground being often extensively water-logged. The 600 yard perimeter walls of the Newarke, the old medieval citadel, remained, offering some security to the south side. The four town gates were still in use [3] but the rest of the medieval stone walls had gone. Mounds and ditches were all that remained of them. The medieval walls more or less followed the lines of the original Roman defences, but documentary evidence suggests that encroachment by housing development involving the widespread removal and use of stone meant that they had little military significance by the 1640s. Indeed, the decay of the town walls is reflected by the absence of any indication of their existence on John Speed's map of 1610, which shows considerable suburban development along the roads leading from the town gates, especially to the east and north of the town. (Speed's map does, however, show the four gates of the town which survived until 1774). Now the watch had been strengthened, the gates repaired, and some gunpowder bought for the magazine in the Newarke. Lord Grey of Groby had secured the town for the parliamentary cause at an early stage and established its garrison. From that point on it had never seriously been threatened by a strong enemy force.

On 18th January 1645 it was decided in London that the sum of £250 a month be assessed on the county of Leicester to pay for the

70

maintenance of its local parliamentarian military forces. [4] On 15th February the parliamentary ordinance was passed to put this into effect and a local committee was appointed to ensure compliance. The following list gives a useful roll-call of locally active parliamentarian partisans, at least from the perspective of London:-

"Thomas, Lord Grey of Groby; Theophilus Grey; Sir Edward Hartopp senior; Sir Arthur Hesilrige; Sir George Villiers, baronets; Sir Martin Lister; Sir Thomas Hartopp; Sir Roger Smith; William Quarles; John St. John; Thomas Babington; Peter Temple; Arthur Staveley; Henry Smith; Thomas Hesilrige; William Hewett; William Noell; Francis Hacker; Thomas Beaumont; William Danvers; Thomas Cotton; John Stafford; Thomas Pochin; William Sherman; and Thomas Goddard, esquires; John Goodman; John Swinfield; and Francis Smalley, gentlemen; William Stanley, Richard Ludlam, and Edmund Craddock, aldermen." [5]

Most of these already served on the main parliamentarian Committee for Leicestershire. By another ordinance issued on 20th February 1645 the monthly sum of £273. 15s. 6d. was also to be raised in the county of Leicester by a similar committee, with almost the same composition, as a contribution towards the maintenance of the Scots' army in England. [6]

In late February 1645 there occurred an incident which sent shock waves through the Leicestershire parliamentarians. A large royalist cavalry force, under Sir Marmaduke Langdale, passing through the county were engaged by a smaller force of parliamentarian dragoons. The results of this action are set out below in accounts from both sides. Firstly the parliamentarian Bulstrode Whitelocke relates that:- *"Between [Market] Harborough and Leicester, a skirmish happened betwixt a party of the King's forces, commanded by Sir Marmaduke Langdale, an eminent commander for his Majesty in the North, and a party of the Parliament's forces. The latter lost about 100 men killed , and 250 taken prisoners; beside a considerable number of horses. The victors lay in Leicester that night ...."* [7]

The second report comes from a Shropshire royalist officer in Langdale's force who took part in the engagement.

"Between Harborough and Leicester, we met with a party of 800 dragoons of the Parliament forces. They found themselves too few to attack; and therefore, to avoid us, had got into a small wood; but, perceiving themselves discovered, came boldly out, and placed themselves at the entrance of a lane, lining both sides of the hedges with their shot. We immediately attacked, and beat them from the hedges into the wood, and out of it, and forced them at last to a downright run-away, on foot, among the inclosures, where we could not follow them, killed about 100, and took 250 prisoners, with all their horses, and came that night to Leicester." [8]

The fact that this force of some 2,500 royalist horse and their own 800 dragoons could just enter Leicester without further resistance and spend the night billeted in the town reveals the open state of its defences at the time. There is no record of the actions of the royalists during their brief stay, nor of the reactions of the governor, Theophilus Grey, his garrison, and the local committee. Langdale's force moved on the following day to the relief of Newark which was once more being besieged by parliamentarian forces, probably including most of the Leicester command.

Whitelocke's account continues:- *"... and there* (i.e. at Leicester) [they] *received orders to collect a sufficient force, and proceed to the relief of Newark ... but, on their passage thither, they were attacked by a party of the enemy, commanded by Colonel Rossiter, near Melton Mowbray, where they had a sharp encounter, and loss on both sides. Of Langdale's party were slain Colonel Tuke, Major Kertlington, Captain Markham, and about 100 others; of Rossiter's about 50, but no officer. He lost one colour, and took two. Langdale got provisions into Newark, and was recruited to 3,000, and Rossiter followed him with 2,000 ".* [9]

The royalist account continues:-

"Accordingly we received the ammunition and provision [at Leicester], and away we went for Newark. About Melton Mowbray, Colonel Rossiter set upon us with above 3,000 men; we were about 2,500 horse and 800 dragoons. We had some foot, but they were still at Harborough, and were ordered to come after us. Rossiter, like a brave officer as he was, charged us with great fury, and rather out-did us in number, while we defended ourselves with all the eagerness we could, and with all gave him to understand we were not so soon to be beaten as he expected. While the fight continued doubtful, especially upon our side, our people, who had charge of the carriages and provisions, began to inclose our flanks with them, as if we had been marching, which, though it was done without orders, had two very good effects, and which did us extraordinary service. First, it secured us from being charged in the flank, which Rossiter had twice attempted; and, secondly, it secured our carriages from being plundered, which had spoiled our expedition. Being thus inclosed, we fought with great security; and though Rossiter made three desperate charges upon us, he could never break us : our men received him with so much courage, and kept their order so well, that the enemy, finding it impossible to force us, gave over, and left us to pursue our orders. We did not offer to chase them, but were contented enough to have repulsed and beaten them off, and, our business being to relieve Newark, we proceeded. If we are to reckon by the enemy's usual method, we got the victory, and had the pillage of their dead; but otherwise, neither side had any great cause to boast. We lost about 150 men, and near as many hurt : they left 170 on the spot, and carried off some. How many they had wounded we could not tell. We got 70 or 80 horse, which helped to remount some of our men that had lost theirs in the fight. We had, however, this disadvantage, that we were to march on immediately after this service; the enemy had only to retire to their quarters, which was but hard-by. This was an injury to our wounded men, whom we were after obliged to leave at Belvoir Castle, and from thence we advanced to Newark." [10]

This repulse to Colonel Rossiter's forces increased the concern of the Leicestershire parliamentarians who realised that, after managing at last to contain the local royalist garrisons which had so plagued them for over two years, the town and county were still wide open to royalist incursions from outside their own boundaries. Attempts were made to strengthen the local political position. The membership of the parliamentarian county committee was reinforced.

"... the following names were added to the Committee for Leicestershire : Sir Edward Hartopp, Mr. Thomas Beaumont, Mr. William Quarles, Mr. Thomas Goddard, Mr. Thomas Cotton, Mr. William Sherman, Mr. William Danvers." [11]

On 20th March it was reported to Parliament that a plot to betray the town to the enemy had been foiled.

"Letters from Derby certify a plot intended by Hastings against Leicester, in which he wrought with some of the town to have it to be betrayed to him; but (thanks to God!) the plot is discovered, and divers of the complotters are in custody, and like to suffer." [12]

Although the political resolve of Leicester might have been strengthened by these two developments it was still wanting in terms of physical defence and adequate number of soldiers. Appeals to London for reinforcements appear to have had little effect. Some work had been done to improve the state of Leicester's physical defences. The Borough Chamberlain's Accounts for 1643/4 record the cost of *'Beare'* (Beer) (£2.11s.11d) paid several times for Carters and others when *"the Towne went wholly out to repair the workes by Mr. Maior's appointment. Payment made to Mr. Daniel Abney* (£15) *which he disbursed about the taking down and setting up again of certain houses which were taken down by Injunction from the Governor beyond the South gate Sentry, by Mr. Maior's appointment."* [13] Payment was also made for repairs to the bridge at Belgrave Gate Sentry.

On 29th March 1645 at a meeting of the Mayor and Aldermen it was decided to levy *" a tax of £20 or thereabouts made to be disposed of for the setting up of such poore peoples houses in St. Maryes Parish as are or shall be taken down by reason of the public affairs, the said houses to be such as by Mr. Abney and Mr. Somerfield shalbe thought fitt and the money to be disposed at their discretion."* [14]

The Self-Denying Ordinance was passed by Parliament on 3rd April 1645 and gradually came into effect. Now, all MPs and Lords, at least in theory, had to resign their army commissions. This affected, amongst others, the Earl of Essex, the Earl of Manchester, Sir William Waller, Lord Grey of Groby, Sir Arthur Hesilrige, and Sir Samuel Luke. The only examples of MPs surviving as army commanders were Oliver Cromwell, Sir William Brereton, and Sir Thomas Middleton, partly through universal recognition of their military abilities and partly through political ingenuity. These exceptions were originally granted on 40 day renewable extensions. Sir Thomas Fairfax and the leadership of the New Model Army required Cromwell as their cavalry commander. Once Parliament had agreed to this in June it was to place him in an exceptionally strong position - and one that was to provide the basis for his future rise to power. He had become the key man; the Army's chief spokesman in Parliament, and Parliament's chief representative in the Army. He was to become a man courted by both parties, and carefully listened to, because he had armed power to back up his arguments. This was to prove critical in the period from 1645 to 1650.

In the meantime any concerns that Thomas, Lord Grey of Groby may have felt about the loss of his command over the Midland Association of Counties might have been affected by a letter he received from Colonel George Booth, a Cheshire landowner and his brother-in-law. Booth, later to become Lord Delamere, was a former royalist who had married Grey's eldest sister, Elizabeth. Staying in Leicester on a visit he wrote on 12th April, 1645 from the town to Lord Grey in London, as follows:-

"My Lord;

Being arrived at this place, which, by reason of your public and private interest in it, lays claim to your utmost endeavours for the preservation of it; I shall make bold to present your Lordship with the weak condition it is in, most obvious to the observing eye. By all men's account, there are not above 200 soldiers in the town, and those as peremptory against discipline as their governors are ignorant of it. I am most confident, nay, durst hazard my life and fortune upon it, that 500 resolute well-managed soldiers, at any time might one day make themselves masters of this town, which if lost will take away all commerce from all the North-west of England; and I can assure you, 'tis God's Providence alone in keeping it from the enemy's knowledge, and suppressing their courage, that is this town's defence; but, when we neglect to serve God in his Providence, by the adhibition [sic] of second means, 'tis just with God to leave us to our own strength, which is nothing but weakness. The grand masters, most sensible of danger, and careful of their own security, have all of them houses in a place of this town called the Newarke, where they are fortifying themselves as strong as may be; which will prove, as I fear, of most dangerous consequence; for, I perceive the townsmen much discontented, conceiving themselves deserted by the Committee to the enemy's mercy. I assure you, my Lord, I espy discontent dispersing itself very fast abroad in this town; and if your lordship's care prevent not, I expect very shortly to hear ill news from this place. Pardon my boldness, excuse my haste, and accept of my profession of being, my Lord, your Lordship's most humble servant,"

`GEO, BOOTH` [15]

Upon receipt of this letter Lord Grey of Groby referred it to the Committee of Both Kingdoms at Derby House in the Strand in order to gain the support of its members for the urgent reinforcement of

Leicester and its increased security. The Committee at London wrote on 25th April to the Leicester Committee asking for their response and instructing them to immediately improve the garrison and fortifications of the town. The response of the Leicester Committee to the Committee of Both Kingdoms, dated 1st May, 1645, was as follows:-

"Right Honourable;

We received your Lordships' letter, on the 25th of April last, about our fortifications; wherein we shall submit to your Lordships' direction. We never had the least thought to desert the town, or any part of it; but have fortified, and still proceed to fortify, all our outworks, and have of late amended them; and never had farther thoughts in fortifying the Newarke, than for a reserve in time of absolute necessity, and as more safety for our magazine, it being a place very easily made a very strong place. Our greatest want is of ordnance and arms; and therefore we humbly desire your Lordships they may be speedily sent to us by this bearer, Commissary Blunt; and that he may have your Lordships' warrant to charge carts, waggons, and horse, for bringing the same hither, giving reasonable pay for it.

We take leave, and are, my Lords, Your Lordships' most humble servants,"

Thomas Hesilrige	*Edmund Cradock*
John Brown	*Valentine Goodman*
Francis Smalley	*John Swinfen*
	William Stanley" [16]

This exchange illustrates the dilemma posed for the defenders of a town likely to be subject to attack. By the middle of the seventeenth century it was difficult to defend adequately an urban area of any considerable size with a long perimeter line whose medieval walls had decayed or been outgrown, particularly when the enemy possessed superior numbers, numerous cannon and siege artillery. In such cases a citadel or strongpoint was further fortified within the larger area to give the defenders the chance of holding out until relief could arrive. Of course, not all the inhabitants of the town and their belongings could be accommodated in the greater security of such a stronghold.

In the case of Nottingham, when a royalist attack had threatened the town in July 1643, Colonel John Hutchinson, the parliamentarian governor, whilst most of his garrison had been sent to the relief of Gainsborough, ordered that the fourteen cannon stationed around the town's perimeter outworks be withdrawn into Nottingham Castle.

"The main reason was, that if the town should be surprised or betrayed (which was then most to be feared), the ordnance would be useless; if any considerable force came against them, with so few men, and it would be difficult, at such a time, to draw off the artillery; if any force they were able to deal with came, it would then be time enough, after the alarm was given to draw them to the works, unless they were surprised. It was not only the town malignants [royalist sympathisers] *that murmured at the drawing up of the ordnance, but Dr. Plumptre, hearing that the forces were to march away, was raging at it; whereupon being answered, that it was more for the public interest of the Cause, in great passion he replied, "What is the Cause to me if my goods be lost?" The governor told him, he might prevent that hazard and secure them in the castle. He replied, "It pitied him to soil them, and he had rather the enemy had them, than they should be spoiled in the removing."* [17]

For some of the supposed 'godly', like Dr. Plumptre, it has been shrewdly observed that "where their treasure was, there their heart was also"!

"... The townsmen, through discontent at the drawing out of the forces, whereby their houses, families, and estates were exposed,

began to envy, then to hate the Castle, as grieved that anything
should be preserved when all could not; and indeed those who
were more concerned in private interests than in the Cause
itself, had some reason, because the neighbourhood of the Castle
, when it was too weak to defend them, would endanger them ...
[by attracting the presence of the violent enemy]." (18)

A similar resentment in Leicester, understandable though it might
be, of the increased fortifications in the Newarke, where some of
the local Committee members had their properties, was to hamper
the preparations for the defence of the town. The Newarke was
described as then *"comprising a circuit of waste ground, the*
Castle hall, [the greater part of the remains of Leicester Castle,
being in a dangerous and ruinous state, had been demolished in 1633
by an order from the Crown directed to a W. Heyrick/Herrick], *a*
fair and spacious Church, [St. Mary de Castro], *and a vast cellar*
by the Castle, as well as an hospital, and many fair buildings,
orchards, barns, and stables." The Newarke had originated as a
walled precinct surrounding the College of the Annunciation of St.
Mary founded by Henry, Duke of Lancaster, in 1353. The College
was abolished in 1547 and the hospital was refounded by James I
with the new name of Trinity Hospital. There was no direct access
in to the town proper as the Newarke Gateway stood outside the
South Gate of Leicester. (The Newarke Gateway was where arms
and gunpowder were stored and it had become known as the
Magazine Gateway, as it still is today). A second gateway, known
as the 'Turret Gateway' (or later 'Rupert's Gateway') led from the
Newarke into the adjacent castle precinct. Inside the Newarke were
the fine church of St. Mary de Castro, the Trinity Hospital, the
Skeffington and Chantry houses originally built for the clergy, and
the more recently built houses of the residents. Significantly, the
area of the Newarke constituted a liberty, separate from the town
of Leicester and exempt from borough rates - a status which it
retained until 1835 and the reforms of the Municipal Corporations
Act. The separate status of the Newarke and the quality of the
houses, as well as its closeness to Leicester, attracted the well-to-
do. The residents of the Newarke, by 1645, included some of

Leicester's leading citizens, such as John Whatton at Skeffington House.

The rest of the line of the town's defences, which had been begun about a year earlier by directions from Lord Grey of Groby consisted of little more than a simple embankment, protected by a fosse or ditch, and strengthened at a few important points such as Belgrave Gate, Gallowtree Gate, and the 'Main Guard' with 'horn works' and some drawbridges, and was still in an unfinished condition.

Lord Grey of Groby did not wait idly for the exchange of correspondence between the Committee of Both Kingdoms in London and the Leicester Committee for the Militia to take place. Upon receipt of the letter from his brother-in-law he immediately set in hand instructions for further improvements to the defences of Leicester, some of which are referred to in the Leicester Committee's letter quoted earlier. The following order was issued on 19th April 1645 and leaves little doubt as to his determination as revealed in the postscript. From the signatures it seems that Peter Temple is acting on his immediate behalf (hence *Vic'*) in this authorisation : Peter Temple, Theophilus Grey and Francis Hacker representing the military, and John Browne, Francis Smalley, and John Swinfen the civilian elements of the local Committee. The Grange Houses referred to were residences which had farm buildings belonging to them. The reluctance of their owners to demolish them is understandable. If left, however, they would provide useful cover for any attacking force.

"By the [Committee of] *Leic.r ffor* [sic] *the necessary defense* [sic] *and safety of the towne and to prevent the enemys approaches to the ffortifications thereof and the danger thereof It is ordered that the Grange howses* [sic] *and all building walls thereto belonginge or adjoyninge lyinge neare the publicke works on the South side of the towne shalbe taken downe and removed and the ground there levelled before Wendsday* [sic] *next. And the owners and inhabitants of the said Granges and*

premises are ordered and required to take downe and dispose the same according to this Order.

Pe : Temple Vic'	**John Browne**
Theo : Grey	**ffr. Smalley**
ffrancis Hacker	**John Swyfen**

If defalt [sic] *be made herein the soldiers are ordered to putt this order in present operation and Colonell* [Henry] *Grey is desired to see it done. xix April 1645"* [19]

The Town Chamberlain's accounts for Michaelmas 1644-45 include payments for the demolition of the Castle malt mill and the Grange. £3.3s. was also paid to workmen for demolishing houses near the South Gate and for other work there.

Meanwhile, in his headquarters at Oxford, the king was keen to begin another campaigning season. He was in a highly optimistic mood. Although considerable territory had been lost to the enemy during 1644, the main field army of the royalists was still intact, and was barely two days' march from London. In addition, the king's Captain-General in Scotland, the gallant Marquis of Montrose, had greatly discomforted Parliament's Covenanter allies during the late winter; and the royal army in the West Country had destroyed Essex's army there during the previous summer in the Lostwithiel campaign.

To King Charles' feeling of confidence was added that of an increased hatred for the enemy. The execution of his old friend and adviser, Archbishop Laud, in January 1645 and the breakdown of the Uxbridge peace negotiations had convinced him that those who adhered to the Parliamentary party *'were arrant rebels, and that their end must be damnation, ruin, and infamy'*. In the past he had often been accused of weakness and hesitation, but now he was resolved to show that he was a man of strength - a true warrior king.

He chose to demonstrate his determination on Wednesday, 7th May, 1645 when he left Oxford with his army at mid-morning. This was to be his third and final march through the midland counties of

England. A direct march on London was not the primary objective. The immediate purpose of the march was the relief of Chester, being besieged by Sir William Brereton, through which town the royalists maintained contact with, and reinforcements from, Ireland. After Chester had been relieved the plan was to restore the royalist presence in the north of England which had been so badly damaged by the Marston Moor defeat.

So what was later to be called the king's *'Leicester march'* began in John Milton's *"bounteous May - flowery May, who from her green lap threw the yellow Cowslip and the pale Primrose."*

The army first stopped at Woodstock where Prince Rupert detached himself from the main force and proceeded to Chipping Norton. Then, on 8th May, at Stow-on-the-Wold in Gloucestershire a Council of War was held which decided that General Goring should take a force of 3,000 horse and 300 foot into the West Country to try to frustrate any attempt by Fairfax, then at Newbury, to relieve Taunton in Somerset. On 9th May the royal army, now minus both Goring's regiments and Rupert's force, arrived at Evesham in Worcestershire. As they travelled northwards through the west midlands both Rupert and the king drew men out of the surrounding royalist garrisons in order to supplement their army which, at a little under 11,000 men, was the smallest that Charles had yet commanded in the war. The emptied garrisons were then fired to prevent the enemy from taking them. For example, Campden House was burnt by its governor, Sir Henry Bard, when he drew out the garrison to join the royal army between Stow and Evesham.

This army, marching through the heart of England with its brightly coloured war standards streaming in the breezes against the clear blue May skies, was a picturesque and awesome sight; yet it was an unwelcome plague to the countryfolk through whose areas it passed. Both sides tended to live off the land whilst on the march, but with the royalists it was 'free quarter' usually in a less restrained and less ordered manner than with the parliamentarians. In this campaign a series of burning buildings marked the progress of the royal army.

The Royalist Army on its *Leicester* march

Charles marched on to Droitwich, where he was rejoined by Prince Rupert on 11th May. Here they stayed until 14th May whilst the main army was stationed at Bromsgrove. During their stay here Lord Astley's Herefordshire men besieged and took a small parliamentarian garrison of some 120 men, under a Captain Gouge, at Hawkesley House.

Meanwhile Parliament, hearing of the king's movements, had set in motion its newly reorganised war machine. Intelligence concerning the movements of the royal army poured into Derby House in the Strand in London from whence the Committee of Both Kingdoms conducted military operations. Instructions were sent to Major-General Browne and Lord General Fairfax to move their forces towards Oxford and so prevent the king's return to his base. Another message was sent to Lieutenant-General Cromwell, who had been observing the king's movements since leaving Oxford, to remain in the pivotal area around Warwick if the royal army continued to move northwards.

The royal army then passed through Staffordshire northwards in the direction of Chester, being joined on their way by forces from the garrisons of Hereford, Dudley Castle, and Ludlow. Whilst he was still in Staffordshire the king was met by Sir John Byron who informed him that Sir William Brereton had abandoned the siege of Chester, leaving the royal army free to prosecute its *'northern design'* without hindrance. Following on the news of Chester, however, came the intelligence that Parliament had sent a strong army into the West Country to crush Goring and that Fairfax *"was himself and his army sat down before Oxford."* [20] Parliament had *"found by experience the three years last past, that the advantage of that place, situate in the heart of the Kingdom, hath enabled the enemy to have ill influences upon the City and Counties adjoining, and to infest all other parts."* The fall of Oxford was therefore considered essential in the struggle *"to put an end to the continuance of this unnatural war."* [21]

The king resolved to relieve the pressure on Oxford, and to strike a possibly fatal blow at Fairfax's New Model Army, before proceeding with the plan to reconquer the North. In order to do this he decided to attempt the capture of an important garrison in the hands of the Parliament. Leicester was chosen as the target for this purpose. The weakness of its defences in terms of both men and fortifications was not unknown to the royalist commanders. The king recalled Lord Goring from the West Country and summoned General Charles Gerard, commander of the royalist army in South Wales, ordering them to rendezvous with him at Leicester. Having issued these instructions he spent a night at Market Drayton and then turned his army eastwards, passing through Stone and Uttoxeter, and thus on into Hastings' territory on the Staffordshire/Derbyshire borders.

Before the king had decided to march on Leicester there had been a separate development which intensified the efforts of the occupants of the town to improve their situation. On 15th May the Leicester Committee had heard the rumour that Lord Hawley, the royalist governor of Bristol, might try to take Leicester. This information had been gained in the following manner. About the 30th April, a Henry Purefoy, who was a Leicestershire man as well as a royalist lieutenant, *"being at Bristol, and coming early in the morning into the governor, the Lord Hawley's chamber, the chamber* [floor] *being matted, and the governor himself in bed and the* [bed] *curtains drawn, he heard the said lord tell* [Bryan] *O'Neale his bedfellow, that he was upon a gallant design the last night for the taking of Leicester, which would be a business of very great consequence; and that the gentry and townsmen invited him thither (or words to that effect); which he marvelled at, the most of the* [royalist] *gentry being either gone to London or in the king's garrison."* [22]

Upon hearing this Purefoy, fearing for the ruin of his home town and county, the following day (being May Day) sent his wife to London to give warning to his parliamentarian relative, Henry Grey, Earl of Kent, urging that Leicester be put in a posture of defence. Following this, on the 13th May, he took the occasion of the prisoner exchange of a Lieutenant-Colonel Hudson to travel first to Banbury and then to his brother's house at Belgrave. He then sent a message to another of his relatives, Colonel Henry Grey, at Leicester, warning him that if the threatened attack came it would be by storming the area near St. Margaret's Church. A party of horse was sent out to Belgrave to escort him into Leicester where he related his story to the local Committee. He was then sent down to London to give evidence to the House of Commons; the House of Lords having already been briefed by the Earl of Kent.

The Leicestershire Committee persuaded the Mayor of Leicester, William Billars, to call a Common Hall (or full meeting) of the Corporation of the Borough at which all members took a solemn oath that they had neither corresponded with the enemy nor assisted him with the supply of arms. Shops were to be closed and an active service list of townsmen aged between sixteen and sixty was prepared. The Newarke fortifications were to be further strengthened and fresh outworks were to be constructed at Grey Friars and Horsefair Leys to protect the quarters of the main defence Guard which covered the London Road to the south. Several houses lying close to the Newarke walls which could be used by the enemy should have been demolished but this was frustrated in some cases by vested interests. Master Wadland, for example, the clerk to the Committee itself, refused to allow a weak point in that part of the Newarke wall abutting on to some of his land to be strengthened as he was unwilling that the ground be cut up. Help was requested from London and from the neighbouring parliamentarian garrison towns such as Coventry, Derby, Nottingham, and Northampton.

At the same time parliament's committee men in the county attempted to carry on their ork as normal. The Leicestershire Committee of Sequestrators ordered on 21st May, *"that Mr. Francis Blithe, solicitor of Sequestrations in this county, employ 16 men as agents under him for gathering proposition and sequestration moneys, etc; and they are to receive 13s. 4d weekly each for pay."* [23] Clearly, it was anticipated that many local royalists were about to be sequestrated. Such royalist families must have received the news of the advance of the king's army towards the county, when it came, with redoubled enthusiasm.

Strengthening the defensive outworks of Leicester

As the royal army moved nearer to the borders of north-west Leicestershire it is not entirely clear where Lord Grey of Groby was or what he was doing. There are some options, however, that may be speculated upon. Since the Self-Denying Ordinance had now taken effect, his military responsibilities in the Midlands might be deemed to have ended; whereas as a Member of Parliament active in the prosecution of the war he might reasonably be expected to be in London. In the capital he could engage in the committee work and general 'politicking' to be expected in the atmosphere of the time. Factions were being formed and reformed at Westminster and it was important to observe the first rule of politics - be there! Thomas Grey also had personal matters to attend to in London. One result of his absence from Leicestershire, however, was to perpetuate the limbo caused by the lack of decisive local parliamentarian leadership. The local committee was split into factions which had previously been expressed as either Lord Grey's adherents versus the others; or Stamford and other absentee *'worthies'* against the Hesilriges and the *'worsted stockingmen'*, with the town corporation members (including the mayor) usually supporting the group which best suited their own interests at the time.

There is just a hint that Lord Grey may have been in the area immediately prior to the siege of Leicester. There were many publications issued by some of the participants shortly after the fall of the town, in an attempt to put their own role and conduct in a good light and to cast doubts upon the behaviour of others. In one of these accounts a parliamentarian officer, Major James Innes, refers to how:- *"it is well remembered, that captain* [Peter] *Temple ... when the lord Grey began to fortify Leicester, upon intelligence given of the enemy's advance out of Worcestershire towards Ashby, repaired at midnight to the Lord Grey's chamber, earnestly persuading him at that instant to remove to Rockingham* [Castle], *with his forces, cannon, and carriages; ..."* [24]

Upon more detailed examination, however, it is clear that the incident referred to above took place not in May 1645 in relation to the fortifications ordered by Lord Grey following Booth's letter in the April and the king's 'Leicester' march from Oxford via Worcestershire, Shropshire and Staffordshire, but on an earlier occasion. Lord Grey had set in hand some fortification o Leicester much earlier and Innes continues his account concerning Peter Temple's conduct:- *"and indeed many times since he hath expressed that fearful disposition; for, in times of danger, pretending business, he usually hastens to London; witnes the last journey that he made up thither, upon the approach of the King's Army into these parts."* [25]

It is likly that this last reference to the royal army's approach is the one relating to the attack on Leicester, given the conjunction of events and timing of the publication of Innes' pamphlet.

On Whitsunday, 25th May 1645 the royalist army marched to Burton-on-Trent. King Charles dined and spent the night at Tutbury Castle with Lord Loughborough and the governor, Sir Andrew Kingston. The following day, whilst the army rested at Burton-upon-Trent, some of Sir John Gell's Derby Horse raided the quarters of Colonel Horatio Cary's Horse Regiment. (Horatio Carey had entered the civil war as a parliamentarian officer in the west country but had changed sides). Gell also sent messages to the Leicester Committee warning them of the royalist advance. Even at this stage, however, it seems that the Committee thought that the king might be heading for Newark rather than Leicester.

Richard Symonds' *Diary of the Marches of the Royal Army in 1645* records how on *"Tuesday, May 27, his Majesty marched to Ashby-de-la-Zouch, the head-garrison of the lord Loughborough; the earl of Lichfield to Packington."* [26]

Symonds, who was of a gentleman's family from Great Yeldham in Essex, was a quarter-master in a troop of horse under Lord Bernard Stuart, who was also Lord Lichfield and son of the Duke of Lennox, in the King's Life Guard of Horse. He adds that *"in this march this day we marched near Shelford, co. Nottingham, a fair seat of the earl of Chesterfield.*" [27] This was probably a morale raising visit by some of the royalist horse to the garrison of Shelford House near Bingham and too far from the main army's line of march unless there was a deliberate feint in the direction of Newark in order to mislead any parliamentarian scouts.

On Wednesday 28th May King Charles led his forces to summon the parliamentarian garrison of 350 horse and foot under Captain Peter Temple at Coleorton to surrender. As members of the Leicester Committee were later to explain, *"... by which sudden coming of the King we were prevented of the assistance of our forces at Coleorton ... they, being not able to bring off their cannon, could not come to us, the garrison standing within cannon-shot of Ashby-de-la-Zouch, for they had shot from Cole Orton into Ashby town. The enemy then summoned Cole Orton garrison; and General Hastings received a preremtory denial to his demand of it; and our horse, issuing out on the rear of the King's army, took and slew 40 of their horse ..."* [28]

According to Symonds' Diary, *"His Majesty marched with his army into Cole Orton, a garrison of the enemy's; then by the abbey of Gracedieu, where Sir Thomas Beaumont lives. There remains an entire court of cloisters, hall, etc. ... His Majesty lay this night at Sir Henry Skipwith's house, called Cotes, in the parish of Prestwold. The headquarters* [of the army] *were at Loughborough."* [29] Whilst the royalist army was quartered at Loughborough and in the surrounding villages it was reinforced by Hastings' own Bluecoats (including three troops of horse totalling 100 men) and 1,200 of the Newark Horse under Sir Richard Willys. Although the arrival of the main royalist field army was a source of great joy and relief to the local beleaguered royalists, both individual and garrisons, it was not welcomed by either its opponents or non-partisans. It was reported that in its progress through Leicestershire the Royal Army did *"very much spoil the country and impoverish it by imprisoning and ransoming the men."* [30] A royalist officer refers to the army in Leicestershire during this march as *"having treated the country but indifferently, as having deserved no better of us ..."* [31]

NOTES:

1. Clarendon, *The History of the Rebellion and Civil Wars in England* (published posthumously, 1702 - 1704)
2. Cited in E. Warburton, *Memoirs of Prince Rupert and the Cavaliers*, London, 1849 Vol. 1, p.503.
3. The four town gates were eventually taken down and sold off in 1774 to ease growing traffic congestion.
4. Journal of the House of Commons, (C.J.), Vol. IV. p. 24.
5. Journal of the House of Lords, (L.J.), Vol. VII. p. 207.
6. Ibid, p. 224.
7. Bulstrode Whitelock, *Memorials of the English Affairs*, London, p. 130.
8. From *The History of the Civil Wars in Germany from 1630 to 1635 : also Genuine Memoirs of the Wars in England in the unhappy Reign of King Charles the First. Written by a Shropshire Gentleman, who personally served under the King of Sweden in Germany; and on the Royal Side during the unhappy Contests in England.* Newark, printed by James Tomlinson, for the Publisher, in 1782. pp. 307 - 310. Cited in John Nichols, Appendix to the *History of Leicestershire*, Vol. III; Part II. *The Civil War in Leicestershire*, p. 41.
9. Whitelock, op. cit. p. 130.
10. Nichols, op. cit. p. 41.
11. Journal of the House of Lords (LJ), Vol. VII., p. 276.
12. *Present Passages of each day's Proceedings in Parliament*, p. 171.
13. Town Chamberlain's Accounts, 1643/4, Records of the Borough of Leicester.
14. Hall Papers XI, No. 326, Records of the Borough of Leicester.
15. Reproduced in Nichols, op. cit. pp. 41 & 42.
16. Ibid. p. 42.
17. Lucy Hutchinson, *Memoirs of the Life of Colonel Hutchinson,* (Everyman's Library 317, Dent, London 1965), p. 126.
18. Ibid. p. 128.
19. Hall Papers XI, No. 334, Records of the Borough of Leicester.
20. Clarendon, op. cit., Bk IX, 32.

21. Letter from the Speakers of Parliament to the Norwich Committee, 19 May 1645'. (Fairfax Correspondence), *Memorials of the Civil War*, ed. Robert Bell (London, 1849), Vol., pp. 225, 226.
22. Nichols, op. cit., p. 46.
23. Carte's Manuscript concerning the Proceedings of the Leicestershire Committee of Sequestrators, 1645. Cited in Nichols, op. cit. p. 42.
24. Nichols, op. cit., pp. 50 & 51.
25. Ibid, p. 51.
26. *Diary of the Marches of the Royal Army during the great Civil War kept by Richard Symonds*, cited in Nichols, op. cit. p. 44.
27. Ibid, p. 44.
28. Nichols, op. cit. p. 47.
29. Symonds, cited in Nichols, op. cit. p. 44.
30. C. S. P. (D). 1644-1645, p. 544.
31. Account by a Shropshire Royalist Officer (see note 6 above), cited in Nichols, op. cit. p. 46.

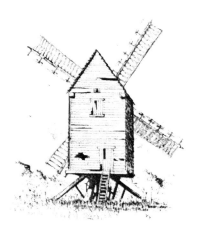

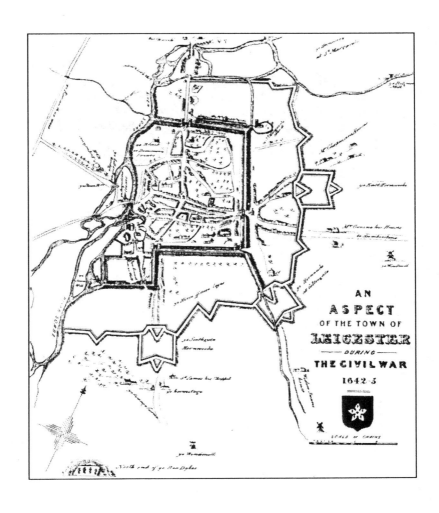

An aspect of Leicester during the Civil War, 1642-1645

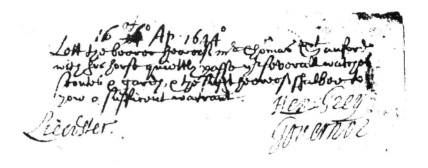

Transcript

16 of Ap. 1644[o]

Lett the bearer heareof Mr. Thomas Stanford
with his horse quiettly passe y[ou]r severall watches
scoutes & gardes, & the sight heereof shalbee to
you a sufficent warrant.

Liecister   Hen. Grey
                                             Governor

Pass issued by Colonel Henry Grey, Governor of Leicester

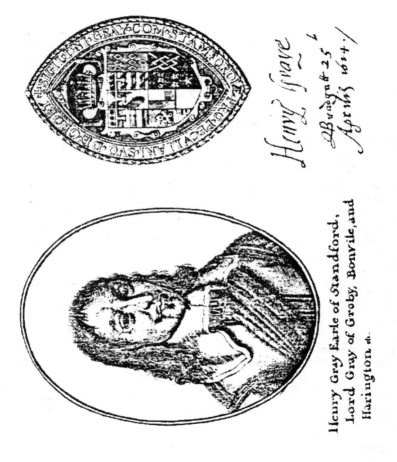

Henry Gray Earle of Standford,
Lord Gray of Groby, Bonvile, and
Harington &.

Engraving of Henry Grey, (Earl of Stamford),
with insignia and signature

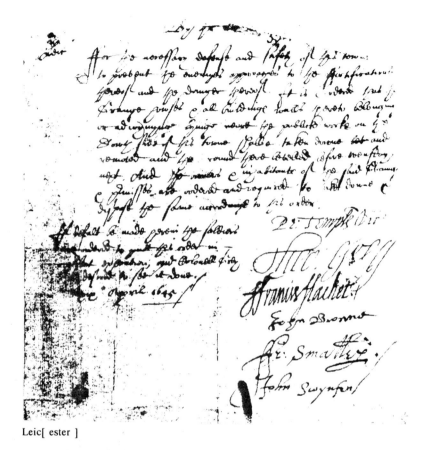

Leic[ester]

For the necessary defense and safety of this Towne to prevent the enemyes approaches to the Fortifications thereof and the danger thereof It is ordered that the Grange howses & all buildinges walls thereto belonginge & adioynynge lyinge neare the publicke worke on the South side of this towne shalbe taken downe and removed and the ground there levelled before Wensday next. And the owners and inhabitantes of the said Graunges & P[re]misses are ordered and required to take downe & dispose the same accordinge to this order.

If defalt be made herein the soldiers are ordered to putt this order in p[re]sent execution, and Colonell Grey is desired to see it done.

xix° Aprili 1645

Pe[ter] Temple Vic[ar]
Theo. Grey
Francis Hacker
John Browne
Fr [ancis] Smalley
John Swynfen

Order for demolition of the Grange Houses - with signature

96

Thomas Grey, Baron Groby (1623-1657)

Sir George Booth

Sir Arthur Hesilrige

99

Lucy Hutchinson

John Hutchinson

101

Dauentry   Brimidgham

The most Illustrious and High borne PRINCE RUPERT.
PRINCE ELECTOR, Second Son to FREDERICK
KING of BOHEMIA, GENERALL of the HORSE
of His MAJESTIES ARMY, KNIGHT of the Nobli
Order of the GARTER.

Woodcut depicting Prince Rupert and the 'Birmingham Butcheries' from a
pamphlet entitled *The Bloody Prince, or a Declaration of the Most Cruell
Practices of Prince Rupert and the rest of the Cavaliers . . .*, dated 1643.

Woodcut of Prince Rupert at Birmingham

102

CHAPTER FOUR

THE SIEGE

"It had for its object the annoyance of some of the most forward and formidable enemies of kingly government."
Richard Symonds

On Wednesday, 28th May, Sir Marmaduke Langdale arrived with the main body of royalist horse to surround Leicester. They signalled their arrival by setting fire to three windmills and one watermill. The defenders of Leicester responded in ways which will be described shortly. The main body of the royalist army arrived with King Charles himself and Prince Rupert on the following day.

"Thursday, May 29, his Majesty marched and pitched down before Leicester city, a garrison of the rebels, commanded by Theophilus Grey, third brother to the earl of Kent."[1]

On the Wednesday the royalist horse had cut off the town, concentrating most of their number on the east side. The river Soar protected most of the west side. The river crossings at St. Sunday's Bridge (north), West Bridge, and the South Bridge at Swan's Mill were all covered, as were the other main exits that lay behind the parliamentarian outworks on the eastern and southern sides. By quartering in neighbouring villages they prevented the delivery of supplies to the town from the countryside. According to Symonds the king encamped most of his army *" in the plains or meadows near Ailstone for two or three days preceding the siege; and the day before it he marched his army and sat down before the garrison of Leicester in St. Mary's field. The day was spent in preparing for the siege, and in parlies and threatenings."* [2]

It was on this day that news reached the king of the capture of Evesham by Colonel Edward Massey. The loss of the strongly garrisoned Evesham, which had occurred on 20th May, was a serious blow to the royalists as it severed their direct line of communication

103

between Oxford, Worcester and South Wales. It may also have strengthened the king's determination to take Leicester and make it an example to others of the price to be paid for resistance to God's anointed sovereign. According to Symonds' account Charles already had reason enough to choose Leicester as a target.

"The siege of Leicester had for its object the annoyance of some of the most forward and formidable enemies of kingly government. Men who had brooded over the real and imagined grievances of the state, till their minds grew intoxicated with the wild reveries of reformation, liberty, and equalization; those, too often, flattering dreams of perfection and prosperity. The people of this little province, early in the reign, shewed a spirit of restlessness; even those who professed themselves to be the teachers of the peaceable doctrines of Jesus, hastened with their appeals to the door of the House of Commons, urging the members, by their heated zeal, eventually to war and desolation. The King, on the other hand, unwilling to lose even a shadow of that prerogative which he had received from his royal ancestors, marched with an army of determined friends towards Leicester, to crush the power which had arisen in that place, and was become extremely injurious to his views and interest. There sat the grand Committees of the Midland district; the most formidable then in the kingdom in aid of the schemes of Parliament. Its central situation commanded the most early intelligence of the movements of the little flying armies and scouting parties which everywhere abounded in its vicinity, and from whence Parliament received daily intelligence and advice in the measures about to be undertaken. At this time some of the leading men of the corporation were men of business, intrigue, and discernment; These formed a part of the committee of safety and intelligence, and were members of the committee for the confiscating of the property of the King's friends ...

"The town of Leicester was chiefly governed by a Committee; viz. Mr. Hewett of Dunton, Mr. Hesilrige, Ludlam a chandler there, Mr. Payne of Medbourne, Newton of Houghton, a receiver,

sometime high constable, Read of Thirlby, Mr. Lewyn, and Stanley, a mercer there by the West gate." [3]

The above account, and others like it, go a long way to refute the claims of some more modern commentators that it was Leicester's 'neutrality' or 'equivocation' which led to its siege and sacking in 1645. Rather, as contemporary records and events demonstrate, the town's position was clearly pro-parliamentarian and was seen as such by both sides.

The alternative view is, in my opinion, difficult to sustain. Alan Everitt, in particular, in his classic contrast of Leicestershire and Northamptonshire during the first civil war makes much of the fact that **"Northampton town, from the outset, was decisively on the side of parliament. There was little of the shilly-shallying of Leicester about it, and within a few months of the beginning of the war it had become the most powerful garrison in the South Midlands.** [4]

This control was facilitated by the departure of the royalist opposition in the county to the new royal court at nearby Oxford - only 40 miles from Northampton - and the early movement into Northampton of the Earl of Essex and his army. Everitt also attributes the reason for the successful seizure of control of the more southern county by the parliamentarians to the fact that **"Northamptonshire seems to have been a more politically-minded county** [whatever is meant by that] **than Leicestershire, and one where family divisions ran more naturally along lines of religious division, instead of cutting across them."** [5] Most attacks on parliamentarian positions in Northamptonshire were staged by royalists from outside the county.

Everitt, along with other commentators, [6] suggests that **"the infamous and disastrous sack of the town was the price Leicester had to pay for its lack of decision in supporting either party during the previous three years. This is the essential lesson of all the rather confused events of 1642-5 in Leicestershire. If the town had unequivocally supported**

parliament, its defences would have been more capable of withstanding Rupert's attack." [7] Against this view it may be argued that it was not lack of commitment to the Good Old Cause but a lack of arms, men, and adequate fortifications that led to the fall of Leicester; and that the latter does not necessarily reflect directly upon the former.

As far as possible, given the situation in the county as outlined in previous chapters, the town had, from the winter of 1642 onwards, made it quite clear that it stood for the Parliamentary Cause. Even prior to this, the 1641 Protestation (or Grand Remonstrance) presented to the king, the election of MPs opposed to the royal policies and the Hastings interest, the lack of response to Henry Hastings' attempt to muster the trained bands for the king with the proclamation of the Commission of Array in 1642; in addition to the evidence from the royalist perspective given by Richard Symonds and others, all make it quite clear where the sympathies of the corporation and most townspeople lay. Despite this, the many requests and pleas to both Houses of Parliament to reinforce the town during 1643, 1644, and particularly in 1645 went unheeded. Indeed, not only had the Earl of Stamford been despatched to the West Country in 1642, but Sir Arthur Hesilrige and Lord Grey of Groby had been increasingly drawn into the national rather than the local military arena and then removed from both by the Self-Denying Ordinance. The effect of this was to reduce further the local political leadership and effective co-ordination of the parliamentary military forces in the Leicester area.

As far as the idea that a more fervent demonstration of opposition to the king being a deterrent to Prince Rupert's attentions is concerned, (and Leicester had experience of *'Prince Robber - the Elector of Plunderland'* in 1642 when he had extorted £500 from the Corporation under threat), one only has to look at the bloody fate of the puritan towns of Birmingham in April 1643 and Bolton in June 1644 to see the weakness of that argument.
The following words from a song entitled, *The Armourer's Widow* survived in the folklore of the Birmingham area into the middle of the nineteenth century to commemorate the visit of the 'royal

106

cavalier', the hero of so many novels by maiden ladies, to Birmingham:-

"When Rupert came to Byrmingeham
We were in a sorry plyght,
Our blood God's earth y stained by daye,
Our homes in blazing ruins laye,
And stained the skye at night.

With matchlock and with culverin,
With caliver and drake,
He battered down our ancient town;
He shot our sons and fathers down,
And Hell on earth did make.

Our daughters' cries, our widows' prayers,
Ascended with the flame,
And called down God's wrath divine,
Upon that Royal Murtherer's line,
And brought his kin to shame." [8]

Was this the fate that Leicester could now expect? The Royal Army which surrounded Leicester in the last days of May 1645 consisted of over 5,500 Horse, over 4,000 Foot and an impressive artillery train including at least six siege pieces. To oppose this vast army the defending forces were pitifully small and their fortifications clearly inadequate.

The Committee members in a published defence of their actions, entitled, *Narration of the Siege of Leicester*, written later in 1645, set out the steps they had taken to remedy the deficiencies that had been identified in the middle of May at the meeting of the Common Hall. A request had been made to the Committee of Both Kingdoms for an order to conscript 1,000 men. Another request was for approval being given to a mutual military alliance with neighbouring counties currently being advocated by Mr. Staveley for the Leicestershire Committee and a Captain White (much disliked by Lucy Hutchinson) for the Nottingham Committee. A request was also made for more cannon. This latter request was approved, but the town was lost before they were delivered. The Committee also wrote to Lt. General Oliver Cromwell, who had been stationed with a force near Warwick, informing him of their condition. He replied that he had been ordered to join Fairfax in besieging Oxford but that he had left behind a considerable party of horse with whom they should keep in touch. This they did, writing to Colonel Vermuyden, the commander of that party, informing him of the approach of the King's Army and craving his assistance. They also *"wrote to all the Committees round about us for aid, whom we never failed, upon any call, to contribute our assistance unto, viz. Northampton, Coventry, Nottingham, Derby, together with Colonel Rossiter, hoping amongst them to have procured 500 men at least; and we engaged to pay them, but could not prevail for a man."* [9]

The perimeter line of the outworks, incomplete as they were, was far too long to be defended by the men available against such overwhelming odds. The Committee attempted, in the short time now available to them, to strengthen key points and to reduce the length of the line. *"We also began to cut off some superfluous works at the Horsefair Leys and the Friers, wherein we saved the* [main] *guard of 150 men, and set on labourers to amend the other works where they were in any way defective, causing the townsmen to shut up their shops, and calling in the country; so that, by the continual pains of the townsmen, women and men, they were very well made up in all places. We then debated the strength of the town, and caused the mayor to give us a list of all that were able to bear arms, from the age of 16 to 60; whereof the list contained about 900 townsmen, besides those that were listed under our own captains."* [10]

They sent out their commissary, Thomas Blunt, to London to collect the additional three cannon that Sir Arthur Hesilrige had sent confirmation of approval for, as well as the purchase of 200 new muskets. These were not to arrive in time either, but 70 carbines were received from Sir Arthur. The Committee also distributed into *"trusty and sure hands, in divers parts of the town"* about 100 barrels of gunpowder and match from the magazine. At this point they say they received news of the king's arrival at Ashby. They had been late in drawing in to Leicester the men from their garrisons in the county. These totalled about 560 men, both horse and foot, of whom only 100 cavalry from Kirby Bellars under Captain Francis Hacker seem to have taken part in the defence of Leicester.

By the time the main party of the royalist horse, under Sir Marmaduke Langdale, had arrived on Wednesday 28th May to cut off the town and to check on the weak points of the defensive line on the eastern side, the size of the garrison had been fixed. There were the regular cavalry of the garrison, presumably Lord Grey of Groby's regiment, now numbering 240 men and led by Captain Thomas Babington of Rothley. To these were now added the cavalry from Kirby Bellars, of the same regiment, under Captain Hacker. The regular infantry of the garrison numbered 480 and were placed under the command of Colonel Henry Grey, assisted by Lieutenant Colonel Whitbroke, an experienced soldier who had seen military service in the Low Countries. These soldiers are likely to have worn blue coats or grey coats. They were supplemented by the 900 townsmen who were issued with arms and 150 recruits from the county, all of whom are likely to have fought in their civilian clothing. The mettle of the conscripts and the recruits was soon to be tested and the Committee were not sure what to expect. *"We had also sent out our warrants into the country to call them in : who came but slowly, being very malignant in most parts of it; many came that meant not to fight : there were not of them above 150 that were willing to take up arms."* [11]

The Committee did, however, have two strokes of fortune to assist them in the forthcoming struggle. Sir Robert Pye of Farringdon, an experienced parliamentarian soldier, had been on his way to join his regiment, which was with Colonel Vermuyden, but had been cut off, in Leicester, from his rendezvous by the royalist advance. The Committee invited him to join them and he freely offered his services. To show their gratitude the Committee presented him with 20 gold pieces. Sir Robert appears to have played a major part in the ensuing events and seems to have been regarded by many commentators as the effective military leader of the defending forces, sometimes being mistakenly referred to as the Governor.

Sir Robert was respected by both sides in the conflict. He was married to Anne Hampden, a younger daughter of the parliamentarian hero and leader John Hampden, who had been, along with Sir Arthur Hesilrige, one of the Five Members and who had died of wounds sustained at Chalgrove Field in June 1643. [12] This had proved a useful connection. Sir Robert sat as a member of the Long Parliament, as did his father. His wealthy father, also named Sir Robert, had written in January 1643 to the King desiring to make his peace with him, declaring that if the war continued for only a few months more destruction and famine must fall upon the kingdom. Sir Symonds D'Ewes noted that when the letter, which had been intercepted, was read in the House of Commons, *"although divers enemies of the House had been put out of the House for less offences, the fiery spirits, out of respect for their chief captain and ringleader, Mr. Hampden, did pass no vote against Sir Robert Pye, the father, neither at that time nor at ay time afterwards."* Notwithstanding the embarrassment caused by his father's position, Sir Robert Pye the Younger had benefited by John Hampden's patronage. Indeed the two seem to have been on the best of terms. In the same month Hampden had written a postscript to a letter addressed to his friend, fellow soldier and MP, Arthur Goodwin, *"I thank you for your favour to Robert Pye, to whom I beseech you to continue it and add your own counsel."* Partly as a consequence of this the younger Sir Robert Pye of Farringdon had now risen from being the captain of a troop of horse to being the colonel of a regiment serving with Vermuyden.

The second piece of good fortune was that a party of 200 parliamentarian dragoons, under a Major James Innes, heading for Nottingham through Leicestershire were persuaded to enter Leicester and assist in its defence. As members of the recently formed New Model Army these soldiers are likely to have worn red coats. With these additions the total number of defenders amounted to just over

2,000 men with which to defend a line of three miles in compass against an army of almost 10,000 royalists.

The leadership of the defence appears to have been shared amongst the members of the Committee and the Corporation, with deference to the professional expertise of Sir Robert Pye and Major Innes once hostilities began. As Major Innes was to explainlater, *"It is true that the lord Grey gave a commission to Theophilus Grey, esq. then eldest captain* [senior captain] *of his Lordship's regiment (the superior officers of the garrison being drawn out upon service) to command in Leicester for some days, when there was not danger of an enemy."* [13] Theophilus Grey was the third brother of the Earl of Kent, the head of the senior branch of the Grey family, but he does not appear to have played a leading role in the ensuing military action. He would have been outranked by Colonel Henry Grey and Lieutenant Colonel Whitbroke in *'his Lordship's regiment'*.

The hostilities began in earnest on the Wednesday when Langdale arrived with the main royalist cavalry force and fired the three windmills and the watermill. On the previous day the defenders of Leicester had witnessed the first appearance of the enemy when an advance guard of some 2,000 royalist horse had drawn near to the walls of the town. To oppose these Captain Thomas Babington had drawn out the cavalry of the garrison under the protection of the town's cannon. He had been subsequently joined, whilst awaiting in this position the attack of the enemy force, by Major Innes and his 200 parliamentarian dragoons who rode in, at some considerable risk, from Humberstone in response to entreaties for assistance from Leicester rather than continuing on to Nottingham. With this welcome reinforcement the defending force maintained a skirmish for a shrt time against the royalist advance guard. Casualties were light on both sides. The parliamentarians recorded the loss of two men killed and a few wounded. Towards evening, the more advanced parties of troops having been safely withdrawn by their commanders, hostilities were suspended for the night. At that stage it was still possible to hope that the attack had been used to cover the progress of the main Royal Army on its way to Newark-on-Trent.

Sir Marmaduke Langdale's Horse set fire to the
windmills outside Leicester

Any such hopes evaporated with the appearance of Sir Marmaduke Langdale's force early on the morning of the following day. Having fired the windmills and the watermill within sight of the walls, he proceeded formally to invest the town by circling it and cutting it off. Numerous parties of cavalier horse, detached for the purpose, rode up close to the defensive lines trying to determine the weakest parts of the defences and the most favourable points to be attacked. Sir Robert Pye ordered out the defending cavalry under Major Innes and Captain Babington again. They drove back the advanced groups of the enemy on to their main body by a vigorous attack. In a second skirmish, which took place in the afternoon, a party of the parliamentarian horse under a Lieutenant Davis, charged a detachment of royalist horse, chasing them as far as the bridge at Belgrave, taking several prisoners and killing others. Skirmishes continued during the day and prisoners were taken on both sides. These encounters generally assisted the morale of the defenders and delayed the royalists from establishing their artillery batteries for the whole of that day. Shots were continually exchanged between the artillery of the town and the relatively light pieces that had accompanied the royalist cavalry. A desultory fire, both of cannon and small arms, continued at intervals during the whole of the following night, especially from the South Sentry from which the enemy were clearly seen to be starting to plant a battery near the South bridge to threaten the defences in that quarter.

Throughout the day, according to the Committee's account, *"our cannon on all hands played roundly whenever they could find a mark within distance and did good execution in our sight; and this continued till night. The night being very light, about 10 or 11 o'clock, we easily discovered he enemy's forces to draw down, and to begin to plant a battery against the Newark wall; we played upon them all night abundantly from our works with our musketeers and cannon shot from the South sentry."* [14]

It had concerned both Pye and Innes as professional soldiers and new arrivals that the perimeter line was still too long for so few to defend. Cannon were few (nine according to some reports) and ouht to be capable of being moved as the sitation dictated, but with a scarcity of suitable draught horses the ability to provide a mobile battery was lacking.

"Sir Robert Pye desired the Committee to take order, that there might be teams and draught-horses for the removing the cannon from place to place, as occasion should require; but not a horse or team was to be seen in readiness for that service. And whereas the Committee promised Sir Robert Pye that there should be 300 men upon the main guard constantly; there were not seen above 20 men." [15]

Another concern was the lack of cover at the defensive lines which left the defenders exposed to enemy fire.

"... the Committee were unprovided of divers materials necessary for the defence of the garrison, [such] *as spades, shovels, and mattocks, to make up the breaches; the works* [being] *altogether naked, there being neither cannon nor musket-baskets to shelter the soldiers."* [16]

Yet another concern of Innes and Pye was the number of buildings outside the defensive line which had been left open to the enemy's use. The reluctance of the Committee to demolish these probably also explains their unwillingness to reduce the perimeter line still further and leave other property unprotected. As Innes later complained:- *"... they had left all places of advantage to the enemy undemolished; as namely, master Chapman's houses near Belgrave-gate; Green's houses near Humberston-gate; the widow Swan's houses, and the Grange, near unto the South-gate; divers houses at the West bridge, and many near to St. Sunday's bridge ... all which places, left thus undemolished, were within six-score paces of the* [out]*works, and most of them within pistol shot."* [17]

It is quite likely that the principal officers of the King's Army had been fully acquainted with information about these weak spots by local royalists who had either left or been expelled from Leicester.

Innes and his dragoons had set out to remedy part of this situation early on the Wednesday evening. A party of them rode out of the North Gate and up to St. Sunday's Bridge over the river Soar. They dismounted on the town side and, with their carbines in their hands, sallied out across the bridge, beat back the cavaliers and set fire to the houses where the royalist snipers had been stationed. They then successfully withdrew back across the bridge having demonstrated to the foot soldiers of the town, who had refused to undertake the mission, how it should be done.

On the Thursday morning, 29th May, the parliamentarians made dispositions of their horse and foot around the defensive line laid out two years previously by Lord Grey of Groby. The three mile perimeter of the outworks was divided into two. One part, from the area of St. Margaret's Church in the north-east corner down to the area of East Gate, including Gallowtree Gate, Belgrave Gate, and Humberstone Gate, was assigned to Colonel Henry Grey and Lieutenant-Colonel Whitbroke. Within this line St. Margaret's Church-yard was referred to as a strong post and both the Belgrave and Gallowtree (Goltre) Gates were protected by hornworks.

The other part, which covered the south side and included the Newarke and the Main Guard, was put under the immediate command of Sir Robert Pye. It seems that Major Innes and his dragoons were also stationed here, along with the largest number of defenders, to hold these vital positions. It was anticipated that the main royalist assaults would be made against the Newarke. It was the nearest thing to a citadel in the Leicester defences. Some accounts of the siege and storming refer to 'the Newarke fort'. The name `Newarke' derived from `*the new worke*', an area of approximately seventeen acres walled in by Henry, Duke of Lancaster circa 1330 and containing a hospital, a church, and the remains of Leicester Castle. It was surrounded on three sides by a stone wall of 600 yards perimeter - the river Soar providing the fourth side. Unfortunately, the walls, particularly the south wall, were in a poor state of repair. The Committee had been in the process of fortifying the Newarke when the response of the Committee of Both Kingdoms to George Booth's letter ordered them not to do so in case the morale of the townspeople was damaged by the thought of the Committee members providing a safe bolt-hole for just themselves. It was the south wall which Master Wadland had refused to allow to be repaired by work to be carried out on his land.

Holes made in the north wall of the Newarke (now part of the gardens of the 'Newarke Houses'), for use as loopholes for firing through, may still be seen. These were most likely unused as they were away from the frontal assault. The holes made for the same purpose in the south wall of the Newarke were larger and were certainly used as this area saw the fiercest parts of the royalist assault when it came. This wall was photographed at the turn of the nineteenth century, but it has since been demolished.

In addition to the manning of the line of outworks on the eastern and southern sides outside the old city walls some defenders were assigned to the northern and western sides of the town alongside the river. These soldiers and armed civilians were placed under the command of Captains Babington and Hacker, who had troops of horse stationed at the North Bridge and the West Bridge, able to ride to support any area that was under strong attack.

The County Committee itself was based in a house overlooking te Market Place at the High Cross in the centre of the town. The Town Corporation was located nearby in the Guildhall close to St. Martin's Church. From these buildings the strategic direction of the defence of the town, such as it might be, was to be determined.
When the main body of the Royal Army with King Charles and Prince Rupert arrived from Loughborough on the following day, Thursday, 29th May, they had marched down the eastern side of the town in three divisions and encamped on the south side in St. Mary's fields. Their artillery was then positioned and the horse and foot allocated to their stations. In the afternoon the king established his headquarters at the manor house, belonging to the Earl of Rutland, in the village of Aylestone to the south of Leicester.

116

The Cavalry skirmish towards the bridge at Belgrave

Prince Rupert quickly identified some existing earthworks, known as the Rawdykes, which faced the southern wall of the Newarke, as a natural location for most of his siege guns. These ancient earthworks extended at this time for some 700 yards across and were about half a mile from the south wall. It is thought that they stretched from the River Soar in the west to the current site of the Leicester Infirmary in the east. The town had already been ringed by royalist cavalry and now strong bodies of foot and further horse were stationed facing the town from various positions to the north, east, and south, particularly at St. Sunday's Bridge. The south wall of the Newarke was, not unnaturally, decided upon as the projected chief point of attack.

Meanwhile the horse of both sides were again involved in skirmishes, during which the royalists were engaged in bringing their cannon up to positions where they could be pointed against the weakest parts of the fortifications. Members of the Leicester Committee claimed that they were guided in this by 'malignant' townsmen who had fled to the enemy camp. At the same time a number of royalist troops established a bridgehead in some of the old houses near St. Sunday's bridge, adjoining the old church-yard of St. Leonards.

Throughout that evening and the whole of the night, Rupert supervised construction of an artillery battery on the Rawdykes facing the south wall of the Newarke. At the same time the defenders, both men and women, soldiers and civilians, worked at improving the defences in anticipation of the coming assault. Also that evening, heartened by the example set by Innes' dragoons the previous day, a party of volunteer townsmen and dismounted cavalry stormed the houses near the St. Sunday's bridge being used by the enemy and forced them to flee. Several houses and the already semi-derelict church of St. Leonard were then burnt down to prevent their further use by the royalists. Another party of the defenders sallied out of a gateway or port in the southern wall of the Newarke and destroyed the Grange houses. These should have been demolished already under Lord Grey of Groby's order of 19th April.

Major Innes and his Dragoons cross St. Sundays bridge at the North Gate and rout the royalist snipers

Despite these heroic forays and a constant firing on the enemy during the night the construction of the battery on the Rawdykes, to hold the royalists' heavy guns, went ahead. By daybreak it was finished and armed. According to some reports it contained six heavy siege pieces. This was not all. As one parliamentarian account records, *"On Thursday, their artillery were drawn up near the town; and, by the direction of some malignants of the town, who had formerly gone out of it, or were put out, their great guns were planted against some of the weakest places of the works."* [18]

There is a story that amongst the royalist soldiers besieging Leicester was the then 17 year old John Bunyan. He was at the time, by his own account, a boisterous and loose-living young man. He was detailed to take up sentry duty opposite some defensive outworks at one point when another member of his company begged to exchange his turn on watch. Bunyan agreed and his replacement was shot in the head by a parliamentarian defender and killed. Bunyan was later to see the hand of God's Providence in this Mercy. One cannot help thinking that the later John Bunyan, the author of *Pilgrim's Progress*, would have been found on the other side of the barricades, fighting for the 'Good Old Cause' of 'God and Parliament'. He was to return to Leicester thirty years later as a well-known dissenting preacher.

An impressive array of young royalist notables were gathered at Leicester for the siege. Many of them had been 'immortalised' in portraits by artists such as William Dobson during their time in winter quarters at Oxford. These dashing 'cavaliers' are featured, resplendent in their armour and the gold fringed deep red sashes of the royalist cause. Amongst those present, and whose images are included amongst the illustrations in this book, are - in addition to King Charles himself - Prince Rupert, his brother Prince Maurice, James Compton the 3rd Earl of Northampton, his brother William Compton, Lord Bernard Stuart (Lord Lichfield and the king's cousin), Sir Marmaduke Langdale, Sir Bernard Astley, Sir George Lisle, Sir

John Byron, his brother Sir Richard Byron, Colonel John Russell, and Sir Richard Willys.

By contrast, no parliamentarian notables were present amongst the defenders of Leicester. Thomas, Lord Grey of Groby and Sir Arthur Hesilrigge, both local MPs and recently active 'roundhead' commanders, had sent some assistance but not their own persons. The 'tawney-orange' or 'deep yellow' sashes of the parliamentarian senior officers in Leicester during its siege and storming were worn by the likes of Colonel Henry Grey, Lt. Colonel Whitbrook, and Major James Innes. It is a reflection of their relative social standing that few such portraits exist to represent the posterity of the brave and greatly outnumbered defenders of Leicester. The exceptions are those of Sir Robert Pye of Farringdon MP, and Captain (later Colonel) Francis Hacker , the latter achieving notoriety with Peter Temple and Lord Grey of Groby through involvement in regicide.

The royalist forces were positioned at particular points in anticipation of the command to attack. Bodies of Foot had bodies of Horse stationed behind them in order to urge them on and to prevent desertion. According to Symonds the following bodies and numbers of royalist Horse were present at the siege and storming of Leicester:

King's Life-Guard, including the King's Own and the Queen's troops	130
Prince Rupert's Life-Guard	140
Prince Maurice's Life-Guard	120
Prince Rupert's Regiment	400
Lord Loughborough's	100
Colonel Horatio Cary's	200
Earl of Northampton's Brigade (Four regiments)	850
Colonel Thomas Howard's Brigade (Seven regiments)	880
Sir Marmaduke Langdale's and Sir William Blackstone's Brigades (usually known as the Northern Horse)	1500
Sir Richard Willey's Newark Horse	<u>1200</u>
	[19]5520

The royalist Foot were divided into four main divisions or 'tertias' (a term originating from the Spanish custom of fighting with three main blocks of infantry). The original three divisions were commanded by Sir Bernard Astley, Colonel Sir Henry Bard, and Colonel Sir George Lisle - all experienced officers. The fourth 'tertia' was composed of Prince Rupert's Bluecoats, under the command of Colonel John Russell, who had joined the army at Stow. In reserve were the redcoated King's Life Guards of Foot, whose task was to protect the royal person, and the redcoated Prince Rupert's Firelocks who guarded the main battery on the Rawdykes.

Sir Bernard Astley's Brigade consisted of elements from Sir Bernard's own regiment with its distinctive green colours emblazoned with hawk lures, the Duke of York's Regiment, Sir Edward Hopton's Bluecoat Regiment, and Sir Richard Page's Regiment. Colonel Sir Henry Bard's Brigade included his own regiment of Greycoats, Owen's Regiment, Sir Charles Gerard's Regiment with its distinctive colours of blue and yellow triangles, and Lord Loughborough's own Bluecoats. Colonel Sir George Lisle's Brigade was an assorted collection of units. Many royalist regiments had by this stage in the civil war been shrunken by death, injury and desertion to virtually company strength. The new brigades became in effect large regiments. Lisle's brigade had a greater variety of regimental coat colours than the others. It included members of Lisle's own regiment, William St. George's Regiment, the Shrewsbury Regiment, Colonel Henry Tillier's Regiment and Colonel Robert Broughton's Regiment. The latter two regiments were Greencoat regiments brought over from service in Ireland. Altogether there were greencoat, bluecoat, redcoat, yellowcoat, greycoat and whitecoat units in Lisle's brigade - a veritable rainbow of musket and pike.

Sir Bernard Astley's division was positioned in two separate bodies. One was stationed on the west bank of the river Soar near the North Mill and St. Sunday's Bridge; the other was in the Abbey Meadows facing St. Margaret's Church. Colonel Sir Henry Bard's division was stationed across the Belgrave Road near the site of the present St. Mark's Church and across the Humberstone Road facing the East Gate which lay behind the defenders' outworks. Prince Rupert's Bluecoats (over a thousand of them) were stationed outside the hornwork commanding Gallowtree Gate and the (London) road to Harborough at the southeast corner of the fortifications and also opposite the defenders' Main Guard emplacement which covered the South Gate and the Horse Fair Leas. Colonel George Lisle's division was stationed between the Rawdykes and the town, facing the south wall of the Newarke. Behind them, in reserve, were the Life Guards of Foot and Horse and Prince Rupert's Firelocks.

The defenders of Leicester were surrounded by overwhelming odds. Would they surrender or would they resist?

NOTES:

1. Symonds, op. cit. p. 44.
2. Ibid, p. 45.
3. Ibid, p. 45.
4. A. M. Everitt, *The Local Community and the Great Rebellion*, Published by the Historical Association, 1969, G.70; pp. 13 - 14.
5. Ibid, p. 17.
6. J. S. Morrill; Jonathan Wilshere & Susan Green, Jack Simmons.
7. Everitt, op. cit. p. 13.
8. *The Armourer's Widow* (Song), included in Thomas A. Vaughton's collection of *Tales of Sutton Town and Chase.*
9. Nichols, op. cit., p. 46.
10. Ibid, p. 47.
11. Ibid, p. 47.
12. There is an account concerning the death of John Hampden which has been drawn to my attention by Robert Dimsdale, a descendant of the Pye family of Farringdon. This account, which has been the subject of some dispute in the past, purports to have been given in a letter by Sir Robert Pye to Sir Edward Harley. (The manuscript was reproduced in the *St. James' Chronicle* in 1761). After describing how his wounded father-in-law had managed to ride from Chalgrove Field back to Thame, Sir Robert Pye's letter continues: *"As soon as he possibly could he sent for me; he was in very great pain, and told me that he suspected his wound was mortal, but what makes it still more grievous to me, says he, is, that I am afraid you are in some degree accessory to it, for the hurt I have received his (sic) occasioned by the bursting of one of those pistolls (sic) which you gave me. You may be sure I was not a little surprised and concerned at hearing this, and assured him they were bought from one of the best workmen in France, and that I myself had seen them tried. You must know it was Mr. Hampden's custom whenever he was going abroad always to order a raw serving boy that he had to be sure to take care that his pistols were loaded, and it seems the boy did so very effectually, for whenever he was thus ordered he always put in a fresh charge without considering or*

examining whether the former charge had been made use of or not, and upon examining the remaining pistoll (sic) *they found it was in this state, quite filled up to the top with two or three supernumerary charges. And the other pistoll* (sic) *having been in the same condition was the occasion of its bursting and shattering Mr. Hampden's arm in such a manner that he received his death by the wound and not by any hurt from the enemy."*

13. Nichols, op. cit., p. 51.
14. Ibid, p. 47.
15. Ibid, p. 50.
16. Ibid, p. 49.
17. Ibid, p. 49
18. Ibid, p. 52.
19. Symonds, op. cit., cited in Nichols.

Sir Robert Pye (Jnr) of Farringdon

126

Captain Francis Hacker

PETER TEMPLE

Captain Peter Temple

128

CHAPTER FIVE

THE STORMING

"...a little after 12 of the clock in the night this violent storm began, and continued till after one."
Richard Symonds

At noon on Friday, 30th May, Prince Rupert *"after he had shot two great pieces at the town"* sent a trumpeter with a summons to the defenders to surrender. The summons was issued to the soldiery, townsmen, and countrymen and offered a pardon to the mayor, William Billars, on behalf of the town and free passage for Major Innes, his troops, and the other commanders of the garrison to march away. The trumpeter read out the summons and was asked to wait while a Council of War was held in the Mayor's parlour of the Guildhall.

One of the Committee members, whose name is not recorded, declared *"We are a part of those who have undertaken the Parliament's cause, a cause so high as I desire to die in no other."* [1] This sentiment was echoed by Captain Hacker, Captain Babington, and other officers of the garrison.

Sir Robert Pye and Major Innes, however, questioned whether the number of defenders was sufficient to withstand such overwhelming odds along such a long line of inadequate fortifications and appear to have advised acceptance of the offered terms. When they had originally agreed to assist in the defence of the town they had been informed by the Committee that they had 1,500 fighting men available but they had found in reality a garrison of 450 soldiers (insufficient to man the circumference of a three mile line), a lack of mobile batteries, and an enemy force far larger than might have been expected. The discussion went on for some time until Pye and Innes agreed to continue in the defence of the town and to contribute their best endeavours, notwithstanding the heavy odds against them.

The mayor, having considered the summons, decided to call a meeting of the Common Hall to make a decision on behalf of the Corporation. In the meantime it was agreed to ask Prince Rupert to give them until the following morning to deliver their answer and henot to raise any further works until he had their response. The reasons that they gave for this later were as follows. Firstly, that all those whom the summons concerned might have the opportunity to agree in advance to its rejection *"the better to unite and engage them."* Secondly, as they assumed that the Newarke would be the target of the main royalist attack they wished to procrastinate in order that the substantial breastwork within it, that was almost finished, be completed. An additional cause of delay was confusion as to whom the response to the summons should be addressed and how it should be styled. Some members thought that the response should be made to King Charles himself rather than to Prince Rupert, who was a foreigner *"that had done so much mischief."* Others disagreed and pointed out that the king had made Rupert his General and that the answer should be given to him who had sent it. This was finally agreed upon but the form of address was shortened to the style *"Sir,"* and the title used was *"the Commander-in-chief of his Majesty's Army."*

At two o'clock the Committee sent their own trumpeter to the prince. The town trumpeter delivered his message, including the abbreviated form of address and the request that Prince Rupert desist from raising any further works during the deliberations of the defenders. It was clear to the prince that the parliamentarians were playing for time and the lack of courtesy shown to him in the style of the response was not best calculated to please someone renowned for his fiery aristocratic temperament. His reaction to the request for a delay in giving a direct answer to his summons until the following morning can best be summarised by a contemporary report.

"His Highness told the trumpeter if he came again with such another errand he would lay him up by the heels." [2]

The Council of War and the Common Hall consider Prince Rupert's surrender summons in the Guildhall

He then sent the town trumpeter back into Leicester. In the meantime he had been engaged in preparing a second battery within six hundred yards of the South Gate in order more effectively to breach the south wall of the Newarke prior to launching a storming assault should his terms be rejected. According to Hollings this battery appears to have been constructed on elevated ground, somewhat to the north-west of the site of the present Infirmary, much nearer the south side of the town than the main battery on the Raw Dykes, somewhere between the Welford Road and Oxford Street, and nearer to the area marked *Grange* on the Siege map. This was, **"like that finished the night before, chosen with sufficient judgement, since the king's troops might thus be moved up within a reasonable distance of the point of attack, protected by the embankments of the Raw-dykes, and by the general inequalities of the ground, from the artillery of the town."** [3]

About half an hour later the man returned again with another note addressed to *"the Commander-in-Chief"* and desiring time to consider the summons until the morrow morning - the Committee displaying a marked stupidity in this action. The incensed Rupert then placed the unfortunate Leicester trumpeter in the custody of his marshal - the royal trumpeter still not having returned from the town. He then sent a drummer to demand a answer to the original summons within a quarter of an hour.

This messenger arrived just as the Mayor and the Common Hall of the Corporation were about to vote on their reaction to the summons. The Mayor, William Billars, informed them of the resolve of the military officers of the garrison to reject the summons and a Committee member urged them to defend the town. One of the townsmen gave his vote in favour of fighting it out, as did a second. Before any more could express their view they were interrupted by the sounds of a heavy artillery bombardment directed at the town. Prince Rupert had run out of patience and given the order to his batteries on the south side of the town to open fire on the Newarke. As Richard Symonds of the King's Life Guard of Horse puts it,

"Then the Prince about three of the clock sent them an answer in lowder termes ... " The other royalist cannon positioned around Leicester joined in. The garrison's cannon fired in response. The meeting of the Committee and Corporation hastily broke up. *"Then all debates ceased, and all were commanded to repair to the works; which was done with much courage and resolution."* [4]

This barrage began at 3 o'clock in the afternoon. *"And now we plied each other both with cannon and musket-shot, as fast as we could charge and discharge; our cannoneers with one shot broke the carriage of one of the battering pieces, and slew the cannoneer; and thus we continued all the day long, and all the night ..."* recorded one of the Committee members later. [5]

According to a story handed down over the years, and quoted by Nichols, a Mr Bent of the Castle Mill in St. Mary's parish, who was a chief gunner in the garrison, during this point in the siege levelled a cannon at the royal tent pitched at the Rawdykes, fired, and struck off the king's hat from his head. [6] Another shot from the garrison artillery is said to have 'dismounted' a royalist gun and slain its gunner. Despite incidents such as this the odds were heavily against the defenders. After three to four hours considerable damage had been done to the city walls and outworks, particularly the south wall of the Newarke.

"... six great peices [sic] *from the* [royalist] *fort on the South side of the towne, playing on a stone wall unlyned, and made ere 6 of the clock a breach of great space, musketts and cannon continually putting us in mind of some thing done."* Reported Symonds in his diary. [7]

Hollings claims that the area of this wall thus battered, unsupported by earthworks, was that leading to Swan's Mill. The loopholes near that part of the wall remaining in his day are featured in the illustrations in the last chapter of this book. The main breach in the south wall of the Newarke appears to have been made in that part of it which was in present day Mill Lane. It is also thought to have been the part

The garrison's artillery fired in response to the royalist bombardment

adjacent to the property of Master Wadland, the clerk to the Militia Committee, who had objected to the construction of any fortification work which would have cut up his land. According to a post-siege account by Major Innes, when the wall was breached the defenders raised a counter line parallel to the stone wall.

The worn and hardpresseddefenders were able to throw up a breastwork five or six yards inside the breach, lining it with woolpacks dragged from the woolstaplers' yards in the area. The women and children of the town are recorded as giving the most active and fearless help. For the next six hours, with shots flying about them and in the face of continued assault, they repaired the breach.

"... the women of the town wrought at it, although the cannon bullets and some splinters of stones fell amongst them, and hurt some of them; yet, to their exceeding commendation, they went on, and made it up, to the enemy's admiration." [8]

The contribution of the women of the town to this and later stages of the defence of Leicester is widely referred to by commentators, including royalists, with considerable respect.

"By Friday night, they [the royalist artillery] *had made wide breaches, which, by the industry of the men and women of the town, were some of them made up again with woolpacks and other materials; but the enemy pressing hard upon them with their numbers, and that round about the town, they were hard put to it, the enemy being numerous without, and they but few within, and the works very large."* [9]

"The night brought on the thunder and lightning of cannon and the rattling of cannon-balls on the houses and in the streets." [10]

John Hollings, writing in 1840, remarks how the angles of the marks of the cannon shot (some of which appeared to have been fired at near point-blank range) on the considerable remains of the south

The defenders (including the women) work to construct the breastwork behind the breach in the south wall of the Newarke using woolpacks

wall of the Newarke, in his time, clearly demonstrate the existence of two separate royalist batteries. **"By following the lines of fire indicated in this manner, additional evidence is gained as to the exact position of the breaching guns of the besiegers. All the features of the spot, which thus vividly gives evidence of a strife from which we are separated by a period of nearly two centuries, will be found well to repay the trouble of a personal inspection."** [11] Unfortunately, as we begin the twenty-first century, over another one and a half centuries even further on, this is no longer so easy to do.

Hollings describes the period before the midnight assault as follows:- **"While the royalists were actively engaged in levelling as much of the defences opposite their guns as might appear necessary to ensure a passage into the interior of the Newarke, the parties entrusted to maintain it had not been idle, having been busily employed as well in returning without intermission the fire of the enemy with their musketry and artillery, as in throwing up what Simmonds [i.e. Symonds] calls *"a handsome retrenchment,"* or breast-work, within four or five yards of the wall, composed of many waggon loads of woolpacks and other materials brought hastily together, and in this labour the women of Leicester are recorded to have taken their share with the most fearless resolution, altogether regardless of the shot flying about them, or the still greater danger from the fragments which were continually struck from the stones in their vicinity. For six hours after the breach had been considered practicable, the firing was continued uninterruptedly on both sides, the royalists being employed almost the whole of this time in making the necessary preparations for a general assault, which had been determined upon by a council of war; and at midnight, all arrangements having been at length completed, the commencement of the threatened storm was announced by a discharge of the whole of the artillery of the besiegers at the same moment."** [12]

King Charles was determined to take Leicester quickly by storming rather than to waste time with a siege. He was urged on in this strategy by Prince Rupert who had previously taken Bristol, Cirencester, Birmingham, and other places by storm. Any doubts the king might have had would have been removed by his experience at Gloucester in 1643. There he had over-ruled Prince Rupert and opted for a time-consuming siege. Gloucester's defences had been inferior to those of Bristol, which had been taken earlier by Rupert, but assaulting a fortified town always cost lives. The king had been upset by the heavy cavalier losses sustained around and on the walls of Bristol. *"As gallant gentlemen as ever drew sword,"* he had lamented, *"lay upon the ground like rotting sheep."* He had, therefore, opted to take Gloucester by a long siege. In the event the siege had been raised by a parliamentarian army under the Earl of Essex which included the London Trained Bands and soldiers from the east midlands led by Lord Grey of Groby. Charles was now determined not to make the same mistake again.

Orders were sent to the commanding officers of the royalist brigades to prepare for a co-ordinated general assault at midnight. Sir Bernard Astley was directed to storm the town from the north side, both across the river and at a drawbridge facing Leicester Abbey. Sir Henry Bard, from the neighbourhood of St. Margaret's, was to take the hornwork along the eastern line, Belgrave Gate, and the East Gate. Colonel John Russell, at the head of Prince Rupert's Bluecoats, was to engage the Main Guard, the chief town battery, outside the Horsefair Leas. Colonel George Lisle, with the largest concentration of royalist infantry, was to storm the breach in the south wall of the Newarke. A further twenty groups of 100 to 200 men were to converge on the walls in different places in an attempt to over-run the town.

Both sides began last minute preparations for the storming that all knew must soon come. The royalists had cut down many bushes and made them into bundles of faggots with the intention of filling up the fosses or ditches in front of the defensive lines so that they might pass the more easily over them. This did not go unnoticed by the defenders. As Symonds records, *"After the breach was made in the wall by our cannon, by six of the clock, they in the town had gotten up a handsome retrenchment with three flankers (including a great Spanish piece) within 4 or 5 yards of the wall."* [13] These included some of the garrison's largest guns and were positioned just behind the hastily repaired breach in the south wall of the Newarke in order to repel the anticipated attack.

Another royalist source, Slingsby, describes how despite hindering fire the defenders *"made a traverse & flank'd it to defend yt* (that) *part."* [14] This seems to indicate that an earthen rampart was thrown up inside the Newarke breach with three projecting bastions, thus giving flanking fire cover.

Symonds continues, *"All the evening was a general preparation to assault the town, and a little after 12 of the clock in the night this violent storm began, and continued till after one."* [15]

The defenders, *"by reason of the smallness of their numbers and the largeness of their works, were enforced to do duty Wednesday, Thursday, and Friday nights together, the enemy keeping them in constant alarm; which did so tire out the townsmen, that they were the more unfit for the resisting the furious enemy; though, to give them their due, they did as much as could be expected, considering the opposition; for, the enemy had about 4,000 foot, who stormed in so many places at once, that the defendants, wanting reserves, were the more easily over-mastered."* [16]

The garrison, subjected to a midnight storming from all sides had to contend with well over twenty simultaneous attacks. The royalists, whose field-word was *'God and the Prince'*, attacked with bodies of horse behind their infantry to force them on and to prevent retreat or desertion.

The Newarke saw the fiercest assault and the hardest fighting. Surging forward into the breach in the south wall the royalist foot of Colonel George Lisle's brigade were subjected to a hail of shot from the parliamentarians and many were slain. Having reached the breach they were engaged at push of pike. Here, in the limited sace, their greater numbers were of no immediate advantage. Four

139

times the royalists were driven back by the defenders. Each time they were forced to rally by their officers and the horse and driven forward again. The fighting was often at hand to hand and the defenders captured enemy colours as they repelled the attacks. As a parliamentarian report records,

"At the Newarke breach was the fiercest assault; the enemy there coming to push of pike : four times they attempted, and were as often repulsed, our men taking two of their colours from them, and plucked many of their pikes out of their hands; and captain Hacker and captain Babington, with their horse [stationed before the inner breastwork], and the cannon from the corner of the wall, made a miserable slaughter of them; amongst the rest colonel [William] *St. George, in a bravery, (to give example to his men), came up to our cannon (facing the breach), and was by it shattered into small pieces, and with him many more; for, after the manner of the Turks, the horse forced on the foot to fight; they beaten on by our musketeers, great slaughter was made of them on the other side of the wall."* [17]

To strengthen the defence a piece *"of our best cannon"* (probably the 'great Spanish piece') was brought up by the parliamentarians (from the Horsefair Leys), loaded with case shot and *"did wonderful execution upon the enemy."*

The conflict at the Newarke throughout was hard and many brave individual deeds were observed. The defenders had had little sleep for three days since they had been on watch for two nights, and had fought and built or repaired the defences by day. Some contemporary observers considered that their performance in defence of the Newarke ranked as one of the most striking examples of courage throughout the entire Civil War.

The artillery fire of the royalists, in addition to being directed against those parts of the south wall of the Newarke in the vicinity of the breach, was spread along a great extent of the southern and eastern

One of the attacks on the Newarke breach

141

defences. Mention was later made in the Corporation accounts for the sum of *"£3. 3s. paid to sundry workmen for taking down divers houses near the South Gate."* Both Nichols and Throsby considered that this was because of damage sustained by these houses during the siege. Also, when the old East Gates were finally taken down, several cannon balls of a large size were found in the woodwork forming part of the structure.

Unfortunately for the gallant and hard pressed defenders the enemy attacks were going better elsewhere than at the Newarke. On the eastern side Sir Henry Bard's tertia attacked the walls with scaling ladders; some near a flanker (a cannon emplacement) and others attempted to scale the hornwork in front of the drawbridge on the east side. The initial attacks were unsuccessful, the defending musketry and cannon fire making a great slaughter of the attackers as they swarmed to mount the scaling ladders.

Sir Henry Bard had lost an arm through wounds sustained at Cheriton in March 1644. Still a young man, he now led his Greycoats in the assault against the works by climbing the ladder one-handed.

Colonel Bard was himself now injured again and his division was compelled to retire, but they then returned with greater success, as a parliamentarian account records:-

"Colonel Sir Henry Bard, at Belgrave-gate, endeavouring to scale, was beaten down by the butt-end of a musket, the bruise whereof was seen by some of us; and his major likewise stricken down by his side; 16 of his men were slain upon the place, and 60 more mortally wounded out of 250, as himself reported; but, setting upon it again, on a second attempt, with hand grenadoes[18] *thrown in amongst our men, entered within the works. Bard then broke down the drawbridge, and made way for the horse to enter ..."* [19]

The Earl of Northampton's Horse then poured into the area between the earthworks (or outworks) and the city walls. Symonds records this part of the action as follows:- *"On the east side of the town*

Colonel Henry Bard's men attempt to break in on the eastern side of the town

Colonel Bard's tertia fell on, some neare a flanker, and others scaled the horne worke before the drawbridge on the east side." [20]

Slingsby adds that:- *"some with Ladders gets over their works, others break ye chains & letts down ye drawbridge & fells down ye works in 2 or 3 several places yt (that) our horse may enter."* [21]

A similar breakthrough occurred at the outworks leading to Galtrey-gate (the modern Gallowtree Gate). The parliamentarian report in Nichols records:- *"... so again at Galtrey-gate, the enemy* [in this case Prince Rupert's Bluecoats] *threw in hand grenadoes abundantly, which terribly burned our men; and, seconding them with squadrons of musketeers, our men were killed and beaten off; and there they also entered. The horse being come in, they rode in a full career in a body of about 600 up the streets, clearing them as they went ..."* [22]

The attackers then fought their way along the North and East defensive lines between the outworks and the city walls. At the same time Sir Bernard Astley's brigade had been attacking from the north side across the river and at a drawbridge in the direction of Leicester Abbey. They stormed through at the North Mills, apparently a place of some strength and importance to the defence, and planting three scaling ladders against the earthworks between St. Margaret's Church and Belgrave Gate, the royalists began to enter from this direction also. The defenders in this area were now attacked from three directions. Lieutenant-Colonel Whitbrook and Captain Farmer, both veterans of campaigns in the Low Countries, were killed. Captain Hurst, another officer of foot in the garrison, was also slain. Colonel Henry Grey, hurrying to the support of his men defending the area around St. Margaret's Church, was sorely wounded in several places and taken prisoner. Meanwhile Captain Francis Hacker and his cavalry were engaged in fierce fighting near the West Bridge.

Colonel Henry Grey is wounded and captured
near St. Margaret's

145

Hollings notes that Throsby had recorded how, " **About the year 1759 two human skeletons were found lying about two feet below the surface, near the North Mill, Leicester; two bullets, which we may conjecture were lodged previously in their bodies, were also found lying by them.**" [23] He also states that several skeletons were subsequently discovered in St. Margaret's Cow Pasture by the workmen employed in forming the bed of the canal - in all probability, like the other two, the remains of some members of Sir Bernard Astley's brigade who had been killed during the attack on the North Mills and had been buried near the spot where they fell.

On the south side towards the east of the Newarke the Main Guard was assaulted by Colonel John Russell's Brigade. Prince Rupert's Bluecoat Regiment of Foot attacked with scaling ladders and were supported by Prince Rupert's Firelocks in their red coats. Major Bunnington, a gentleman-pensioner in Prince Rupert's Firelocks, was shot in the eye just as he reached the top of one of the ladders. The assault succeeded, however, and as Symonds records:- *"... They set up the Prince's black colours* [distinctive German-style black wedges and circles on a white field] *on the great battery, where the Earl of Northampton's Horse ... were let in at the ports, and they scowered the line and town; in the mean time the Foot got in and fell to plunder, so that ere day fully opened scarcely a cottage was unplundered."* [24]

There were rumours later, from parliamentarian sources, of betrayal; in that someone opened the East Gate to the enemy once they had penetrated the outworks. There is a reference to *"one Smith, a lieutenant, who let them in as soon as he could,* [and] *is since made a captain by colonel Hastings."* [25]

Clarendon records the progress of the assault on Leicester in the following terms:- *"... the battery began to play, and in the space of four hours made such a breach* [at the Newarke] *that it was thought counsellable* [sic] *the same night to make a general assault with the whole army in several places, but principally at the breach; which was defended with great courage and resolution,*

insomuch that the King's forces were twice repulsed with great loss and slaughter, and were even ready to draw off in despair when another party, on the other side of the town, under the command of Colonel Page, seconded by a body of horse that came but that day from Newark, and, putting themselves on foot, advanced with their swords and pistols with the other, entered the town, and made way for their fellows to follow them : so that by break of day, the assault having continued all the night, all the King's army entered the line." [26]

As the royalists poured through the outworks and into the town the resistance at the Newarke continued. The king was obliged to send in his own Life Guard of Foot in their red coats and with their distinctive royal company colours to stiffen the shaken and badly mauled soldiers of Lisle's brigade. As one commentator records:- *"It is said that, at the breach, many women fought with the most resolute courage, and spurned the danger."* [27]

The royalist officer from Shropshire recorded how:- *"The inhabitants to shew their over-forward zeal to defend the town, fought in the breach; nay, the very women, to the honour of the Leicester Ladies (if they like it), officiously did their parts ..."* [28]

At one point the royalists had entered the breach and had beaten the parliamentarian musketeers back from the loopholes of the wall, but they were themselves forced back by a timely charge of horse. The latter were assisted in this by Major Innes and his dismounted dragoons, armed with carbines, who had come to the Newarke breach as they fell back from the Main Guard. Innes then succeeded in repulsing the enemy attacks through the breach five times whilst the regular garrison troops and many of the townsfolk retired into the buildings of the *'Newarke fort'*. At the breach the defenders captured two more royalist colours. Participants later commended the bravery of a German dragoon, who had dismounted and voluntarily taken the place of the slain principal gunner of the garrison's *'great piece'*, keeping it in action facing the breach, until he was transfixed beside it by a pike.

The defence of the Newarke breach was heroic right up to the very end

Slingsby recorded that the royalists entered the breach three times but were each time repulsed. The attackers at last effected another entrance at the breach, being reinforced by the party of horse newly arrived from Newark in Nottinghamshire, who had dismounted and entered the conflict fresh, fighting with swords and pistols, against the now very weary defenders. This force would appear to have been reinforcements for the 1,200 Newark horse, under Sir Richard Willys, who had already joined the king before the siege began. The town's defenders still fought step by step and contested every yard of ground with the royalists. Eventually, attacked from behind by royalist horse and foot who had arrived from the northern and eastern parts of the town as well as those pouring in through the breach in the south wall, the parliamentarians were forced to give way.

According to Symonds:- *"The garrison were at length driven from the fortifications, at and near the old castle in the Newark, to St. Martin's Church and church-yard, where they made a stand; but were soon after driven thence, from street to street, avenue to avenue, into the market-place ..."* [29]

Heath's Chronicle records this stage of the fighting as follows:- *"The works being seized, there remained a work of greater bloodshed, the Market-Place, where the defendants had drawn up their artillery, and for three hours space maintained their fight at the cross therein."* [30]

Small skirmishes were also taking place all over the town but the main centres of resistance were located in the *'Newarke fort'*, the area around the High Cross in the Wednesday Market Place, and St. Martin's Church and churchyard. Those defenders, both soldiers and townspeople, who had been driven back from the southern perimeter and the Newarke wall retreated, fighting, up Highcross street. The enemy pursued them, to be received by volleys of musketry from house windows and by hails of assorted tiles, stones, and other missiles from the house tops. The defenders from the eastern side of the town also fought on as they retreated up the High Street.

151

There is an oral tradition in Leicester that several people lost their lives in St. Martin's churchyard (now the site of Leicester Cathedral). Fighting persisted there for an hour and some of the defenders are said to have gained admittance into the church, and from there annoyed the king's forces by sniping and throwing objects from the battlements and leads. It appears from the following item in the parish book of the time that the royalists broke into the church to drive them out:- *"Paid Francis Motley for mendinge* [sic] *the locks of the church doors broke by the King's army 3s."* [31]

There is also a record of a charge in the churchwardens' accounts for that year, according to Throsby, for the payment of Wm. Hastwell, mason, for *"Leyinge downe many graves, which weare taken up at the burienge of several great officers of the King's army, which was slaine at the stormeinge of the town."* One royalist officer who was buried in St. Martin's Church had died of his wounds at the Red Lion Inn. [32]

Those defenders who escaped from the churchyard fell back to the High Cross where the main stand was being made under the cover of the remnants of the garrison's cannon and cavalry. The parliamentarian horse rode out under either Major Innes or Captain Babington (depending upon which version one accepts) and charged the royalist cavalry, who were driven back from the market place to the South Gate. On rallying there, under, in turn, the protection of their own and more numerous infantry and cannon, the royalists forced a parliamentarian retreat back to the High Cross. Here, according to a parliamentarian report:- *"... our horse, that all this while had backed our foot, and kept them to their duty, now were themselves put to it, and behaved themselves resolutely, and held the fight in the town almost an hour after, betaking themselves to places of strength, enforced to ask quarter for their lives; and some of them escaped, having gotten the enemies' word which was `God and the Prince!"* [33]

The royalists now, in ever greater numbers, converged upon the town's defenders at the market place from all directions. The

The fighting in St. Martin's churchyard

The last stand of the parliamentarians at the High Cross
in the Market Place

154

parliamentarians eventually had no option but to throw down their weapons and ask for quarter. At first this was refused; some defenders, soldiers and townsfolk alike, being killed in the heat of the moment. According to the rules of war of that time the garrison of a town that had refused a summons to surrender had no automatic right to be granted quarter. In particular there was one house in Leicester which appeared to have been more strongly defended, and for longer, than most. This was a house where some of the members of the local parliamentarian County Committee had been meeting. It was said that some Scottish soldiers attached to the garrison had retreated into it and fired upon the attackers right up to the last minute. Some seven or eight royalist dragoons were killed by shots from this place. The royalists stormed the house, set it on fire and put all of its inmates to the sword without mercy. It seems that the Presbyterian Scots soldiers were viewed as particular enemies by the 'cavaliers' in much the same way as the Catholic Irish soldiers on the other side were viewed by the 'roundheads'.

A little earlier the defenders occupying the *'Newarke fort'* had been surrounded and had agreed to surrender on conditions of personal safety and exemption from plunder. This proved to be a pious hope in the circumstances. The parliamentarian chronicler, John Rushworth, records how the members of the garrison had capitulated *"upon Composition, ... that neither clothes nor money should be taken away from any of the soldiers of that fort ... Nor any violence offered to them."* But, he continues, *"the King's soldiers, contrary to the articles, fell upon the soldiers, stripped, cut, and wounded many of them."* [34]

At the time of the trial of the king later, in January 1649, a Humphrey Brown, a husbandman of Whissendine in Rutland, swore as a witness:- *"That at such time as the town of Leicester was taken by the forces of Charles the First, being in or about June 1645, Newark fort, in Leicester, was surrendered to the King, upon condition, that neither cloathe [sic] nor money should be taken from any of the garrison. which had surrendered; nor any violence should be offered to them; and that, as soon as the fort was*

The ill-treatment of the parliamentarian prisoners, taken at the Newarke fort, with *the king on horseback in bright armour*.

upon such consideration so surrendered, the King's soldiers, contrary to the articles, fell upon the soldiers of the fort; did strip and wound may of them; whereupon one of the King's officers rebuking some of those soldiers, this deponent did hear the King say, `I do not care if they cut them three times more, for they are mine enemies'; or words to such effect. And that the King was on horse-back, in bright armour, in the said town of Leicester." [35]

NOTES:

1. John Nichols, Appendix to the *History of Leicestershire*, Vol. III; Part II. The Civil War in Leicestershire, p. 47.
2. Richard Symonds, *Diary of the Marches of the Royal Army During the Great Civil War Kept by Richard Symonds'*, ed. C. E. Long, Camden Society. Vol 74., London, 1859, p. 44.
3. John Hollings, *The History of Leicester during the Great Civil War*, Leicester, 1840. p. 49.
4. Nichols, op. cit., p. 48.
5. Ibid, p. 48.
6. Ibid, p. 42. (footnote)
7. Symonds, op. cit., p. 44.
8. Nichols, op. cit., p. 47.
9. Ibid, p. 52.
10. Ibid, p. 45.
11. Hollings, op. cit., p. 52.
12. Ibid, p. 52.
13. Symonds, op. cit., p. 44.
14. Slingsby, *The Diary of Sir Henry Slingsby*, ed. D. Parsons, London, 1836, pp. 147-8
15. Ibid, p. 44.
16. Nichols, op. cit., p. 52.
17. Ibid, p. 48.
18. 'Hand grenadoes' were essentially hand thrown bombs made of pottery with a wooden tube inserted as a fuse (or 'fusee') filled with fine gunpowder which acted as a time fuse. The grenades themselves were not only explosive but scattered 'wildfire' (hence the expression "to spread like wildfire"), an early equivalent of modern napalm. Timing was critical in their use in order to prevent the 'grenado' from exploding in one's own hand or being thrown back by the enemy.
19. Nichols, op. cit., p. 48.
20. Symonds, op. cit., p.44.
21. Slingsby, op. cit., pp. 147-8
22. Nichols, op. cit., p. 48.
23. Hollings, p. 61.
24. Symonds, op. cit., p. 44.

25. Nichols, op. cit., p. 53.

26. Clarendon, Book IX, p.33.

27. Nichols, op. cit., p.45.

28. Ibid, p. 46. In the war between King and Parliament which rent the fabric of English society in the middle years of the seventeenth century, the women of England often played an active part. Some, indeed, displayed a courage so far above the traditional role of their sex as to surprise, and frequently disconcert, their men. Alison Plowden in *Women All On Fire - The Women of the English Civil War* cites the following comment from a chronicler of the siege of Chester, also in 1645. ***"Our women are all on fire, striving through a gallant emulation to outdoe our men and will make good our yielding walls or loose*** (sic) ***their lives."*** The women defending Chester were doing so for the royalist cause; parliamentarian examples even by Alison Plowden were those of Bristol and Gloucester. Unfortunately she fails to mention the heroic role of the women in the defence of Leicester.

29. Symonds, cited in Nichols, p. 45.

30. Heath's Chronicle, cited in Nichols, p. 42.

31. Nichols, op. cit., p. 46.

32. John Throsby, *Select Views of Leicestershire - from original drawings - containing seats of the nobility and gentry, town views and ruins, accompanied with descriptive and historical relations.* Published 1789. pp. 119 - 123.

33. Nichols, op. cit., p. 53.

34. John Rushworth, *Historical Collections of Private Passages of State*, Part IV, Vol. II, p.1411.

35. Ibid. p. 42.

King Charles I in armour

Prince Rupert of the Rhineland Palatine

161

Prince Rupert summoning the garrison of Leicester to surrender to the army of Charles I, May 30th 1645

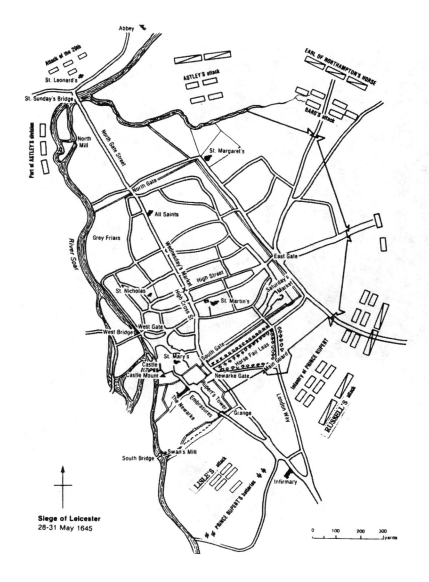

Abbey
Attack of the 29th
St. Leonard's
St. Sunday's Bridge
Part of ASTLEY's division
North Mill
North Gate Street
St. Margaret's
ASTLEY'S attack
EARL OF NORTHAMPTON'S HORSE
BARD's attack
North Gate
All Saints
Grey Friars
River Soar
Wednesday's Market
High Street
East Gate
St. Nicholas
High Cross St.
Saturday's Market
St. Martin's
West Bridge
West Gate
South Gate
Horse Fair Leas
Infantry of PRINCE RUPERT
St. Mary's
Castle
Castle Mount
Newarke Gate
Main Guard
RUSSELL'S attack
Rupert's Tower
The Newarke
Embrasures
Grange
London Way
Swan's Mill
South Bridge
LISLE'S attack
PRINCE RUPERT'S batteries
Infirmary

Siege of Leicester
28-31 May 1645

0   100   200   300
.1yards

Map – The Siege of Leicester – 28-31 May 1645

163

Prince Maurice

164

James Compton, Third Earl of Northampton

Sir William Compton

Colonel John Russell

Sir Richard Willys

Lord Bernard Stuart, Lord Lichfield (pictured on the right)

Sir Richard Byron

John, First Lord Byron

171

S.ʳ Marmaduke Langdale, the firſt Lord Langdale,
From a Picture of him in the Poſſeſsion of Marmaduke Lord Langdale,
at Holme on Spaldingmore 1774

Sir Marmaduke Langdale

Sr Bernard Astley
Col. & Son of Sr Jacob Astley

From a Painting at Sir Jacob Astley's House
call'd the Palace at Maidstone in Kent.

Vol. 2. P. 546

88

Sir Bernard Astley

Sir George Lisle (Engraving)

Sir George Lisle (Oil Painting)

175

Colonel William Legge

Colonel Sir George Gerard

177

Hon. Persiana Bard

178

CHAPTER SIX

THE FALL

**"Turn thou us unto thee, O Lord, and we shall be turned;
Renew our days as of old."**
Lamentations Chapter 5, vs. 21.

The accounts of the losses suffered in the storming of Leicester and of the nature and extent of the atrocities that followed its surrender vary; and not always strictly according to the allegiance of the commentator.

Bulstrode Whitelock records that, *"The king's forces, having entered the town, had a hot encounter at the market-place; and many of them were slain by shot out of windows; that they gave no quarter, but hanged some of the committee, and cut others to pieces. Some letters say that the kennels* [gutters] *ran down with blood; that Colonel Grey the governor, and Captain Hacker, were wounded and taken prisoners, and very many of the garrison put to the sword, and the town miserably plundered. The King entered the town on Sunday, June 1; and sent part of his forces into Derbyshire."* [1]

The royalist *Mercurius Rusticus* more matter-of-factly reports that: *"May 30, his Majesty's army sat down before Leicester; and in the morrow morning early took it by storm, and in it the whole Committee, Sir Robert Pye, and many hundred prisoners, many horses, much powder, arms, and ordnance, and great store of wealth."* [2]

Heath's Chronicle tells how:- *"... the committee-men, with Sir Robert Pye, colonel Hacker, and colonel Grey* [were] *taken prisoners, and put into custody; only Sir Robert had some more respect shewed him. The town was plundered, and some of the inhabitants for the present secured; the spoil, part of it carried*

179

*away to the King's adjacent garrisons of Newark, Ashby-de-la-
Zouch, and Belvoir."* [(3)]

Richard Symonds relates how:- *"... the foot got in, and fell to
plunder, so that ere the day fully opened scarcely a cottage was
unplundered. There were many Scots in this town, and no
quarter given to any in the heat. More dead bodies lay just
within the line far than without or on the grass. I told 30 and
more at the breach, as many within as without. Every street
had some."* [(4)]

Two accounts in particular give a detailed and relatively balanced
account, coming as they do from partisans who give credit, however
grudgingly, to the opposing side.

The first account is from the Shropshire royalist officer who took
part in the siege and storming.

*"This was but a short siege; for the King, resolving to lose no
time, fell on with his great guns, and, having beaten down their
works, our foot entered after a vigorous resistance, and took
the town by storm. There was some blood shed here, the town
being carried by assault, though it was their own faults; for,
after the town was taken, the soldiers and townsmen obstinately
fought us in the market-place; insomuch that the horse were
called to enter the town and clear the streets. But this was not
all; I was commanded to advance with the horse, being three
regiments and to enter the town; the foot who were engaged in
the streets, crying out, `horse! horse!' Immediately I advanced
to the gate, for we were drawn up about a musket shot from the
works, to have supported our foot in the case of a sally. Having
seized the gate, I placed a guard of horse there, with orders to
let nobody pass in or out; and, dividing my troops, rode up by
two ways towards the market place; the garrison defending
themselves there and in the churchyard with great obstinacy,
killed a great many men; but, as soon as our horse appeared
they demanded quarter, which our foot refused them in the first
heat, as is frequent in all nations in like cases, till at last they*

threw down their arms and yielded at discretion; and then I can testify to the world that fair quarter was given them. I am the more particular in this relation, having been an eye-witness of the action, and because the King was reproached in all the public libels, with which those times abounded, for having put a great many to death, and hanged the Committee of the Parliament and some Scots in cold blood, which was a notorious forgery; and I am sure there was no such thing done. I must acknowledge I never saw any inclination in his Majesty to cruelty, or to act any thing which was not practised by the general laws of war, and by men of honour in all nations. But the matter of fact in respect to the garrison was as I have related; and if they had thrown down their arms sooner, they had had mercy sooner; but it was not for a conquering army, entering a town by storm, to offer conditions of quarter in the streets. Another circumstance was that a great many of the inhabitants, both men and women, were killed which is most true; and the case was thus. The inhabitants, to shew their over-forward zeal to defend the town, fought in the breach; nay, the very women, to the honour of the Leicester ladies (if they like it), officiously did their parts; and after the town was taken, and when, if they had been possessed of any discretion with their zeal, they would have kept their houses and been quiet, they fired upon our men out of their windows, from the tops of houses, and threw tiles upon their heads; several of my men being wounded so, and 7 or 8-killed. This exasperated us to the last degree; and finding one house better manned than ordinary, and many shot fired at us out of the windows, I caused my men to attack it, and resolved to make them an example for the rest; which they did; and breaking open the doors, they killed all they found there without distinction; and I appeal to the world if they were to blame. If the Parliament Committee, or the Scots' deputies were here, they ought to have been quiet, sincethe town was taken : but they began it with us, and, I think, brought it upon themselves. This is the whole case, so far as came within my knowledge, for which his Majesty was so much abused. We took here colonel Grey and captain Hacker, about 300 prisoners, and about 300 more were killed. This was the last day of May, 1645." [5]

181

The second account comes from a parliamentarian publication entitled *Perfect Relation of the Taking of Leicester* dated 9th June 1645. Much of the information in this report seems to have come from Major James Innes, on parole to seek a prisoner exchange, who was now at Northampton.

"Sir; To satisfy your request in your letter touching the condition of Leicester, I have endeavoured to inform myself from the most moderate nd understanding men that were sufferers in that general loss, and eye-witnesses of the whole carriage of that sad business, that are since fled hither [Northampton] for refuge ... At their first coing in they [the royalists] slaughtered many, until ours had lain down their arms and yielded themselves prisoners; and then they fell to their plundering work, and catching of men to be their prisoners, executing their accustomed cruelty to men and women, to find out their money and best goods. The gentlemen of the Committee, Sir Robert Pye, and Major Innes were carried before the Prince to their inn [the Red Lion], who disposed them to several houses as prisoners; the last two, upon their parole, were set at liberty, to procure exchange. The Committee were yet kept prisoners in the town. Many other gentlemen of the country and officers of the garrison were sent, with the best of the plunder, to their several garrisons of Newark, Lichfield, and Belvoir; 140 cartloads of the best goods and wares in the shops were sent away by Saturday noon with a convey of horse.

I find some of the pamphlets speaking of the horrid cruelty of the insulting enemy putting man, woman and child to the sword. I know their tender mercies are cruelties; but (give the Devil his due) there were indeed many slain at the first entrance, and some that made little resistance, and some women and children amongst the multitude, by the rabble of common soldiers; but I cannot learn of any such order given to destroy all, as is said by some. And it is the general opinion of many that have since got out of the town, that in the conflict and since there were not slain of the Parliament's party, soldiers and others, above 100, and some of those in cold blood after they had granted quarter of life; picking out some active men, and setting common soldiers to quarrel with them and slay them; but of these not many. It is confidently believed that not above 300 are slain on both sides. The town was full of wealth, which the countries had brought in for safety. They took there nine pieces of ordnance, great and small, above 1,000 muskets, near 400 horses and arms, and about 50 barrels of powder, besides what was spent in the service." [6]

This account also includes the following passage:- *"All speak* [at the taking of the town by the Royalists] *of their cruelty to the Scots, slaying divers of them in cold blood after quarter given to them; but this is said to be by the Irish in the King's army, and English Papists their adherents."* [7]

Whitelock confirms much of the above analysis when he records on 7th June 1645 that, *"letters from Leicester informed that the Committee men and the Scots there were not killed in cold blood, as was before reported; but that the King's forces killed divers who prayed for quarter, and put divers women to the sword, and other women and children they turned naked into the streets, and many they ravished."* [8]

The nineteenth century Leicestershire historian, James Thompson, paints the following graphic picture of the immediate aftermat of the storming of Leicester.

"At daybreak all the direful and revolting scenes witnessed in a town taken by storm followed the surrender. The women were exposed to the unmeasured brutalities of a licentious soldiery. The shops were broken into and rifled of their contents. Dwelling houses were entered, and the money, valuables and goods of the inhabitants - which had been increased in amount by the large stores brought into the town for security -were taken away by the plunderers. The record room of the borough was invaded, and robbed of its charters. The mace and seals were stolen by the king's soldiers. Every street presented some scene of blood or outrage. Dead and

dying men were on the pavement - naked women thrown down in the public streets. The curses and ribald conversation of the drunken cavaliers mingled with the groans of the dying and the screams of the outraged or widowed women. Such were the scenes and such the sounds which greeted the eyes and the ears of men in Leicester, when the morning opened on the last day of May, 1645". [9]

It is said that during the storming of the town King Charles urged the defenders to lay down their arms and to seek quarter. Accounts vary as to just where and when this occurred. One story is that as he watched the storming from the Raw Dykes he repeatedly said (as if to himself), *"Dear and loving subjects, cry quarter: dear and loving subjects, obey!"* [10]

Another version is that he rode through the streets of Leicester towards the High Cross in the closing stages of the fighting crying much the same message out loud to those still resisting. This image contrasts strongly with that attested to by Humphrey Brown, the Rutland farm-labourer quoted earlier, who recalled the king's alleged reference to the brutalising of parliamentarian prisoners, *"I do not care if they cut them three times more, for they are mine enemies."* It has been commented, however, by some who have studied the character of Charles I that it is quite probable that both stories are true.

The king spent the night of the fall of Leicester at the Countess of Devonshire's huse at Leicester Abbey. During the night parties of royalist horse faced the town in order to prevent any of the defenders from escaping under the cover of darkness. Some of the parliamentarian horse had already escaed, having discovered the royalists' watchword, *'God and the Prince'*. One of these was Francis Hacker who, according to Major James Innes' account, had ridden out through the breach in the Newarke wall towards the end of the confused fighting there. Unfortunately for him he was discovered by royalists at Belgrave and brought back to Leicester. At dawn on the Saturday morning about ten of the defenders broke out on the river side (i.e. the west) and were pursued. Hollings' account, unlike that of Innes, combines the two incidents and seems the more ikely, although it has the same end result. **"Captain Hacker, who had, early in the morning, with a few others, made his escape over the river [** i.e. Soar] **at the Pike head, was not more fortunate than his companions in arms, since, after being closely pursued, he was taken near Braunstone** [a village to the west of Leicester], **and subjected to the same confinement as the rest."** [11]

Some of the captured officers and soldiers could expect to be exchanged for royalist prisoners held by the parliamentarians. Some of the wealthier townsfolk could expect to ransom their freedom. Others, either notorious for their zeal for the temporarily losing cause or too poor to bribe their greedy captors, might rather fear for their lives and/or limbs. A parliamentarian source spoke of the *"many ... bloody outrages committed, the like scarce to be paralleled,"* for *"after they had entered the town, they killed many that begged for quarter, and put divers women inhumanly to the sword ... they turned divers women and children out of their houses into the open streets, almost naked and succourless, and some of them they committed to prison, where they be now in great misery."* They also *"hanged Master Raynor, an honest, religious gentleman, and one Mr. Sawer in cold blood."*[12]

The plundering was also extensive. *"They dealt also extremely cruelly with the town, plundering all they had, and putting many to great ransoms when they had taken away all their moneys and goods, and compelling many to march along with them, in case they were not able to give them their demand; insomuch that it is to be feared, unless some course be taken for their relief, Leicester cannot provide victuals for themselves, much less to accommodate a garrison; and divers in the country are in the same estate; for, some that we know of £40, £50, £80, and £100, a year revenue are turned into rags, plundered house and field, and almost all the well-affected thrust out of the town, whole families, wives and children, without any compassion."* [13]

185

The royalist soldiers plundered the town extensively after its capture

This lack of adherence to the articles of surrender was confirmed even by the royalists themselves. The King's Secretary for War, Sir Edward Walker, admitted that *"the town* [was] *miserably sackt* (sic) *without regard to church or hospital,"* [14] and this was echoed by Clarendon : *"... the conquerors pursued their advantage with the usual license of rapine and plunder, and miserably sacked the whole town, without any distinction of persons or places, churches, and hospitals as well as other houses* [being] *made a prey to the enraged and greedy soldier."* [15] These atrocities, according to Clarendon, were nevertheless *"to the exceeding regret of the King: who well knew that, how disaffected soever that town was generally, there were yet many who had faithful hearts to him."* [16]

Whatever Charles' role in, and attitudes towards, these excesses it is unlikely that he would have had much influence over the behaviour of his troops anyway, because atrocities in the heat of the action are almost bound to be committed in stormings of this nature where the royalists are said to have *"lost three for one in the assault"* [17] including around thirty officers.

This was the initial reaction of even the parliamentarian newsheet *The Moderate Intelligencer* towards the behaviour of the royalist victors at Leicester. *"There was much hurt done in the town its confessed,"* said the issue of 5th June 1645, *"but not anything to speak of more than what was done in heate ... Some women were seen dead, which was casual rather than on purpose."* The following week's issue, however, roundly condemned the king and advised him to *"call to mind, if he have time, the cruelties done to his poore subjects the weeks past, there* [at Leicester], *and in the counties about. Consider how ill gotten goods prosper. Let somebody tell him that his commanders, when they entred* (sic) *Leicester, and in particular the late governour* (sic) *of Campden House* [Sir Henry Bard], *gave command to ravish all, and that he brag'd* (sic) *he had done it the same day several times."* [18] (It had been said earlier by Clarendon of Sir Henry Bard's occupancy of Campden House, before he wantonly burnt it upon joining the king's 'Leicester March', that it *"had brought no other benefits to the public than the enriching the licentious governor thereof, who exercised an illimited* (sic) *tyranny over the whole of the country."*) [19]

As to the actual number of those slain at Leicester *The Moderate Intelligencer*, which was usually fairly accurate in its reporting, claimed that the defenders lost 300 men and the royalists some 400. [20] The royalist *Mercurius Aulicus* refuted this figure for parliamentarian losses and insisted that only 120 'rebels' were slain, *"which may fully stoppe their shameful mouths that offer to talke of cruelty in his Majesties soldiers."* [21] The Leicester Committee in their own report later talked of a total of 719 bodies requiring burial which accords closely with the figures in *The Moderate Intelligencer*. From the return of actual burials taken immediately after the storming the total loss of both sides was given as 709, allowing for a further ten who died later as a result of the injuries they had sustained. The number of royalists killed is recorded as 200 at the places of assault, but those who died later from their wounds were not included in this figure. The royalists lost between twenty-eight and thirty officers, including Colonel St. George. The parliamentarians lost five principal officers, including Lt. Colonel Whitbrooke; though other officers were taken prisoner, some of these later being exchanged for leading royalist prisoners. In total, two colonels, four majors, and three other senior officers were buried in St. Martin's Church, the main church of the borough, and many soldiers in the church-yard there. Another ten officers were buried at St. Margaret's Church. It is likely that the rank and file were buried in mass graves.

The Town Chamberlains' Accounts record an *"Item paid several men for burying fifty dead corpses within Mr. Abney's Ward and the Newarke, when the towne was taken by the kings forces, by command of the Chief Commander* [i.e. Prince Rupert]." [22] In 1951 an archaeological excavation uncovered a mass grave in the herb garden behind Trinity Hospital in the Newarke. This may well have been one of the graves in which those killed in or near the breach, during the fighting there, were buried.

As *The Moderate Intelligencer* reported, not only Leicester itself, but also the county appeared to have suffered at the hands of the royalists, to the extent thought Nehemiah Wallington, that *"the losses will not be repaired there* [for] *seven years"* and that *"in the ruins of Leicester you may behold a large map of misery, the townsmen, from the richest to the poorest, being all of them despoiled of their goods."* [23] For instance, *"... at Wigston two miles from Leicester, they .. most barbarously murdered Mistress Burrowes and two of her children, her husband a godly and religious divine then prisoner in Leicester, if not slain."* [24]

Some of the more polemical parliamentarian sources drew comparisons between the royalists' treatment of Leicester and the notoriously savage sacking of Magdeburg by the Imperialist forces of the Catholic League and the Hapsburg Emperor during the Thirty Years War in Germany. This latter event had become a byword for the horrors of war at the time. The Imperialists had succeeded, after a long siege, in capturing the Lutheran stronghold of Magdeburg in May 1631. The fall of the city was attended by a massacre of the garrison, and of armed and unarmed citizens - men, women, and children alike - in streets, houses, and churches; at least 20,000 perished; wholesale plundering, pillaging, and a general conflagration completed the havoc. The sack of Magdeburg by Count Tilly's cosmopolitan and papist Imperial Army was etched deeply into the psyche of, and evoked the greatest indignation and revulsion from, the Protestants of Europe. In the September of 1631 Gustavus Adolphus, the Swedish king with an army in Germany (including many Scots and also some Englishmen), and a popular Protestant hero, advanced into Saxony where he avenged the carnage of Magdeburg by defeating Tilly's army decisively on the Breitenfeld, near Leipzig. When, it was asked, would the Lord of Hosts grant similar retribution for the slaughter of the godly by the malignants at Leicester?

For the moment, however, King Charles was in good spirits. He wrote to his wife, Henrietta Maria, from Leicester Abbey on Saturday, 31st May, the following letter (originally in cypher) : -

189

"My dear heart,

"I had written to thee from Tutbury Monday last, by the ordinary of Oxford. They stopped my letter, nor am I confident how soon, or if this will come to thee, but I must not stay longer from giving thee thanks for thine of the 19th of May, which assures me of thy health, as likewise to tell thee of the good success which it hath pleased God to give me this day, of taking this town, which was well defended, for the few men that were in it. It was assaulted at a breach and two other places; at the first we were thrice repulsed, because of a strong intrenchment made before the breach, but the other two being weakly manned, our men entered without much opposition, which soon made amends for the strong resistance in the other place, where our men showed as much courage as was possible which got that success their fellows procured than by their successful entrance.

"The number of prisoners, quantities of arms, and ammunition, are not yet certain, but that assuredly they are very considerable. I am now hastening to the relief of Oxford, where, if it shall please God to bless me, according to these beginnings, it may make us see London next winter.

"I am momently, and by good hand, assured that Montrose's late good success is the cause of the Scot's sudden retreat.

"God bless thee, sweet heart.

Leicester Abbey, Saturday 31st May." [(25)]

On the following day the king levied a fine of £2,000 on the already despoiled and impoverished inhabitants of Leicester,

"Charles R.

"Our will and pleasure is That forthwith you cause to be leavyed uppon ye inhabitants of our Towne of Leicester ye summe of two thousand pounds sterling. And that you cause ye same to be payd unto our trustie and wel beloved John Ashbourne Esqr.

190

our Treasurer at Warrs for ye use of our Army. And your dilligent performance hereof shall be taken by us as an expression of your desire to redeeme and expiate your high offences. It being an effect of our clemency that wee afford you ye means of doing it. In this way whereas you may iustly [sic] *expect from us all rigour and severitie. Given at our Courte at Leicester ye first day of June in ye one and twentith yeare of our raigne.*

By his Maiesties Command

George Digbye

To ye late Maior, Aldermen and Corporation of our Towne of Leicester." [26]

In addition to this official fine Leicester had already been thoroughly sacked and plundered. Some 140 wagon loads of looted goods and property were removed to Newark-on-Trent as well as the personal pilfering which filled the pockets and bags of the royalist soldiers. The ceremonial mace, the town seals, and borough archives were *"taken away by unruly soldiers."* [27] Te archives were later recovered, but the search for the mace and seals was to prove fruitless. A meeting of the Common Hall held later on 22nd August decided *"that a Newe Mace shalbe* [sic] *bought about the size of the old mace as neare to the price as conveniently"* together with new *"silver and gilte bosses"* engraved with the Town Arms. A Corporation Seal, a Seal of Office and a Mayor's Seal were also to be procured in order that civic business could be formally resumed. The cost of the new mace proved to be £24. 6s. 6d. [28]

The royalist cause was very much encouraged by the capture of Leicester. The parliamentarians, on the other hand, were seized by fear and apprehension. Both Houses of Parliament were now in the utmost consternation, and conference succeeded conference. The Earl of Northumberland reported from the Committee of Both Kingdoms on 2nd June:-

"That, upon the report of the taking of Leicester, the said Committee do think it fit that Sir Thomas Fairfax with his army before Oxford should rise and take the field" [29] and, *"on consideration of the King's being at Leicester, and the danger to the associated counties thereby; the Committee of Both Kingdoms were to consider of the disposal of the armies under Sir Thomas Fairfax, as may be most advantageous for the publick; and the blocking up of Oxford was left to Major-General Browne."* [30]

Heath's Chronicle records that:- *"The Royal party were as good as sure that the day was their own; which they made appear, even in London, by all public signs and discourses. The King himself, deceived also with this lightning before his ruin, which he construed for the greatest sunshine of his felicity, was of the same opinion; the result thereof appeared in a letter written to the Queen, June the 8th, where he used this expression;*
'I may, without being too sanguine, affirm, that since this rebellion my affairs were never in so hopeful a way!'" [31]

Whilst the king remained at Leicester he was anxious to strengthen the fortifications, which, incomplete previously, had been badly weakened by the siege and storming:- *"... he augmented some parts, and repaired others; but his enemies, being as desirous to recover as he was to preserve it, raised the siege of Oxford, and with Fairfax at the head of the army, marched towards Leicester; and the King, being ignorant of the movement, left Leicester on the 4th of June, and marched with his army to the relief of his garrison at Oxford.* [Sir Marmaduke] *Langdale's regiment* [the Northern Horse] *were in discontent near Leicester, because they might not advance northwards; but the King quieted them with a promise that they should march thither within 15 days."* [32]

The king had appointed Lord Loughborough as his Governor of Leicester on 2nd June, with Sir Matthew Appleyard as his deputy. A garrison of 1,200 men was left to continue the improvement of the town's defences in case of an attempt by the parliamentarians to retake it. Hastings' efforts to increase his garrison had limited success. Some reports say that up to 400 local royalists, aged between 16 and 60, came in from the county to swell his numbers. Of the original defenders of the town a parliamentarian source records that:- *"Few of the 800 soldiers, horse and foot, taken prisoners at Leicester, would by any means take up arms for the other party, though they were daily solicited both by threats and promises; only one Smith, a lieutenant, who let them in as soon as he could, is since made a captain by colonel Hastings, and he persuaded about 40 foot soldiers to take up arms with him; but some of them have since deserted him, and got to Coventry."* [33]

The parliamentarian newsheet *Mercurius Brittanicus* reported, following the fall of Leicester:- *"that snivelling coward Hastings, ... fortifies* [Leicester] *so earnestly as if he meant to command the whole country, and then woe to the carriers of Derby; for this Goblin of Ashby-de-la-Zouch means to play the Devil at Leicester."* [34]

The royalists quickly repaired the breaches in the Newarke. The account of Edward Walker, a royalist officer, indicates that a plan was also made to reduce the line of defence by fortifying the south part of the town, but it is not clear how much progress was made in this regard. [35] A parliamentary newsheet reported on 3rd June, *"we understand that the Kings Forces are demolishing part of the workes at Leicester and that they are raysing new ones at a place called newarke, which place is strong of it selfe by nature, and where the enemy intends to keep the town with a small garrison of men."* [36]

Another parliamentary journal reported on 13th June that the new royalist governor was, *"pulling down two parts of Leicester, to make the other two parts impregnable, if he can."* [37]

It is uncertain whether this work was ever completed. It is possible that systematic demolition of houses lying outside the defences was undertaken, but there is a lack of evidence for widespread destruction of property in the northern or eastern suburbs or for the construction of a shorter defensive perimeter line.

No sooner had the king left Leicester for Oxford than royalist soldiers burned the Countess of Devonshire's house at Leicester Abbey, which had been his residence after the siege. It is ironic that Lord Loughborough could not save his kinswoman's property which had been previously protected from Lord Grey's threats by order of Parliament.

On 7th June it was recorded in London that, *"the Countess of Devon had a pass to transport herself, with two servants, a coach and four horses, and two saddle nags, beyond the seas."*

The same report also recorded that, *"... the ord Grey of Groby was ordered to have the benefit of two assessments for the twentieth part discovered by him to the Committee at Haberdasher's hall."* [38]

This was money voted by the House of Commons as part of the arrears owed to him for his service to the Parliament. Lord Grey was not at Leicester during its siege and storming, but he was losing no time whilst in London in advancing his financial interests through obtaining shares in the assessment of fines and sequestrations laid upon those identified by him as 'malignants'. He was to find this an increasingly lucrative practice.

On 3rd June the Committee of Both Kingdoms wrote to Sir Thomas Fairfax desiring him to send a trumpeter to Leicester in order to determine the number and 'quality' of the prisoners held there, how many wounded, and to think of exchanges. A week later *"One hundred pounds were voted to Major Innes as a gift from the House of Commons. The same sum was also given to Sir Robert Pye junior, as a gratuity from the Parliament, and in recompense of his losses at Leicester."* [39]

It was reported to London frm Northampton that on:- *"Sabbath-day, June 8, there came in divers soldiers, both horse and foot, from Leicester, that had been prisoners about a week, and were exchanged for so many of the Evesham prisoners sent hither, in all 100 horse and foot soldiers; the like number to be released here for them; and they inform us there were 300 released on Thursday last, for so many from Warwick, Coventry, and Stratford. Here are yet about 100 more, most of them lately taken in this country, of the King's party; which will release more, the enemy not knowing what to do with so many prisoners."* [40]

On 13th June it was agreed in London:- *"that Mr. Job Grey, a prisoner in Leicester, should be exchanged for Sir William Riddell, a prisoner in the Tower; Mr. John Angell, a minister, and the confracter of Wigston* [Wyggeston] *hospital, for Daniel Ambrose, doctor in Divinity; and Sir Robert Pye for Colonel Tillier* [also a prisoner in the Tower of London]." [41]

Recriminations amongst the parliamentarians followed the fall of Leicester and attempts were made to fix the blame for its loss on others. Absentee grandees, such as the Earl of Stamford, blamed the local Committee men for inadequate preparations for the attack, as did the professional army officers, particularly Major James Innes. In the words of Joshua Sprigge, Fairfax's chaplain, *"many discourses were raised, each one venting his discontent according as passion directed his affections."* [42] In attempting to follow the course of actual events it is necessary, therefore, to take into account the varying perspectives of the writers.

In their own defence the members of the Committee issued *A Narration of the Siege of Leicester, etc.* in which they rejected the charges of lack of zeal and disloyalty to the Cause to which they had given so much and for which they had hazarded all that they had. Despite their own best efforts they had been left unsupported by the local nobility, such as the Earl of Stamford, or the neighbouring parliamentarian garrisons, whom they had sent to for aid and whom they had never failed to assist, or by the Parliament's field armies. Even when they had tried in April to further strengthen the defences by fortifying the Newarke, to act as a refuge and a citadel from within which they could stand a siege until relief came, they had been instructed by the Committee of Both Kingdoms to stop doing so.

"But now it is visible to all, that what we would have done, the enemy now doeth; and Sir Henry Bard told some of us that he heard that we began to fortify the Newark, which if we had finished, the King's army would never have come to Leicester." [43]

It will be recalled that the work of fortifying the Newarke had been stopped following Colonel George Booth's letter of 12th April to Lord Grey of Groby. Lord Grey's brotherin-law had been travelling back from London to his estate in Cheshire. He had commented on the weakness and indiscipline of the Leicester garrison, advised against the strengthening of the Newarke where *"the grand masters..." "... have all of them got houses,"* and that the town could be captured by 500 determined men. Booth was clearly concerned about the possible disruption of trade between London and his properties in the north west of England if the town was captured. He did, however, exaggerate the proportion of committee men with houses in the Newarke. The committee men pointed out that *"Townes-men who were of the committee subscribed the Order for fortifying the Newarke, though their houses stood in the Towne."* [44] They accused Booth (a former - and later to be again - royalist officer) of inexperience and explained that he had been falsely deceived about the amount of discontent in the town relating to the fortification of the Newarke because he had stayed at a *"malignant Inne"* during his visit and had not talked to the Committee about the matter.

They also stressed the bravery of the garrison's officers during the fighting, including Lt. Colonel Whitbrooke, Captain Hurst, and Captain Farmer who had been killed, Captain Hacker, and Colonel Henry

Grey who had been sorely wounded whilst gallantly leading the defence of the town in the St. Margaret's area.

Major James Innes, a professional soldier, joined in the criticism of the local Committee and its militia officers. He suggested that they were inept and cowardly. He claimed that they and the townspeople had only resisted due to the presence of Sir Robert Pye, himself and his dragoons, and the handful of Scottish soldiers. Reports of the deaths of Captains Hurst and Farmer he claims are greatly exaggerated; that Theophilus Grey was only made acting Governor because his brother was the Earl of Kent and at the time of the temporary appointment no-one expected an attack from the major royalist field army; that the garrison officers and committee men had failed to demolish points of advantage to the enemy, which he then proceeded to o. Almost all the other contemporary commentators, however, record the death of Captains Hurst and Farmer. Innes specifically criticises Colonel Henry Grey, who he claims was deliberately wounded in the back by the royalists when he was running away from them in order to mark him as a coward. Innes claims that he was told this by their royalist captors. This strongly conflicts with the version of events recorded by Hollings from other sources when he states that, **"Colonel Grey having hastened with part of the cavalry of the garrison to check the further progress of the enemy, after being severely injured by two sword cuts in the face and a pike wound in the back, was taken prisoner by Major Trollope, and his whole party routed and dispersed."** [(45)]

Innes also attacks Captain Peter Temple for cowardice, saying that he deliberately left it too late to bring his cavalry in from Coleorton to assist in the defence of Leicester, unlike Captain Francis Hacker who had come in with his command from Kirby Bellars. Innes points out that on previous occasions Temple had seen discretion as the better part of valour.

"It is well remembered, that captain Temple ... when the lord Grey began to fortify Leicester, upon intelligence given of the enemy's advance out of Worcestershire towards Ashby, repaired

at midnight to the lord Grey's chamber, earnestly persuading him at that instant to remove to Rockingham [Castle], with his forces, cannon, and carriages; and indeed many times since he hath expressed that fearful disposition; for, in times of danger, pretending business, he usually hastens to London; witness the last journey that he made up thither, upon the approach of the King's Army into these parts. [46]

Major Innes, by all accounts, appears to have been a very competent officer and to have behaved very courageously during the siege and storming himself. It is noticeable, however, that he makes no criticism of the absent notables such as the Earl of Stamford, Sir Arthur Hesilrige, Lord Grey of Groby or those who had failed to send aid to the defence of Leicester. He seems to have been annoyed that he and Sir Robert Pye had been misled about the strength of the garrison and the defences of the town when they had been persuaded to stay and give their assistance. His attacks on the officers of the garrison seem somewhat harsh given the odds they had to cope with and the generally vigorous nature of the resistance of the parliamentarian soldiers and townsfolk as vouched for by commentators from both sides of the conflict. Perhaps his criticisms reveal disagreements - strategic, tactical, or personal - between some of the leading defenders which may have been present earlier.

Fortunately, the search for scapegoats did not continue for long. Within a few short weeks the situation nationally had been recovered and a more considered view could be taken. Leicester, as it had been garrisoned and fortified in late May 1645, could not have been held against the king's main field army, with siege cannon, no matter who had been in command. Although earthworks (sometimes referred to as 'outworks') had been thrown up around the perimeter, strategic hornworks or 'sentries' constructed, the city gates repaired and closed, and some outlying houses thrown down, there had been insufficient resources made available to the town to make it really defensible; particularly after the prohibition on making the Newarke a real stronghold. The gap in the south wall of the Newarke was a notorious weak spot. Medieval city walls, even where they still existed intact, were not meant to withstand siege cannon for long. In fact, after five hundred years or so of peace they were not really fit to withstand any determined assault.

Moreover, until almost the last days, preparations for defence on the ground were largely left in the hands of the Corporation and the Leicester Committee whom professional soldiers like Sir Robert Pye and Major James Innes blamed, but who were understandably reluctant to destroy the houses of friends and neighbours in preparation for a siege that might never happen. Prince Rupert may or may not have been a good general, opinions vary, but even a poor one, with the artillery and the numbers of men at his command, could have made short work of Leicester. This he did. There was no long drawn-out siege such as at Gloucester, Newark and Oxford. For a couple of days he had pounded the south side of the Newarke walls, battered a breach in them, and then, when his summons to surrender was refused, sent in his troops in overwhelming numerical superiority to storm the town from all sides. In a matter of hours it was all over, despite fierce resistance in the streets as well as at the fortifications.

Credit for their bravery should go to the gallant defenders, be they soldiers or townsfolk, men or women. If any blame is to be apportioned it should be directed to those who kept the town short of resources to build stronger fortifications, whilst at the same time prohibiting the improvements to the defences of the Newarke, and failed to send the reinforcements of horse, foot, and artillery that were needed as the royal army turned towards the east midlands.

As John Hollings comments, **"When it is considered that this obstinate resistance was maintained by men** [and women] **nearly worn out by watching for two nights previously, as well as by constant and laborious exertions during the preceding day, many of whom moreover had been without refreshment or relief for four and twenty hours, it must be acknowledged that the defence of the Newark fort, as it is called, by the soldiers of the parliament, is not unworthy of being** reckoned among the most striking instances of the stern and enduring courage, for which that party was during the Civil War remarkable, and of which the well-known sieges of Bristol, Gloucester, and Taunton afford so many parallel examples." [47]

Lucy Hutchinson chronicles the impact of the fall of Leicester in the following terms:- *"... the king ... broke out* [of Oxford] *, and joining Prince Rupert's horse, came, after several attempts elsewhere, to Leicester, which he took by storm. The loss of this town was a great affliction and terror to all the neighbouring garrisons and counties, whereupon Fairfax closely attended the king's motions ..."* [48]

NOTES:

1. Bulstrode Whitelock, *Memorials of the English Affairs*, p.143.
2. *Mercurius Rusticus.*
3. Heath's Chronicle, p. 78.
4. Symonds, op. cit., p. 44.
5. Cited in Nichols, op. cit., p. 46.
6. Ibid. p. 53.
7. Ibid. p. 53.
8. Whitelock, p. 144.
9. James Thompson, *The History of Leicester* (1849), pp. 393 & 394.
10. Ibid. p. 393.
11. Hollings, op. cit., p. 62.
12. *A Perfect Diurnal*, No. 97. (1645)
13. Nichols, op. cit., p. 48.
14. Walker, *Historical Discourses*, p. 128.
15. Clarendon, op. cit., Book IX, 33.
16. Ibid.
17. Walker, op. cit., p. 128.
18. *The Moderate Intelligencer*, 14 June 1645, Thomason Tracts, E. 288.
19. Clarendon, op. cit., Book IX, 32.
20. *The Moderate Intelligencer*, op. cit.
21. *Mercurius Aulicus*, 8 June, 1645.
22. Town Chamberlains' Accounts, 1645, Records of the Borough of Leicester.
23. Wallington, *Historical Notes of Events*, Vol. II, p. 263.
24. *A Perfect Diurnal*, No. 97 (1645).
25. W. Kelly, *Royal Progesses and Visits to Leicester.* (1884)
26. Records of the Borough of Leicester - CCCCLXVIII Original Letters, No. 70. [1st June, 1645]
27. Ibid. [Hall Book, 31 May, 1645]
28. Ibid. [Hall Book, 22 August, 1645]
29. L.J., Vol. VII., p. 403.
30. Ibid and C. J., Vol. IV., p. 160.
31. Heath's Chronicle, p. 48.

32. L. J., Vol. VII., p. 428.
33. *A Perfect Relation of the Taking of Leicester*, 9th June, 1645. Cited in Nicholls, p. 53.
34. *Mercurius Brittanicus*, No. 86. June, 1645.
35. Walker, op. cit., pp. 127-8.
36. *A Diary or an Exact Journal of the Houses of Parliament, 3rd June 1645'.*
37. *The Exchange Intelligencer* No. 5, June 13, 1645.
38. C. J., Vol. IV, p. 166.
39. Cited in Nichols, op. cit., p. 54.
40. *A Perfect Relation of the Taking of Leicester'*, 9th June, 1645. Cited in Nichols, p. 53.
41. L. J., Vol. VII., p. 421.
42. Joshua Sprigge, *Anglia Rediviva,* London, 1647, reprinted 1857, 27.
43. *A Narration of the Siege of Leicester*, 1645, Cited in Nichols.
44. *An Examination Examinied, etc.* 1645.
45. Hollings, op. cit., p 55.
46. Cited in Nichols, pp. 50-51.
47. Hollings, op. cit., p. 54.
48. Lucy Hutchinson, op. cit., p.224.

Great Seal – King Charles I

The Siege and Sacking of Magdeburg, Germany – 1631

CHAPTER SEVEN

REDEMPTION

"Be strong, fear not :
behold, your God will come with vengeance,
even God with a recompense;
he will come and save you."
Isaiah Chapter 35. Vs. 4.

Parliament had been unable to prevent the storming and sacking of Leicester, although an order was sent from the Committee of Both Kingdoms to Sir John Gell instructing him to join his Derbyshire forces with those of Nottinghamshire *"to obstruct the King's forces in the siege of Leicester."* [1] But by the time Gell had assembled his force the king had taken the town and was again on the move.

After leaving Leicester the Royal Army passed southwards through Great Glen, where Prince Rupert's cavalry had been quartered, to Market Harborough. Here a review revealed just how much their forces had been weakened by the action at Leicester *"by the loss of those who were killed and wounded in the storm, by the absence of those who were left behind in the garrison, and by the running away of very many with their plunder,"* [2] the town of Leicester having been *"full of wealth which the counties had brought in for safety."* [3] The number of the remaining foot totalled some 4,000 which, as Clarendon observed, *"was not a body sufficient to fight a battle for a crown."* [4] The royalist horse numbered some 3,600. Whilst the army was at Market Harborough the king heard that Fairfax had abandoned his siege of Oxford. From Market Harborough the royal army marched to Daventry, where it stayed for five days. All this time Fairfax and the New Model Army were drawing nearer.

At eleven o'clock on the night of 10th June, Sir Samuel Luke wrote an urgent letter to his father. In this the Parliament's Scoutmaster-

General gives the following information:- *"... I gave Sir T. Fairfax notice of the party drawing out to go to Oxford and also of its retreating back, and yet I cannot see any hope of King-catching or cavalier-catching.*

P.S. Acquaint Lord Grey that I hear the King has summoned pioneers to fortify Holmby that he may hunt more securely." [5]

The message for Lord Grey indicates that he was still involved and interested in the activities within the area.

Unknown to the king the two armies were only six miles apart on 12th June. The next day, King Charles was hunting deer in Fawsley Park, about three miles south of Daventry, when he learned of the approach of the 14,000 strong parliamentarian army (of whom some 6,000 were cavalry). Fairfax's force was larger than the king had expected and had already reached Northampton.

Upon receiving this news Charles pulled his army back some eighteen miles to Market Harborough, intending to return to Leicester where he could receive support from Newark and reinforcements already due from South Wales, under Sir Charles Gerard, and from the west of England, under Lord Goring.

Fairfax moved north from Northampton, however, on 12th June following the king's withdrawal to Market Harborough. By 13th June the New Model Army had reached Kislingbury where they were joined by Lieutenant-General Oliver Crmwell, with his Ironsides, to lead the parliamentarian horse. This greatly cheered their whole army.

On the night of the 13th Fairfax entered Guilsborough. His advance guard under Henry Ireton had gone four miles further north and taken prisoner some twenty members of Langdale's Northern Horse, who had been drinking ale and playing quoits at an inn in a small village, located on the Northamptonshire side of the border with Leicestershire, called Naseby. The following day the battle of

Naseby, which was to determine the outcome of the first civil war, was fought.

Accounts of the battle of Naseby are generally well known and are not central to this work. Two brief summaries, one from each side, should suffice to give its essence.

The royalist Mercurius Rusticus records how:- *"June 14, was that fatal battle at Naseby down in Northamptonshire, where his Majesty's army (till then victorious) was now, by the uncertainty of war, much worsted, his foot, ordnance, and baggage, most lost. ... The whole number on both sides slain was conceived not to exceed 400; but more wounded. Above all the rebels' cruelty was remarkable, in killing upon cold blood at least 100 women, whereof some of quality, being commanders' wives; and this was done under the pretence that they were Irish women."* [6]

The Scotsman, Robert Baillie, sums up the course of the battle succinctly from the other perspective:- *"Rupert, on the King's right wing carried doune the Parliament's left wing, and made the Independent Collonells Pickering and Montague [under Ireton] flee lyke men; but Cromwell, on our right wing, carried doune Prince Maurice; and while Rupert, in his furie, pursues too farr, Cromwell comes on the back of the King's foot, and Fairfax on their face, and quicklie makes them lay doune their armes. Rupert, with difficultie, did charge through our armie. The King, in persone, did rally againe the body of his horse; but they were again put to flight. The victory was entire."* [7]

The cruelties referred to in the royalist account relate to the treatment meted out by the victorious parliamentarian troops to what John Vicars, one of their publicists, called the *"whores and camp sluts that attended that wicked army."* [8] The Roundhead foot, in the immediate aftermath of the battle, set about plundering the royal baggage park. They found sheltering there a crowd of raggedly dressed women, whom they took for Irish Catholics because they spoke an unfamiliar language, had `cruel countenances', and tried to defend themselves with kitchen knives. These were almost certainly not Irishwomen, but the Welsh-speaking women of poor Welsh conscripts in the royalist infantry. A hundred of these unfortunate women were put to the sword. Officers' wives and some camp followers who had also taken shelter in the baggage park were, if not killed, deliberately slashed in the face or had their noses slit so as to never again be attractive to men. To these puritan soldiers of the New Model Army in their self-righteous bloodlust, any woman, whether lady or slut, who chose to follow the evil royal army could only represent Sin Incarnate. This great victory, won in the heart of England, was visible proof to the Puritans that God was with their cause. Many of them believed literally that they were fighting God's enemies, just as the Children of Israel had done in the Old Testament. Unfortunately, the parliamentarian triumph at Naseby was stained by such needless atrocity.

In part the violent and cruel actions of the parliamentarian foot at the close of the battle may be attributed to the desire for revenge for the atrocities committed by that very royalist army in Leicester only two weeks earlier, including their treatment of the townswomen there. The 'roundhead' foot also pillaged their 4,500 prisoners and the 1,000 'cavalier' corpses all across Naseby field. They were, in fact, plundering the plunderers, since, as an eye-witness pointed out, *"No royalist prisoner, but had forty shillings on him after Leicester."* A letter from Sir Samuel Luke to his father, dated 12th June, spoke of captured royalist soldiers being in possession of considerable quantities of plunder and money; one sergeant having £20.

John Vicars links these two elements in the following polemical terms:- *"One great encouragement to our common soldiers to fall on the more courageously, was the rich plunder the enemy had (their purses and pockets being too full of money and the plunder of poor Leicestershire), which God now made a means of their ruin and destruction in this fight; for indeed our soldiers got very great plenty of gold and silver out of most of their pockets that were slain. Prince Rupert, or rather Prince Robber, had brought into the field many Irish women, inhuman whores, with skeans, or long Irish knives, about them, to cut the throats of our wounded*

The soldiers of the New Model Army committed their own atrocities on the royalist baggage train at the close of the Battle of Naseby

men, and of such prisoners as they pleased (the wives of the bloody rebels in Ireland, his Majesty's dearly beloved subjects), to whom our soldiers would grant no quarter. About 100 of them were slain on the ground, and most of the rest of the whores and camp-sluts that attended that wicked army were marked in their faces or noses with slashes and cuts, and some cut off; just rewards for such wicked strumpets." [9]

King Charles, with Prince Rupert and the Life Guard of Horse, had fled from the field in the direction of Leicester at about one o'clock in the afternoon, seeing that the battle was lost. Cromwell had sent his cavalry in pursuit having first warned them that any trooper dismounting to plunder would be put to death. The chase was relentless. The first eleven of the fourteen miles to Leicester were littered with 300 cavalier dead, chopped down from behind in their flight. King Charles and Prince Rupert paused briefly at Wistow Hall, Richard Halford's house, to hurriedly exchange their conspicuous royal saddles for plain ones. They passed through Leicester, with Cromwell in hot pursuit, and headed for Ashby Castle. Lord Loughborough was left to hold Leicester as best, and for as long as, he could. By the evening Cromwell had surrounded the town with his cavalry.

Richard Symonds recorded that:- *"The horse escaped to Leicester this afternoone and were pursued by a body of the enemyes horse and loose scowters to Great Glyn* [Great Glen]*, and there the Earle of Lichfield* [Lord Bernard Stuart with his troop in the King's Life Guard of Horse, of which Symonds himself was a member] *charged their loose men with halfe a score horse and beat them back.* [Then comes a list of those killed] *Towards night this dismall Satterday, his Majestie, after the wounded were taken care of in Leicester, and that the two Princes were come safe to him, and had taken order with that garrison, had left two regiments of horse there, viz. The Queenes and Colonel Caryes, he marched that night (for now we had left off running), to Ashby-de-la-Zouch."* [10]

The royal evacuation from Leicester was aided by some of the local people including, according to John Throsby the 18th century Leicestershire historian:- *"Thomas Throsbie, my great grandfather, who, in his sovereign's distress, went voluntarily to Leicester with his team, when grey in years, accompanied by his son to assist the king's army in their flight from Leicester, after the fatal battle of Naseby. Surely the driving of a baggage-wagon was, in that case, an amiable, if not an honourable service; it was in the aid of the distressed."* [11]

After the battle the scattered and confused royalist foot soldiers who had escaped either death or capture were reduced to a starving and desperate condition. An incident is recorded in the north west Leicestershire village of Ravenstone where an exhausted straggler from the defeated army stole a loaf of bread from a farmhouse. He was detected by a stout maid-servant who slew him upon the dunghill in the farmhouse yard with the 'muddle' she was using to stir her washing.

Lord Grey of Groby was not in Leicester at the time of the fall of the town to the royalists; nor does he appear to have been with the avenging army under Sir Thomas Fairfax which was victorious at Naseby. He would, of course, since the coming into effect of the Self-Denying Ordinance, have had no official military command role. The former soldiers of his command are likely to have taken part at Naseby or in the recapture of Leicester, unless they were still prisoners in the town. Also, in the absence of their commander, a detachment of Lord Loughborough's Bluecoat Horse fought on the royalist side under Langdale at Naseby, whilst Sir Robert Pye's Regiment of Horse formed part of Cromwell's division in that action.

The speed with which the fortunes of war had been reversed was remarkable. The military victory at Naseby had political spoils attached to it. For example, the victorious parliamentarians discovered in the king's coach after the battle his personal correspondence which revealed, for all the world to see, his dealings with the Irish and the French in an attempt to raise foreign troops to fight for his cause in England. This was a major propaganda coup for the parliamentarians.

The defeat at Naseby, although admittedly suffered against superior odds, had wiped out for the time being the only effective royalist field army in England. The king decided to lead what men were left to him, apart from the garrison of Leicester who would be used to buy time, to Hereford where he hoped to be joined by forces commanded by Gerard from South Wales and Goring from the West of England.

From Ashby-de-la-Zouch the king moved on through Lichfield, Wolverhampton, Kidderminster, Bewdley, and Bromyard, arriving at Hereford on 19th June, having completed a march of some 120 miles in only five days.

Meanwhile Sir Thomas Fairfax and the main parliamentarian force arrived outside Leicester on 16th June to join Cromwell's cavalry in the second siege of the town in less than three weeks.

"On Monday the 16th the whole army came before the town, when the general sent a summons to lord Hastings, to deliver it to the use of the Parliament; who very resolutely refused them: and thereupon command was given for a present storm." [12]

Lord Loughborogh was at first defiant, but after a heavy artillery bombardment, which included the use of the siege guns used formerly by the royalists and captured at Naseby, lasting three hours, a breach was made in the walls on the Newarke side. Even a commander with the single-minded loyalty of 'blind' (for the royal cause) Hastings had to realise that his position was untenable.

A parliamentarian pamphleteer wrote:- *"we stormed it, playing with our Ordnance very hot on the Newarke side, which we conceived was their greatest strength. And in a short time we made a breach in their workes, which strucke such terror into the hearts of the Enemy, that the Governour sent to us to desire a Parley, and offered to surrender on very faire termes."* [13]

212

Heath's Chronicle records that:- *"On the 17th, being Tuesday, great store of ladders were brought against the town of Leicester, a battery raised, and two demi-cannons and a whole culverin taken at Naseby were placed upon an old work against the Newark, being the very same guns which the King, not many days before, had used against the same place. Whereupon the Lord of Loughborough [after the bombardment and the opening of the breach], seeing the resolution of the enemy, sent a trumpeter out that day with letters, desiring a parlay concerning the surrender of the town; which began that evening, and concluded in an agreement. "* [14]

The parliamentarian commissioners who negotiated with Lord Loughborough were Colonel Pickering and Colonel Rainsborough. Under the articles of surrender the garrison marched out on the morning of Wednesday, 18th June, on fair and honourable terms, without arms and with only staves in their hands. Cavalry officers were allowed to retain their arms. Lord Loughborough was allowed to go to Ashby but the other officers and soldiers were to march to royalist-held Lichfield. All prisoners previously taken by the royalists and still held in Leicester were released. There was considerable rejoicing in the town. The parliamentarian spoils included some 2,000 stand of arms, 500 horses, 14 pieces of cannon, 30 colours, 50 barrels of gunpowder and other ammunition and stores.

Richard Symonds relates that, *"The day before we came to Hereford* [i.e. on 18th June] *His Majestie had intelligence that Fairfax had appeared before Leicester, and that Lord Loughborough had yielded it upon conditions. To march away the soldjers, sans armes, officers with swords. Two regiments of horse, vizt. Queenes and Caryes; the men marched, but horses and armes the enemy had. 1,500 foot marched out of Leicester with those gentlemen and wounded men that came in I suppose."* [15]

The day following the recapture of the town was a day of public thanksgiving. There were church collections in London for the relief of Leicester. Despite all this and a substantial grant from Parliament to make good the town's losses, to provide corn for the poor, and to finance traders in giving work to the poor, it was to be many years before the financial health of the town recovered from the events of May and June 1645. Later, during the Preston campaign of 1648 in the second civil war, when troops under Cromwell passed through Leicester, the town was unable to meet their needs for footwear. Only when they reached Nottingham were they able to be supplied - with stockings from Coventry and shoes from Northampton. The Corporation of Leicester received an award of £1,500 from Parliament which was raised from the estates of royalist 'delinquents'. The Clerk to the Leicester Committee, Master Wadland, who had refused to allow a weak point in the Newarke south wall abutting on to some of his land be strengthened, was sacked and not less than 40 of the 72 members of the Common Hall were removed for supposed royalist sympathies in the recriminations that followed the retaking of Leicester.

Reference has already been made to recriminations amongst the local parliamentarians towards the end of the previous chapter. John Nichols refers to the first attempt at self justification. This was entitled *A Narration of the siege and taking of the town of Leicester, the last of May, 1645, by the King's forces; together with other proceedings of the Committee, and answers to some aspersions cast upon that Committee.* It was produced by some of the Committee members as a defence of their actions and was printed by *G. Miller, dwelling in Black Friars, 1645.* In response, as noted earlier and included in Nichols, the *Narration ...* was added to by *A more perfect and exact relation of the taking of the said town and garrison,* etc. by Major James Innes.
John Hollings, however, refers to two additional pamphlets which were omitted by Nichols in his work. The first of these was entitled *A more exact Relation of the Siege laid to the Town of Leicester, how it was maintained and how won, and what quarter was given by the king's forces delivered to the Honourable House of Commons by Sir Robert Pye, governor* [?] *of the said town , and Major James Ennis* [sic]. The second was issued again by

the members of the Leicester Committee who had been present during the siege and storming and was entitled *An Examination examined, being a full answer to Major Innes' Relation of the taking of Leicester.*

The following passage, from the *Narration...* gives the essence of the Committee's justifications for their actions and the refutation of the 'aspersions' cast by their critics.

"Many aspersions are laid on the Committee of Leicester, both by the Earl of Stamford at the House of Commons door and other places, and also by one Lilly in a printed book, much to our disparagement. We desire that any of them be made good. "We have served the Parliament in the Committees from the first ordinance, and we who were not officers never received a penny of money, nor a meal's meat, at the state's charge: some of us, however inconsiderable to others, have contributed large sums on the propositions; and have spent hundreds of pounds in the Parliament's service; our estates are plundered, our persons imprisned, and we rewarded with being called rascals, pedlars, base fellows, at the door of the House of Commons; and by Master Lilly betrayers of the town, and knaves, in print. We know no reason; we appeal for justice; if traitors or knaves, we beg no favour; and, if we are rascals and base fellows, we are unfit for the Parliament's service. It was the Cause of God and the kingdom that made us undertake the work at the beginning, and when others of greater estates deserted it." [16]

This was the authentic voice of what was known as *'the worsted stockinged committee men'*, who were often looked down upon by the (absentee) 'grandees' (who were more likely to be able to afford and to wear silk stockings) but who formed the backbone of the parliamentarian administrative support and sinews for the war effort in the localities during the first Civil War.

It took a long time to repair the damage done to Leicester. Money was spent on the demolition of the outworks and the other additional fortifications that had been erected. Progress on repairing streets was slow: several parishes were reported as being defective in this respect in 1647-8. The Corporation claimed that over 120 dwelling houses had been demolished when the defences were being strengthened on the orders of Sir Thomas Fairfax after the recapture of the town, that the poor people who had lived in them were thus homeless, and that its charges in poor relief were consequently much increased.

Accordingly, the Borough submitted a petition to the House of Commons:- *"The owners of the said howses* [sic] *and grounds* [which had been dug up and spoiled] *are much impoverished and weakened in their estate and disabled to maintain themselves and become chargeable to the places where they live. The burthen whereof growes so great that your peticioners* [sic] *are not able to beare the same beinge extraordinarily plundered and wasted by the Kinges forces at the takinge of this Towne and many poore widdowes whose husbands were slayne at the same tyme and they thereby disabled to subsist and mayntayne themselves and their poor famylies are very chardgable* [sic] *to your peticioners to provide for and keepe."* [17]

A grant from the money raised by fines on forfeited royalist estates, including those of the Ashby-de-la-Zouch 'delinquents', was therefore requested to meet that additional expense. The Corporation also felt obliged to lower or waive rents on properties that had been damaged in connection with the siege and storming and sought compensation in this respect too. Some guide to the extent of property damage is given by the town chamberlain's accounts of 1644-45. Allowance is made for the loss of rents from some 46 houses and 10 tenements. Property in the Newarke and the Castle liberties, however, as well as in Braunstone Gate across the West Bridge which lay in the liberty of Bromkinsthorpe, would not have been included in the borough's tally. The Bishop's fee, which contained 35 houses in the 1670 hearth tax, was also excluded. This liberty lay in the eastern suburb but was confined to Humberstone Gate and perhaps a small part of Gallowtree Gate.

The greatest loss within the town itself occurred in the Southgate area (viz. 30 houses, 4 tenements, a 'backhouse' and a barn) and presumably represents the demolition recorded in the town chamberlain's accounts of 1643-44 and 1644-45. Both the Grange and the Hermitage were included within the Southgate area. In that first accounting year beginning Michaelmas (i.e. 29th September) 1643 houses outside the southern defence were recorded as being demolished and the town as a whole went out to repair the defences. The following year the southern defence line was apparently shortened not long before the siege occurred. This necessitated the levelling of all the houses that still remained outside the South Gate. It may be significant that this southern suburb, in marked contrast to the nearby Newarke, was the poorest part of Leicester and its citizens presumably powerless compared with their wealthier brethren outside the North and East gates of the town. In the Abbeygate area 5 houses were recorded as *'decayed rents'*. These properties lay over St. Sunday's Bridge and may include those dwellings deliberately fired by the defenders at the beginning of the siege. St. Leonard's church in the Abbeygate was probably finally destroyed at this time. It was never rebuilt, although the graveyard continued in use for burials. Other losses also appear on the peripheral parts of the town. The highest of these (4 houses and 3 tenements) was at Belgrave Gate where the royalists under Colonel Sir Henry Bard had forced their first entry. Others included St. Nicholas Parish (1 house and 1 tenement), Northbridge end, North Gate, All Saints Parish, over (beyond) the West Bridge (all 1 house each), and Parchment Lane (1 tenement). In addition there were 2 further houses and a tenement listed as *'unlocated'*. Even allowing for the lack of evidence for the area of the Bishop's fee (i.e. Humberstone Gate) there seems to be no indication of wholesale destruction of buildings in the eastern suburbs. Other areas had not fared so well as we have seen. As late as 1648-49 the town chamberlains' accounts still made allowance for 18 houses in the Southgate area. It is not clear how many of the dwellings referred to above were demolished during the fighting or destroyed as part of defensive operations of either the parliamentarian or royalist garrisons.[18]

217

Individual citizens also suffered from the consequences of the siege and storming of Leicester. Examples given below, drawn from the Borough Records, illustrate the extent to which lives were disrupted. William Harley, a cordwainer (boot and shoemaker) by trade and with a wife and three children to maintain, reported that all his goods had been plundered by the royalist soldiers. He requested admission as a freeman of the borough so that he could be elected a member of the Cordwainers' Company. John Stocker, a joiner by trade, who had served as a gunner's mate in the defence of the town, had seen his house near the South Gate demolished and he also sought admission as a freeman of the borough in compensation. William Sumner, a tailor, had lost not only his house and fruit trees, but his son had been killed by the enemy, his wife driven to distraction, and his possessions plundered. In order to maintain himself and his remaining family he now sought work as a 'butcher'. An earlier entry shows that he had been allowed to work as a 'botcher' rather than a 'taylor' (i.e. a repairer rather than a maker of attire; c.f. a 'cobbler' and a 'cordwainer' in respect of footwear). Robert Warburton had been apprenticed to his father in the trade of blacksmith. His father had been slain in the defence of the town during the storming. The son no sought not only a new master, but requested credit for that part of the seven year apprenticeship that he had already served.

A Captain Atkinson, a soldier who had served in the town when it was attacked - acting, as he comprehensively described it, *"for defence of the King, Parliament, and this Corporation"* - and had subsequently settled in Leicester, requested and received the status of Freeman of the Borough. This is very likely to have been the *"Captain Adkinson, a valiant Scotchman"* who had distinguished himself in a successful skirmish against Hastings' men in August of the previous year, *"about the bridge between Leicester and Belgrave,"* when he had *"charged them gallantly, his men playing their parts stoutly, though much overpowered* [i.e. outnumbered] *by the enemy."* This incident was reported in '*A Perfect Diurnal, No. 54., or Diary of Parliamentary Proceedings*' on 10th August, 1644. Captain Rowland Hacker, the royalist brother of Francis Hacker, was mortally wounded in that skirmish.

A John Turlington submitted a petition to the Mayor and Burgesses. He was *"Constable in Mr. Abney's ward when the town was taken by the King's party."* (Mr. Daniel Abney's ward was one of the two southern wards.) Turlington had been imprisoned by the royalists and, having applied for his liberty, was forced *"upon payne of death"* to bury the dead, relieve the sentries, etc. He subsequently submitted a bill to the Town Chamberlains for 44 shillings but had only been paid 10 shillings to date. He humbly requests payment of the rest - *"for I did nothing but Mr. Byllers* [Billars] *that was Maior* [Mayor] *was Acquaynted with itt"* and *" was oute for my goods. I lost three mylch kyne* [milk cows] *in serving my office, so that I am in great want , so hoping you will take itt into consideration I humbly take leave, Your poore petitioner, John Turlington."* [19]

Another petitioner, an ex-soldier whose name is unrecorded, was in gaol at the time of submitting his petition. He stated that he was a freeman of the Borough who had served as a Gunner and a Gunner's mate in the garrison *"almost ever since the first fortifying thereof."* During this time he sold beer, sometimes under licences granted by various mayors and *"the rest of the said tyme being Importuned thereunto by many of the Cheife* [sic] *souldiery of the Garrison (your peticioners house having bene appointed to be the place for a Company of Guards)."* He had continued to sell beer without a license (allegedly under pressure from the soldiers) for which offence he had been imprisoned. He petitions for his release and promises never to offend in like manner again. [20] Many other individuals must have experienced personal disasters, but most of them remain anonymous.

Meanwhile, the war continued. Bulstrode Whitelock records how, on 20th June:- *"... Sir Thomas Fairfax's army, notwithstanding their hard service, marched from Leicester, and sate before Ashby-de-la-Zouch; and on the 24th, Sir Thomas Fairfax*

*prosecuted the King's forces towards Hereford; and left Colonel
Needham governor of Leicester."* [21]

This John eedham had been before the outbreak of the civil war a
close neighbour of Colonel John Hutchinson and Captain Francis
Hacker in south Nottinghamshire.

Even though Fairfax's army had followed the king away from Ashby
there was continued skirmishing between the members of Hastings's
home garrison and the local parliamentarian forces in eicester and
their re-established outpost at Coleorton. The royalists were forced
to continue their constant raiding to feed and re-equip themselves
whilst the Coleorton garrison sought to contain them with sporadic
attacks. A number of parliamentarian letters refer to minor successes
achieved over the 'rob-carriers', but they must still have managed
to keep themselves supplied.

There appears to have been outbreak of plague in the Ashby garrison
in late June which forced the defenders to move out of the castle
itself and into the outer fortifications. At one time the number of
soldiers seems to have been reduced, for one reason or another, to
sixty men.

Mercurius Veridicus reported in early June that, *"Two of the Derby
troops of horse are come to Leicester, for the better security of
that town, and to keep the enemy from robbing near unto it.
They marched to Ashby-de-la-Zouch, and took horse sufficient
to make up another troop from Hastings out of the meadows.
We hope Sir John Gell's and other horse, which were once in a
body, will be ready and fitted for action when the Scots army
leave those parts."* [22]

The following month it was reported that, *"The sickness continueth
at Ashby-de-la-Zouch. It is most certain that the garrison
soldiers, and the lord Loughborough himself, are come out of
the house, and do quarter in the Park."* [23]

A month later *Mercurius Veridicus* added, *"We will trouble you in discoursing but of one more of the king's garrisons at this time, which is Ashby-de-la-Zouch, which is closely besieged; the town is much visited with the sickness; and in the garrison or fort are said to be not above 60 men."* [24]

Ashby was not the only local royalist outpost to be experiencing difficulty after the disaster of Naseby. Whitelock records how in August, *"Captain Allen, with 95 dragoons from Burleigh House, fell upon 200 of the Newark and Belvoir horse, commanded by Sir Robert Dalison; routed them, killed 5, took several officers, and 50 prisoners; 80 horse, and rescued the countrymen and plunder which they had taken."* [25]

On 30th August 1645 the Committee at Leicester was authorised *"to compound with such gentlemen of the country as had assisted or countenanced the King or his party; the money to be employed for the service and maintenance of the garrison and forces in the town."* [26] Compounding involved the fining of `delinquents' or `malignants' by a proportion of their estate as a form of rent and began to be used regularly by the parliamentarians as a more convenient form of income than sequestration which had involved wholesale confiscation of assets.

The Scots army referred to by *Mercurius Veridicus* in July had, under its commander Lord Leven, moved through the midlands, via Nottingham, south Derbyshire, Staffordshire, Warwickshire, and Worcestershire, by-passing royalist Worcester, en route to beginning a six week siege of royalist-held Hereford. This army was little less of a plague to the localities it passed through than the king's army had been. Leicestershire was, mercifully, spared its attentions. The Scots *"art of perfect plundering"* reported *Mercurius Aulicus "makes their brethren never invite them to stay two nights together, particularly at Nottingham* [where] *the very Presbyterians were ready to petition against their insolent pillaging ... Nay, Burmingham* [sic] *in Warwickshire would not confide in them, but after one night acquaintance extolled Tinker*

Fox [Colonel John Fox, a noted Edgbaston-based parliamentarian plunderer of royalists] *for a very small plunderer ... No wonder, therefore, that the Committees of Warwicke and other counties met at Alcester to consult about the Scots."* [27]

King Charles had left Hereford on 1st July to move into South Wales and join with Gerard's forces there. He had then set out northwards with the intention of linking up with his successful Scottish general, the Marquess of Montrose. Elsewhere Fairfax and the New Model Army had joined Massey's forces in the West of England in an attempt to destroy Lord Goring's royalist army there.

The king's progress northwards had been rapid, but he was soon back in the east midlands. On 25th August it was reported that, *"From Newark the King marched into Lincolnshire, where his army committed many outrages. The next day he again lay at Belvoir castle; and the next day at Stamford."* [28]

While the Scots army in England was busy besieging Hereford, the king had marched as far as Doncaster in Yorkshire. Here he abandoned his journey to Scotland and decided instead to return on a circuitous route through the midlands. On 1st September Lord Leven received intelligence that the king was advancing to the relief of Hereford from the direction of Worcester. The Scots withdrew to Gloucester, where the sight of these ferocious and ill-clad 'foreigners' caused almost as much apprehension among the local population as it had at Hereford. At the arrival of the king it was reported that *"Hereford and the whole country were transported with exaltation and triumph."* [29] This feeling of relief was no doubt short-lived as Wallington records that the Royal Army immediately *"fell to their wonted course of plundering the country, and some of the houses where the Scots quartered they pulled down, others they burnt down, but plundered them all. Honest men, that had never so little showed themselves for the Parliament were fain to fly, and their wives and children turned out all."* [30]

The king spent the following three months in South Wales and the north-east Midlands, during which time he decimated Gerard's army by despatching it to Chester in a vain attempt to relieve the Nottinghamshire royalist Lord Byron who was besieged there again. He also attempted to raise recruits and to rekindle the flame of hope in those who by now saw only too clearly that his cause was lost. On 10th July Fairfax and Massey had reduced Lord Goring's military power by inflicting a demoralising defeat on his western royalist army at Langport.

Fairfax had followed this up on 10th September by taking Bristol from Prince Rupert, who had been despatched there by his uncle from Hereford to take command of its defence. Having promised to hold Bristol for the king, Rupert was forced to surrender this key city and valuable port after a heavy bombardment and storming. For failing to hold Bristol the prince was relieved of his command and his regiment cashiered by the king. Charles, now at Newark, sent a curt and angry written order to Rupert and his brother, Prince Maurice, telling them *"to seek your subsistence somewhere beyond the seas, to which end I send you herewith a pass."* This affront to his honour was too much for Prince Rupert to bear. With a handful of friends he cut his way recklessly through enemy held territory from Oxford, where he had been allowed to retreat with his men and baggage, to meet his ungrateful uncle face-to-face at Newark. He explained that Bristol had proved impossible to hold and that no treachery or disloyalty had been involved in its loss. It was to no avail; the king was implacable. Rupert and Maurice returned to Oxford, shortly to give up the fight and to leave for the continent. The people of Leicester would not have been sorry to hear that they had left the country!

On 5th November the king returned to his winter quarters at Oxford, having finished, as Clarendon relates:- *"the most tedious, and grievous march, that ever king was exercised in, having been almost in perpetual motion from the losse of the battle of Naseby to this hour, with such a variety of dismal accidents as must have broken the spirits of any man who had not been the most magnanimous person in the world."* [31]

Lucy Hutchinson provides a view from the opposite perspective:-
"This summer [1645] *there was another kind of progresse made in the warre than had bene before, and the new parliament Armie prosecuting it so much in earnest that they made a shew to block up the King in his maine Garrison at Oxford, he breaks out, and joyning Prince Rupert's horse, came, after several attempts otherwhere, to Liecester* [sic], *which he tooke by Storme, the loss of which Towne was a great affliction and terror to all the neighbouring Garrisons and countries. Whereupon Fairfax, closely attending the King's motions, came within a few dayes, and fought with the King and overcame him in that memorable battle at Naseby, where his coach and cabinett of letters were taken; which letters being carried to London were printed, and manifested his falsehood, when, contrary to his professions, he had endeavour'd to bring in Danes and Lorainers and Irish Rebells to subdue the good people here, and given himself up to be govern'd by the Queene in all affairs both of State and religion. After this fight Fairfax tooke againe the Town of Liecester* [sic] *and went into the West, reliev'd Taunton, tooke Bristoll* [sic], *and many other Garrisons."* [32]

Roy Sherwood sums up the events covered in this chapter fittingly when he states that, **"the net success of Charles' peregrinations around Wales and the Midlands during 1645 was the relief of Hereford. Without doubt this, the last campaign of the ill-starred monarch, was the most disastrous."** [33]

So ended the year of the king's so-called *'Leicester march'* of 1645 with its consequences for town, county, and country.

NOTES:

1. Calendar of State Papers (Domestic), 1644-1645, p. 548.
2. Clarendon, op. cit., Book IX, 35.
3. *A Perfect Relation of the Taking of Leicester*, 9th June, 1645. Cited in Nicholls, p. 53.
4. Clarendon, op. cit., Book IX, 35.
5. *Letter Books of Sir Samuel Luke*, (1644 - 1645), 706.
6. *Mercurius Rusticus*, 1645.
7. *The Letters and Journals of Robert Baillie*, ed. David Laing, (Edinburgh 1841 - 1842), Vol. II., pp. 286 & 287.
8. John Vicars, *Magnalia Dei Anglicana*, Part IV, p. 164.
9. Ibid.
10. Richard Symonds, op. cit., p. 194.
11. John Throsby, op. cit. Supplementary Volume to the Leicestershire Views *Excursions* - Published 1790. p. 90.
12. Heath's Chronicle, op. cit., p. 80.
13. A Copie of a Letter of the Taking of Leicester on Wednesday the 18th of June (1645)
14. Heath's Chronicle, op. cit., p. 80.
15. Richard Symonds, op. cit. p. 196.
16. *A Narration of the siege and taking of the town of Leicester, the last of May, 1645, by the King's forces; together with other proceedings of the Committee, and answers to some aspersions cast upon that Committee.* Printed by G. Miller, dwelling in Black Friars, 1645. (King's Pamphlets in the British Museum; Small quarto, 213b.)
17. Hall Papers XI, No. 464. Petition to House of Commons, Records of the Borough of Leicester.
18. Paul and Yolanda Courtney, *A Siege Examined : the Civil War archaeology of Leicester* in *Post-Medieval Archaeology* Vol. 26 pp. 58/59.
19. Hall Papers XI, No. 455. Records of the Borough of Leicester.
20. Hall Papers XI, No. 520. Records of the Borough of Leicester.
21. Whitelock, op. cit., p. 147.

22. *Mercurius Veridicus*, July 5, 1645.
23. *The Parliament's Post*, August 19, 1645.
24. *Mercurius Veridicus*, September 27, 1645.
25. Whitelock, op. cit., p.160.
26. C. J., Vol. IV., p. 257.
27. *Mercurius Aulicus*, July 18, 1645.
28. Whitelock, op. cit., p. 153.
29. *Military Memoirs of Colonel John Birch,*
    (later Parliamentarian Governor of Hereford) p. 133.
30. Wallington, *Historical Notes of Events*, Vol. II., p. 270.
31. Clarendon, op. cit., Book IX, 132.
32. Lucy Hutchinson, *Memoirs of the Life of Colonel Hutchinson*, Oxford University Press, London, 1973 Edition. p.160.
33. Roy E. Sherwood, *Civil Strife in the Midlands*, Phillimore & Co. London & Chichester, 1974. p. 206.

Sir Thomas Fairfax, Lord General of the New Model Army

227

Lt. General Oliver Cromwell

228

The Battle of Naseby – June 1645

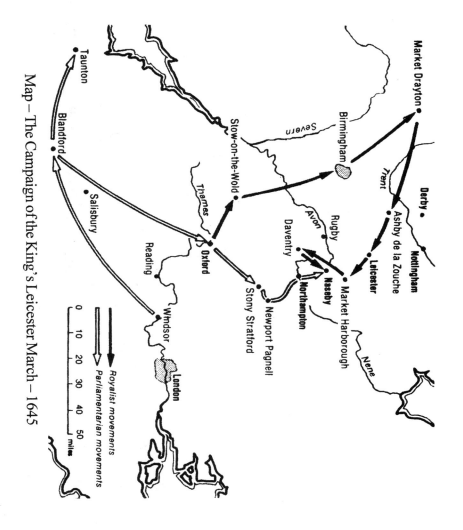

Map – The Campaign of the King's Leicester March – 1645

Scale:
0 10 20 30 40 50 miles

→ Royalist movements
→ Parliamentarian movements

Locations shown: Market Drayton, Derby, Nottingham, Ashby de la Zouche, Leicester, Birmingham, Stow-on-the-Wold, Rugby, Daventry, Naseby, Northampton, Market Harborough, Newport Pagnell, Stony Stratford, Oxford, Reading, Salisbury, Blandford, Taunton, Windsor, London

Rivers shown: Severn, Trent, Avon, Thames, Nene

CHAPTER EIGHT

AFTERMATH - REGICIDE AND REPUBLIC

"Fret not thyself because of evil-doers, Neither be
thou envious of them that work unrighteousness, For
they shall soon be cut down like the grass, And wither
as the green herb."

(Psalm 37 vs. 1 & 2)

Before the king had retreated to winter quarters once more at Oxford
the royalists had managed to reinforce the garrison at Ashby-de-la-
Zouch by between 500 and 600 men towards the end of October.
This meant that by November offensive raids were being carried
out again by Lord Loughborough from Ashby Castle. Indeed, on
16th January 1646 the garrison sallied out and captured a mortar
which was being conveyed by the parliamentarians to their forces
besieging Newark. Five days later 300 men were sent from Ashby
in an attempt to help raise the siege of Chester. It appears that, for
all the boasting of the parliamentarian commentators, the force based
at Coleorton was not very effective when it came to containing the
'De La Zouchians'.

In Leicester itself the Corporation responded to the wish of
Parliament that Thomas Cook (or Coke), the borough MP elected
by the burgesses of Leicester to the Long Parliament with Lord
Grey of Groby in 1640, be replaced because of his suspected royalist
sympathies.

"Whereas Thomas Coke Esquire was lately elected one of the
Burgesses for the said Borough of Leicester for the present
Parliament begunn at the Cittie of Westminster the third day of
November in the sixteenth yeare of the reigne of our Soveraign
Lord the King's Majesty that nowe is and being soe chosen and
in due manner retorned into the Lower House for the
Government of the Kingdom of England accordinge to the forme

of the Statute in that case made as amongest the records of the Parliament aforesad remaininge in his Majesty's High Court of Chancery more plainly appeareth and the said Thomas Coke sithence [sic] by the judgement of the House of Commons is adjudged incapable to sitt any longer there s a member of the same duringe the present Parliament." [1]

Cook's replacement was chosen in November 1645; the parliamentarians still maintaining the fiction that their actions were being done in the name of the king.

"An Assemblie of the Mayor, Bayliffes and Burgesses of the Burrough aforesaid by virtue of a warrantt from John Stafford Sherriffe of the County of Leicester grounded on his Majesty's writt to them directed for the choseinge of a Burgesse of Parliament in the place of Mr. Thomas Cooke late Burgesse of the Burrough aforesaid and rendered incapable of that service as by the said writ and warrant may appeare.
Peter Temple Esquire was then freely chosen a Burgesse for this Burrough of Leicester to serve in the present Parliament and was then sworn a ffreeman [sic] of this Burrough and tooke the oath of supremacie and allegiance." [2]

This change strengthened Lord Grey of Groby's position in Leicester by adding his erstwhile military subordinate (the commander of the Coleorton garrison) and personal supporter to his growing circle of influence at Westminster. Evidently Major Innes' hostile comments about Peter Temple's military conduct had not harmed him.

The effects of that disastrous campaign of summer 1645 as far as King Charles was concerned soon began to be seen. During the winter of 1645/46 at Oxford he still thought that he might achieve victory. If he could not gain it upon the battlefield outright he schemed that he might achieve it by encouraging a split between the Presbyterian and Independent wings of the parliamentarians. Events, however, were now moving too swiftly for this to be a successful strategy.

The published contents of his cabinet taken at Naseby had revealed that Charles had intended to introduce foreign mercenaries, notably the French and Irish, into the struggle on his side against the English Protestants, and that he was prepared to abolish the anti-papist laws. This caused considerable disquiet among many of his followers who, being aware of the obviously declining fortunes of the king's cause, now began to wonder whether their loyalties had been misplaced. They also began to consider whether a public withdrawal from his cause at this time might protect them from subsequent post-war sequestration, compounding and other forms of retribution or recrimination. The steady stream of royalists compounding for their estates in an attempt to keep them became a flood, and soldiers began to desert from the remaining royalist forces and garrisons by the score, some actually 'turning their coats' and joining the parliamentarian armies.

The king's few remaining strongholds began to capitulate. During the winter royalist garrisons in the midlands fell in quick succession with the parliamentarian chronicler Vicars recording each one with righteous enthusiasm. In November, for example, General Poyntz assaulted the Nottinghamshire garrison of Shelford House, the defenders of which, according to Vicars:- *"... chose rather to die in their obstinance than to aske for quarter, upon which their desperate pertinacy (there being about 180 of them in the house) most of them suffered by the edge of the sword."* [3]

Vicars also records that on 18th December Hereford was *"surprised and taken by a brave stratagem."* [4]

Royalist garrisons continued to fall throughout the winter and into the New Year. On 2nd February 1646 Belvoir Castle surrendered. Vicars records that Belvoir in Leicestershire:- *"... being one of the strongest and fairest buildings in the Kingdome ... is reduced to the obedience of the Parliament, Sir Jarvis Lucas, the Governor thereof, with all the Commanders, Officers and Souldiers therein, having permission to march away to Lichfield, upon more honourable termes, indeed, then they deserved."* [5]

Chester surrendered the next day. Ashby Castle, cut off from both Lichfield and Tutbury, was now the sole surviving royalist outpost in Leicestershire. Undaunted, the Ashby garrison continued to show defiance. Whitelock records on 1st January that, *"A party of the King's from Ashby took the minister of Morley and of other towns* [in Derbyshire], *and carried them away prisoners; but Sir John Gell rescued them, and took others of the enemy prisoners."* [6]

On 24th January the parliamentarian *Mercurius Academicus* incorrectly reported Ashby Castle as having been taken. The confusion arose because of a successful raid made upon Ashby by the Leicester forces in late January. The attack was recorded by John Vicars, in characteristic style, as follows:- *"A party of about 80 horse and 40 dragoons were sent out of Leicester, under the command of Major Meeres, a very valiant and discreet gentleman, by night, unto Ashby-de-la-Zouch, who carried on the design exceedingly bravely, and marched with such expedition and privacy, that they came to Ashby about 11 of the clock that night, altogether undiscovered, which was about 12 miles march; whither being come, they suddenly surprised the centinels* [sic], *fell-in at the turnpike, broke the chain, and entered the town, took near 100 of the enemy's horse, being the greatest part of the horse of that garrison, whereof 50 were already saddled, and fitted to have gone forth upon some design of theirs, all of them excellent horses, and some worth 20, 30, and 40 pounds a horse. They took store of arms, and more other pillage, released divers prisoners, and some countrymen, whom the enemy had taken for ransoms; and thus having plundered the town, in part requital of the many mischiefs and plunderings of that garrison to the parliament's friends, all these our friends returned to Leicester without the least molestation; the enemy (who was in the great house or close), either not receiving the alarm, or not daring to come forth at all against them. And thus they came safely back again to Leicester, with all their horse, prize and pillage"* [7]

In retaliation for this raid the Ashby garrison attacked and beat up the quarters of the enemy at Coleorton. Such gestures were becoming increasingly futile, however, given the odds, Eventually talks began between Lord Loughborough and Colonel John Needham concerning the conditions that might be agreed for the giving up of Ashby Castle to the parliamentarians.

Colonel Needham, who had been appointed as Governor of Leicester in June by Sir Thomas Fairfax, had been confirmed in that office by both Houses of Parliament with Owen Cambridge as his major and deputy. On 28th February 1646 articles of agreement were entered into between 'Colonel-General Hastings' and 'Colonel Needham', concerning the *"rendition and slighting of Ashby-de-la-Zouch."*

Vicars records the surrender of Ashby Castle in the following terms:-
"Upon the 4th of this instant March, we received certain intelligence and confirmation of the surrender of the strong garrion of Ashby-de-la-Zouch to Leicester forces. The conditions of surrender were, that Hastings, alias the lord of Loughborough, together with his brother [Ferdinando] *the earl of Huntingdon and colonel* [Isham] *Perkins* [the Governor of the castle]*, should have their estates unsequestrated, protections for their persons, and passes to go beyond the sea; the rest of the officers to have liberty to compound for their sequestration, and passes (if desired) to go beyond the seas also; and the garrison to be slighted* [to prevent it being used again] *: too good conditions indeed for such a desperate and wicked Rob-carryer as Hastings was, but that the kingdom may be glad to be rid of such wretches. The surrender was made accordingly on Monday the 2nd instant. We took therein five pieces of ordnance, about 300 arms, little ammunition, and no great store of other provisions; a great mercy and mighty preservation of the peace and tranquillity of all those adjacent parts about it, for which let God have all due praise and glory."* [8]

The fall of first Belvoir Castle and then Ashby Castle saw the end of the first civil war in Leicestershire. Henry Hastings, Lord Loughborough, the chief protagonist of the royalist cause in this period now left the area, ostensibly to pass *'beyond the sea'* into exile - at least for the time being.

As another interesting postscript there is a reference in the Harleian Catalogue as a loose paper, which can no longer be traced, to an original pass granted by Colonel John Needham, governor of Leicester for the Parliament, to a Mr. Richard Symonds [whose account of the siege and storming of Leicester from the royalist viewpoint has been noted], his two servants, with their horses and arms, dated at Leicester on the 5th day of March, 1646.

The first civil war was now drawing rapidly to an end. During March Sir Thomas Fairfax had taken Woodstock House, the last of the ring of garrisons that had protected the king's capital, and was laying siege to Oxford itself. This was the final blow as, in February, Lord Byron had surrendered to Brereton in Cheshire, and Lord Hopton, who had replaced Lord Goring as commander of the King's Army in the West, had surrendered a month later.

On 21st March Sir Jacob Astley, now Lord Astley, marching from Worcester with 3,000 men to join the king at Oxford:- *"... being set upon near Stow on the Wolds in Gloucestershire, by Raynsborough, Fleetwood, and Sir William Brereton, was so much overpowered by their conjunct strength; that he with all his men, after a sharp dispute and some loss were made Prisoners; this being the last encounter that the Royallists* [sic] *were able to make with those insolent Rebels."* [9]

There is a story that Sir Jacob, who had commanded the royalist foot at Edgehill and Naseby, made a shrewd prediction at the time of his capture. Sitting on a drumhead at Stow-on-the-Wold the white haired sixty-seven year old Roman Catholic veteran said gently to his 'Roundhead' captors, *"You have done your work, boys, and now you may go play - unless you will fall out among yourselves."* It was to prove a prophetic statement.

To add to the king's misfortunes he had failed to secure the sought for and controversial military support from France and elsewhere abroad. His military options had run out. As a result *"his Majesty, observing at Oxford the ill Posture of his Affairs, resolved to betake himself to the Scotch Army before Newarke."* [10]

In the early hours of 27th April 1646 the king left Oxford disguised as 'Harry', the servant of Master Jack Asburnham (the king's Treasurer at Warrs). The king's party passed through the parliamentarian lines with the aid of a pass signed by Fairfax which gave permission for Asburnham, with servants, to ride to London and *'make his composition'* with the Parliamentary authorities - that is, to buy himself out of the war. Through the French ambassador the king had received a verbal assurance from Lord Leven's Scots army in England. This promised that he would be received by them "in safety and honour" and with no wrong done to his conscience. The Stuarts had been Kings of Scotland long before they had reigned in England. Charles calculated that he might expect to obtain better conditions of surrender from his Scottish subjects than from the English rebels. On 5th May he gave himself up to the Scots at the Saracen's Head Inn at Southwell, near Newark in Nottinghamshire. He was soon to regret his decision.

As soon as Newark had fallen to the Scots on 8th May they struck camp and moved with the king up to Newcastle-upon-Tyne whilst negotiations as to who would make the final settlement with Charles were undertaken. The Scottish Presbyterian nobles had enriched themselves wth church land at the time of the Reformation in Scotland and so had a strong motive for supporting the Kirk system and the Covenant. The king was an Episcopalian; even one who was suspected of favouring Roman Catholics. The men of importance in Scotland therefore needed a Presbyterian king who would guarantee their estates, put down dangerous social and religious opinions like those beginning to spread amongst the Independents in the New Model Army in England, and do his best to see that Scotland was not dominated by England. The Scots proved unable to come to a deal with Charles, however, on the question of the nature of the state religion.

During the king's journey to Newcastle and his stay there, the last elements of royalist military power in the Midlands were dying out. At the end of April the garrison of Tutbury Castle surrendered, to be followed by that of Banbury on 9th May. Dudley Castle surrendered on 13th May, as did Hartlebury in Staffordshire on 16th May, and Ludlow, the last royalist stronghold in Shropshire, on 20th May. Now only three Midlands garrisons of any importance remained in oyalist hands; these were Lichfield, Worcester, and Oxford. The king wrote to all commanders of these and to *"... all other Commanders of any Townes, Castles, or Forts within the Kingdome of England or Dominion of Wales"* from Newcastle on 10th June 1646 ordering them *"... upon honourable terms and conditions to quit those TOWNES, CASTLES, and FORTS intrusted by us to you, and to disband all the forces under your severall commands."* [11]

This signalled the formal end of the first civil war, although the remaining garrisons continued to resist for some time. The garrison at Oxford, after much haggling over terms, finally complied with the king's order and surrendered to Sir Thomas Fairfax on 25th June. It was some time before the garrison commander at Lichfield was finally convinced that the king no longer possessed an army with which to relieve the garrison, but he did eventually capitulate, upon *"honourable terms of surrender,"* on 10th July.

Worcester had been the first town in England to declare for the king. Defended furiously by Colonel Henry Washington, it was the last town to yield. It was not until the news reached the garrison that Fairfax had taken Oxford and was marching upon Worcester to assist Major-General Whalley in his siege that Washington finally agreed to surrender. At 5 pm on 23rd July 1646 the victorious parliamentarian soldiers entered the last major garrison in England to hold out for the king.

Within nine months of his surrender to the Scots at Newark, Charles was handed over by them to the English Parliament on payment of £200,000 deposit and security for a similar sum to be paid at a later date. With their 'thirty pieces of silver' secured the Scots marched back north of the border. The king, now a prisoner of Parliament, was conveyed to Holdenby (or Holmby) House in Northamptonshire. En-route to Holdenby House he slept in Leicester, on the night of 12th February 1647, at the Angel Inn. Four months later he was taken from the custody of Parliament by members of the New Model Army.

The Second Civil War broke out on 30th April 1648 when English Royalists in the North seized both Berwick-upon-Tweed and Carlisle with the help of the Scots. The following day, May Day, in the midst of a meeting of the Army Council of the New Model Army at Windsor, came the dramatic news that the Adjutant-General in Wales, Fleming, had been killed in a royalist uprising there which coincided with a mutiny of disbanded Parliamentarian soldiers. The whole of South Wales was up in arms. Many political Presbyterians throughout England and Wales, who like the Scottish army had fought on the side of Parliament in the First Civil War, had become pro-royalist in the Second Civil War in opposition to the Independents in Parliament and the New Model Army.

Fleming had been popular in the Army and the news moved the Army Council to a historic resolution against the person whom they regarded as being responsible for the renewed horrors of war.

"We were led to a clear agreement amongst ourselves, not any dissenting, that it was the duty of our day, with the forces we had, to go out and fight against those potent enemies, which in that year appeared against us, with a humble confidence, in the name of the Lord only, that we should destroy them. And we were also enabled then, after seriously seeking His face, to come to a very clear joint resolution that it was our duty, if ever the Lord brought us back again in peace, to call Charles Stuart, that man of blood, to an account for the blood he had shed, and mischief he had done to the utmost against the Lord's cause and people in these poor nations." [12]

Following the defeat of the Scots and Royalists at Preston, and the latter in South Wales, Colchester, and elsewhere during the Second

Civil War, and a subsequent political purge of members of the House of Commons in early December 1648 (known as 'Pride's Purge'), King Charles I was brought to trial. This was done *"In the name of the Commons in Parliament assembled, and all the good people of England"* for *"high treason and high misdemeanours."* [13] Generally he was accused of having *"traitorously and maliciously"* plotted to enslave the English nation and of levying war on his subjects. He was to be judged by the Commissioners of a High Court of Justice especially appointed for the purpose.

The trial of the king took place in late January 1649 in the Great Hall of Westminster. As part of the trial process a committee was appointed from amongst the membership of the Commissioners to hear witnesses give condemning evidence against the accused in his absence. By this process it was hoped to convince the waverers in their own number, of whom there were many, and to indicate to the public that they did not lack evidence to support the charges against the king. The thirty-three witnesses were heard by the appointed Committee (of which Oliver Cromwell was not a member but Lord Grey of Groby was) on 24th January. On 25th January their depositions were read out at a public session of the High Court in the Painted Chamber. They demonstrated beyond doubt, if there had been any room for doubt, that the king had been seen in arms against the parliament and had invited foreign armies to enter England. They included the evidence of Humphrey Brown, the farm labourer/husbandman from Rutland, that, at the capture of Leicester, the king had not only permitted the parliamentarian prisoners to be stripped and cut about by his men, but when a royalist officer had tried to stop this barbarity he had said, *"I do not care if they cut them three times more, for they are mine enemies,"* the king being all this while *" on horseback, in bright armour, in the said town of Leicester."* The depositions of the witnesses put beyond doubt not only his personal participation in the war, but also his intention of continuing it, even during recent Treaty negotiations with representatives of Parliament. They may have helped a little to strengthen the wavering resolution

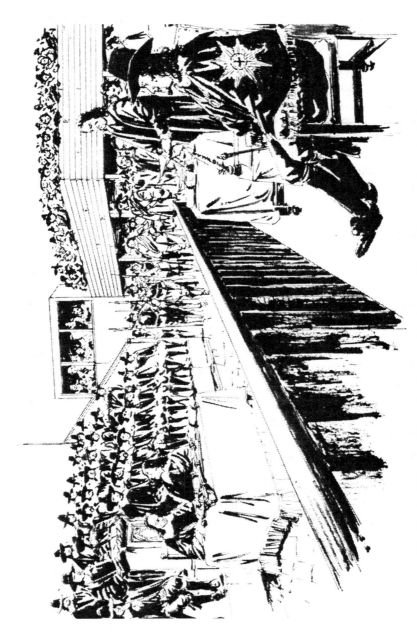

The Trial of Charles I involved several Leicestershire parliamentarians, including Thomas, Lord Grey of Groby, Peter Temple, Francis Hacker, etc.

of the more hesitant Commissioners and to impress any members of the public in the Painted Chamber or who read the newsheets being issued at the time.

On 27th January the expected guilty verdict and the death sentence were pronounced. There were sixty-eight Commissioners present, including Lord Grey of Groby. On 30th January the sentence was carried out and King Charles was beheaded. The Monarchy and the House of Lords were abolished shortly afterwards and a republican form of government known as the 'Commonwealth of England', with a Council of State, was established instead.

The Death Warrant, [14] which still survives, carries the signatures of fifty nine Commissioners set out in seven irregular parallel columns, with matching seals, at the foot of the warrant. The first four sigatures appear in the first column. John Bradshaw's name comes first, (*Jo. Bradshawe*) as President of the High Court of Justice. The second signature (*Tho. Grey*) is that of Lord Grey of Groby, in a clear bold hand, taking the precedence due to his rank in the social hierarchy. He was the only prominent member of an aristocratic family among the regicides. Next comes the signature of Oliver Cromwell (*O. Cromwell*), written as large as that of Lord Grey of Groby. The Lieutenant General of the Horse in the New Model Army was to become head of state himself, as Lord Protector, in 1654. The final signature in the first column is that of Edward Whalley (*Edw. Whalley*) and is written in a much smaller hand than the previous two. Whalley, from Nottinghamshire, was a cousin of Cromwell.

The sixteenth signature, written clearly and in the third column, is that of Peter Temple (*Pe. Temple*), the former linen-draper and militia captain from Leicester, who had been elected as a borough MP by the burgesses of Leicester to replace Thomas Cook in 1645, following the recapture of the town. Sir Arthur Hesilrige, although a commissioner (or member) of the court, did not sign the Death Warrant as his duties kept him at Newcastle-upon-Tyne where he was the Governor. He had been one of the Five Members, along with John Hampden, whom Charles I had tried to arrest in Parliament before the outbreak of the Civil War. He was a leading parliamentarian, a known republican, and a close ally of Cromwell at this point. There is little doubt that he would have signed the Death Warrant had he been in London.

Other Leicestershiremen who signed the Death Warrant, in addition to Thomas, Lord Grey of Groby and Peter Temple were Thomas Horton, Henry Smyth (or Smith), and Thomas Wayte (or Waite). Thomas Horton had originally been a servant and falconer to Sir Arthur Hesilrige at Noseley in south Leicestershire. He had joined Sir Arthur's troop of horse (nicknamed 'the Lobsters' because of their three-quarter cuirassier armour) at the outbreak of the Civil War. He had risen to the rank of colonel by 1649. His signature (*Tho. Horton*) is the forty-first and appears in the sixth column. Henry Smyth (or Smith) of Withcote was a lawyer and a relative of Edward Smih of Edmundthorpe, both in east Leicestershire. His signature (*Hen. Smyth*) is the nineteenth and appears in the fourth column. The fifth Leicestershireman to sign the Death Warrant was Thomas Wayte (or Waite) who was M.P. for Rutland and had been Governor of the Burley-on-the-Hill garrison during the Civil War. He later, at the time of the Restoration, claimed to have been duped into signing the Warrant (*Tho. Wayte*) in fifty-sixth place out of the fifty-nine sgnatures, in the seventh and final column, just after the openly hesitant commissioner John Downes.

John Cook, of Husbands Bosworth near Market Harborough, did not sign the Death Warrant. He was not a commissioner, but as the Solicitor-General at the time he prepared the charge and conducted the prosecution at the king's trial. He later said of it, *"I went cheerfully about it as to a wedding."*

Those who signed the death warrant made themselves formally and fully responsible for the king's death. The warrant was directed to three officers of the Army to see that it was put into effect. One of these was Colonel Francis Hacker, the Leicestershireman and protégé of Sir Arthur Hesilrige, who had led the garrison's cavalry during the battle for Leicester. Ironically from a family of

Nottinghamshire royalists (his brother, Rowland, was killed fighting in Henry Hastings' forces), Hacker was responsible for guarding the king and seeing that Charles Stuart was put to death by the severing of his head from his body between the hours of ten in the morning and five in the afternoon on Tuesday, January 30th 1649. Lucy Hutchinson said of him that *"Hacker ... was such a creature of Sir Arthur's* [i.e. Hesilrige's] *that, without questioning justice or honesty, he was more diligent in obeying Sir Arthur's than God's commands."* [15]

As the news of the verdict and the sentence spread a feeling of shock fell upon London. The death sentence against the king was not the work of the people of England in whose name it had been pronounced. Rather it was carried through by a small, resolute and armed minority in the face of a stunned nation. Yet this minority was convinced that it was doing the Lord God's work on behalf of the people of England. Lucy Hutchinson wrote that:-

"The gentlemen that were appointed his judges and divers others, saw in the King a disposition so bent on the ruin of all that opposed him, and of all the righteous and just things they had contended for, that it was upon the conscience of many of them that if they did not execute justice upon him, God would require at their hands all the blood and desolation which should ensue by their suffering him to escape, when God had brought him into their hands." [16]

John Hutchinson, according to his wife, had been put in as a commissioner *"very much against his will, but looking upon himself as called hereunto, durst not refuse it, as holding himself obliged by the covenant of God and the public trust of his country reposed in him, although he was not ignorant of the danger he run as the condition of things then was."* [17]

Oliver Cromwell justified their actions as taken in respect of *"This man against whom the Lord hath witnessed."*
Lord Grey of Groby did not stay in London to witness the execution

of the king. He left, after signing the Death Warrant, to return to Bradgate. He had played a leading role in the sequence of events from the time before the Army had moved from Windsor to Whitehall, through the Purge of the Long Parliament, and culminating in the trial and the sentencing of the king. According to Noble:-

"He sat in the Painted Chamber, January the 8th, 15th, 17th, 18th, 20th, 22nd, 23rd, 24th, 26th, 27th, and 29th; and he sat every day in Westminster Hall, when his majesty was brought before them, and signed the warrant for execution. His presence probably was absolutely necessary to give some sanction to the infamous proceedings, and to overawe such as might be refractory." [18]

In relation to Cromwell's assumed influence over the other signatories, and the sequence of events in general, it seems that Lord Grey of Groby's role is likely to have been previously underrated. [19]

To summarise: both of Leicester's Members of Parliament, one of its leading military defenders, and four others from Leicestershire were instrumental in exacting full retribution for the *'large map of miserie'* caused by the siege, storming and sacking of the town by the Royal Army in the summer of 1645. Both Thomas, Lord Grey of Groby and Peter Temple went on to serve on the new Council of State which was set up to run the country under the republican Commonwealth when both the Monarchy and the House of Lords were abolished later in 1649. Lord Grey was a founder member of the Council of State; Peter Temple became a member in 1650. Thus Leicester was firmly identified with the new regime.

The change of regime at national level from monarchy to commonwealth was reflected locally through changes in emblems on the state coat of arms, borough mace, and so forth. The puritan revolution was also marked by a continuing change in the sort of person active in local administration. Such changes had already been noted, often in critical terms, in local petitions to Parliament which lamented the absence from the work of the County Committee of many of the local aristocracy and greater gentry and the growing activity instead of the *'worsted stocking men'*, to use Lucy Hutchinson's term.

The Commonwealth, according to Clarendon, brought into local power *"a more inferior sort of the common people ..... who were not above the condition of ordinary inferior constables six or seven years before"*.[20] After making the usual allowance for the natural exaggeration of the embittered royalist emigré and snob, there is still some truth in Clarendon's statement. The most dramatic changes at local level came only in the last months of the Rump Parliament, however, and even more spectacularly during the period of the `Saints' or `Barebones' Parliament in 1653.

By the spring of 1650 the requirement to take the Oath of Engagement had given sme indication of those who were loyal to the new Commonwealth. It was applied to justices of the peace, constables, tithe collectors, church wardens, etc. Some were reluctant to take the oath for a variety of reasons and delayed as long as they could. In the summer of 1650, however, the process was reviewed countrywide by Bulstrode Whitelocke and his fellow Commissioners of the Great Seal and there were widespread dismissals of those who had failed to take the Engagement by then. The extent of the purge varied considerably in the counties from place to place. In Leicestershire only three J.P.s were removed and only one additional appointment made.

Throughout the Commonwealth period there was a considerable degree of defection by the old traditional county governing families.[21] Not only did they cease to support the decaying County Committees but also the Militia Committees which must have included all the really prominent men in the counties who were actively committed to the new regime. The officers appointed by the Militia Committees reflected even more strikingly the Commonwealth's lack of appeal to men of the old governing class. Many of these new officers were drawn from the ranks of the minor gentry, others from tradesmen and shopkeepers.

Leicester and its county experienced examples of changing policies that were affecting the country generally. In March 1651 the borough corporation discussed depopulation and enclosures, always a pressing local issue, and during the following year they supported a petition to Parliament on the subject. The times were unpropitious, however, and Leicester appears to have been the only town to join the lonely traditionalist voices in opposition to 'improvers' and 'inclosures'. The Earl of Stamford continued to be such an 'improver'. In addition to continuing the work of draining Wildmere Fen in Lincolnshire, which he had begun with royal agreement in the 1630s, he obtained £1,500 out of delinquents' estates for improving the navigation of the river Welland. There was nothing new about such policies. Peculiar to the period of the new regime, however, were the frequent purchases of Crown and ecclesiastical lands and fee-farm rents. Many corporations bought whatever they could lay their hands on, stretching their resources to the limit, or borrowing from their wealthier members.

There were several changes in the borough and the county after the establishment of the Commonwealth. The new regime introduced changes, some as early as from the end of the first civil war in 1645, affecting matters of religious observance, the appointment of clergy and ministers, and the raising and disbursement of revenue.

In 1649, when there were rumours of a popular movement to throw down the enclosures of the neighbouring Leicester Forest, the Corporation took the matter up. A petition was drafted, setting out the economic and social evils attending enclosure, and proposing the establishment of machinery to check it, consisting of a committee without whose assent enclosing was not to be permitted. They set out as follows,

"Reasons against depopulacion [sic] and decaye of tillage"

"1. Itt unpeoples ye Nacion, abates strength and courage

2. It ympoverisheth Citties, Borroughs and markett Townes

3. It makes many poore, Idle, and wanderers

4. Our grounde beinge a deepe Soyle that the wayes wilbe unpassable, as experience in some allreddye appeares

5. This was the second Countye appointed by Parliament to continue for tillage.

6. The Countyes of Leicester and Northampton are as a Magazeene for Corne, both for the North and west

7. Depopulated townes, doe not serve the Comon Wealth with men, Horse, Carriages, or quarters for Souldiers by the decaye of tillage".[22]

A local minister was instructed to submit the petition to Parliament, *"which hath still a watchful eye and open ear to redress the common grievances of the nation"*. The agent selected to present the borough's case was the Rev. John Moore, the minister of Shearsby, a prolific pamphleteer, who for several years attacked the local depopulating landlords. But it proved a slow and uphill struggle. The suggestion of sending a petition *"against depopulacion in regard there is many feilds* [sic] *against inclosure"* was first considered by the Corporation in March 1651. On 13th October, 1653 it was agreed that it should be copied out and *"hands to be gotten to the same, and then sent up to London by Mr. Moore, Minister of Shearsby"*.

Half a century earlier it is probable that such local concern would have been followed by the passing of Depopulation Acts and the issue of a Royal Commission. In the long years since the meeting of the Long Parliament, however, the whole attitude of public policy towards the enclosure movement had begun to change. Confiscations, sequestrations, compositions, sale of fee rents, and war taxation had effected a revolution in the distribution of property. As land changed hands, customary relationships were shaken and new interests were created. Enclosure was being pushed forward by means of law suits ending in Chancery decrees. It was not to be expected that City merchants and members of the Committee for Compounding, some of whom had found land speculation a profitable business, should hear with enthusiasm a proposal to revive the old policy of arresting enclosures by State interference, at which the gentry had grumbled for more than a century.

In these circumstances, it is not surprising that reformers should have found the supposedly *'open ear of Parliament'* closed to agrarian grievances. Nor was it only the political and economic environment which had changed. The revolution in thought had been equally profound. The theoretical basis of the policy of protecting the rural population who derived their living from the land by preventing enclosure had been a conception of landownership which regarded its rights and its duties as inextricably linked. Property was not merely a source of income, but a public function too. Its use was limited by social obligations and the necessities of State. With such a doctrine the classes who had taken the lead in the struggle against the monarchy could no longer compromise. The view of society held by that part of the Puritan movement which was socially and politically influential had been expressed by the Grandees, such as Cromwell and Ireton, in their retort to the radicals in the Army during the Putney Debates. It was that the freeholders really constituted the body politic, and that they could use their property as they pleased, uncontrolled by obligations to any superior, or by the needs of the mass of the community, who were mere tenants at will, with no fixed interest or share in the land of the kingdom - *"just the interest in breathing"*!

Naturally, this change of ideas had profound effects on society. Formerly a course commending itself to all public-spirited persons, the attempt to prevent enclosure was now discredited as the programme of religious and political radicals. Later, when in 1656 Major-General Whalley introduced a measure to regulate and restrict the enclosure of common land, apparently based on the lines proposed by the Leicester petition, there was an instant outcry from Parliament that it would *'destroy property'*, and the bill was refused a second reading.

Similarly, the issues of the fee farm rents (from former Crown estates), farming out the excise in the county, and the diversion of monies by the government which had traditionally gone to support local charities were all issues which exercised the Corporation and people of Leicester, again without much satisfaction.

In 1651 a letter was written to the Boroughs MPs, Lord Grey of Groby and Peter Temple, by the Mayor and the Aldermen *"to acquaint them howe generally the farminge out of ye Excise in this Countye is disliked and to praye their assistance for releife* [sic] *therein"*.[23] Some time later a letter from a solicitor on behalf of the mayor described how he had waited about in London trying to get the business of fee farm rates seen to. After getting a requisite order drawn up and signed he had attended a meeting of the Commissioners at Worcester House to secure *"a stopp made of those fee farme rents mencioned in the order"*. He explained that other fee farm rents were available to be contracted for by purchasers who were likely to be preferred before petitioners. These *"with your own fee farm rentes will come to a little more than the summe allowed, and for the overplus the Corporacion are to be purchasers, which will be but a small matter. These are the best rentes that I could make choice of that are not as yet contracted for. I am to waite upon my Lord Grey upon Thursday morninge, and in the afternoone the Committee have promised his lordship to meete and give the bussines* [sic] *as speedy a dispatch as may bee"*.[24]

One of the features of the new regime at the local level was interference in matters of religious observance and the appointment of ministers. Another aspect that caused concern was the award of many local Crown revenues to the Army or to the highest bidder, as illustrated in the above extract concerning fee farm rents. For a time the Corporation protested, mainly in vain, that some of the dues for local charitable foundations, such as the Wyggeston's Hospital, the Trinity Hospital, and the Honour of Leicester (relating to the ancient rights, customs, privileges, and properties of the Duchy of Lancaster in Leicester), of which Lord Grey of Groby was the Steward, had gone towards the maintenance of regiments. Sometimes they were successful in getting the payment restored.

For example, the Chamberlains' Accounts for the Borough for 1650-51 show the following, *"Rents of fee farmes and cheife [sic] and payd this to the Trustees for the Trinity Hospitall Leicester, and which were heretofore paid to the Crowne and synce to the Common Wealth of England, and were lately sould by the Trustees by order of parliament amongst other things towards the sayd Trinity Hospital paye"*.[25]

In December 1651 the county of Leicester contributed the sum of £1,400 out of a nation-wide tax of £90,000 a month for six months towards the maintenance of the army. It was this level of taxation that was making both the new regime and the Army unpopular in many parts of the country. Lord Grey of Groby had to work actively to maintain his position both nationally and locally through cultivating his contacts.

On 1st March 1652 lists of names of the Justices of the Peace for all the counties in England and Wales were issued. These documents are of interest because they indicate those who were attached to the then government of the Commonwealth. The names of Speaker Lenthall, Captain-General Cromwell, Lord President Bradshaw, Bulstrode Whitelocke and the other commissioners of the great seal, the chief justices, some judges, and most of the great officers of state, were named in the commission of each county.

251

The names of those listed for the county of Leicester are as follows:

"John Bradshaw, Lord President
William Lenthall, Speaker of Parliament
Oliver Cromwell, captain-general
Bulstrode Whitelocke)
Richard Keble   ) lords commissioners of the great seal
John Lisle   )
Henry, earl of Kent
Henry, earl of Stamford
Thomas, lord Grey de Groby
Bennett, lord Sherard
Thomas, lord Fairfax
Henry Rolle, chief justice of the upper bench
Oliver St. John, chief justice of the common bench
John Wilde, chief baron, of the public exchequer
Philip Jermyn, one of the justices in the upper bench
John Puleston and Edward Atkins, two of the justices of the common pleas
Edmund Predeaux, attorney-general
Sir Arthur Haslewrigge, baronet
Sir Thomas Hartop, knight
Thomas Chapman, sergeant at law

John St. John	*Thomas Waite*
Thomas Beaumont	*Thomas Hasbridge*
Christopher Packe	*James Abney*
Richard Newdigate	*William Hewett*
Henry Smyth	*Arthur Stavely*
William Quarles	*William Danvers*
Peter Temple	*Gamaliell Purefoy*
Casibilian Burton	*Henry Danvers*
John Browne	*Francis Hacker*
Thomas Brudenell	*Thomas Pochin*
Simon Rugeby	*John Goodman*
William Hartoppe	*John Pratt*
William Bainbridge	*Henry Markham "*[(26)]

The reign of the 'Saints' in Leicester was drab rather than cruel. The Mayor, Aldermen, and Justices had the difficult task of enforcing, as far as they could, their ideal of a uniform and moderate puritanism in a society that included some ungodly backsliders and a number of intemperate zealots. They fined people for working, or allowing their children to play, on the Lord's day, for ringing church bells contrary to the ordinance, for drinking the king's health, for playing *"shove grote"*. They also imprisoned people for writing *'lybells in a songe ..... against Generall Cromwell"* and circulating the same. They impounded heretical books and committed Quakers to prison for refusing to recognize the authority of 'magistrates' in church and state. The reaction of the local gentry to the members of the local puritan regime in Leicester might well have been that of the free living Sir Toby Belch to Malvolio in Shakespeare's *Twelfth Night*. *"Art [thou] any more than a steward? Dost thou think because thou art virtuous, there shall be no more cakes and ale?"*[27]

At the same time the Corporation attempted to improve the material benefit of the town which had suffered so much from the storming and sacking in 1645 and the following poor harvests. They sought to increase their corporate powers and approved a scheme, which was not particularly successful, for bringing water from the Castle Mill to the High Cross, and preparing their case for a new charter which would extend their full jurisdiction over the suburbs of St. Margarets, St. Leonards, the Castle and the Newarke.

Following the execution of the king the symbols of the monarchy were replaced over a period of months by those of the Commonwealth. Another new mace, this time bearing the new arms, weighing 87 ounces and costing £48 3s. 6d., had to be purchased. It was to be carried on official occasions by Hugh Dawes the Corporation mace bearer. The 'late Kings Armes' were taken down from the mayor's parlour, the rich new chimney-piece being scoured and the arms of the Commonwealth were substituted. The royal arms were similarly removed from the 'Towne Hall' and the Gainsborough. On 23rd December 1650 the mayor and the justices received the following instruction which was swiftly relayed, *"According to speciall directions from the Councell of State of the third day of December instant you are desired upon sight hereof presently to give order to the Constables, Churchwardens and third barowes in the severall divisions and wards of your Borrough to take away and deface the Armes and pictures of the late Kinge in all Churches, Chappells and publicke places in your Borough before the sixth day of January next comynge according to the Act of Parliament in that behalf ....."*[(28)]

Thirteen staves were ordered for the Constables and Beadles; topped with knobs bearing the State Arms and the Town Arms. The new State Arms were set up on the city gates at a cost of four shillings. Five frames for the new state arms were produced and these arms were emblazoned by a Robert Bradshawe at the Town Hall, the East Gate and the West Gate.

The Corporation also regularly incurred expenditure relating to providing hospitality, entertaining local and national dignitaries, ad celebrating the triumphs of the Commonwealth regime. Payments were made *"to the Sergeants and drummers when proclamacion was made against the Scots King"* [i.e. Charles II], for *"beere given to the generalls army when they marched to Worcester"*, for *"wyne, suger* [sic] *and nutmeggs when the Maior and divers Aldermen went to visit Coll: Temple and Capt. Smyth att Mr Barnes"*, for *"a quart of sacke to drinke with Coll: Hacker when he came from Worcester fight"*, for *"2 gallons of Clarett, 2 gallons of white* [wine], *two galloons of sacke, three pound of Suger, and a bankett* [sic] (a banquet?) presented to Lord Generall Cromwell when he went to Worcester. Similar expenses were incurred in relation to entertainment at `the Crane' involving wine, beer, tobacco, and pipes on separate occasions for *"Lord Grey about takeinge of horses charges upon the Towne, and about foote to be raysed att two severall tymes"*, Colonel Hacker and divers gentlemen, Colonel Fairfax and Colonel Hacker, Sir Arthur Haselrigg, and again for *"two gallons and 5 pints of sack, two gallons of white wine, two pounds of biskett and 1 lb. of suger when the Maior and Aldermen went to visett the Lord Grey att the Crane, August 1651"*.[(29)]

254

On 18th June 1651 the mayor and aldermen dined with several ministers, consuming wine, beer, and tobacco, this being *"a daye of thanksgiving"*. Similar events are recorded for *"14 gentlemens dinners, and for wyne, strong beare and tobacco, att a dinner there upon the daye of thanksgiving for the great victory att Worcester"* and for *"14 gentlemens dinners and fower* [sic] *others and for wyne, strong beare and tobacco, att a dinner upon the daye of thanksgiving for ye regaining of Leicester"*.[(30)]

The change of regime had also had its impact throughout the wider county. One of the areas in which it was most noticeable was that of religious observation and the appointment of clergy to the 'livings' of the established church. The civil war, the resultant execution of the king and the creation of the puritan Commonwealth marked not only the removal of bishops and the Book of Common Prayer, but also the end of any realistic attempt to maintain the conformity and comprehensiveness of the Church of England as a national institution with membership analogous with that of the national or local state. The state church, whether the Arminian version of Anglicanism favoured by Laud or the Presbyterian version under the Covenant, could no longer include the radical Independents, Baptists, and other sectaries who were so important to the 'revolutionaries' of the Rump, such as Lord Grey of Groby, and their supporters. This does not mean that attempts were not made to enforce conformity and to deter dissent, as has already been noted, particularly by the Presbyterians whenever they thought they were in the ascendent. Indeed, John Milton, in his poem *On the New Forcers of Conscience under the Long Parliament*, as an Independent charged that *"New Presbyter is but old Priest writ large"*. Yet even when monarchical and episcopal authority were restored in 1660 there had come into being a large body of Christians who were outside the established Church of England, and who were to become known from then on as 'dissenters'.

The civil war itself had many and varied effects upon the clergy of Leicester and Leicestershire. Many parish priests had supported the king with their prayers and their money. Some had supported *'the Lord's anointed'* in more active ways. Foremost amongst these was Henry Ferne, Rector of Medbourne, who had been appointed Archdeacon of Leicester in 1641. He had joined Charles I when the royal standard was raised at Nottingham and preached before him on several occasions, becoming a royal chaplain. He had then poured out pamphlets in the royalist cause, for which he was denounced by Parliament. He had been with the king at Oxford and at the siege of Leicester in 1645. Later he had been with the besieged royalist garrison at Newark when it had surrendered. When he had been deprived of his living at Medbourne in 1646 the loyal Archdeacon had rejoined Charles during his captivity at Carisbrooke Castle. After the king's execution Ferne had retired to his native Yorkshire.

Other royalist clergy had actually taken up arms themselves. The most prominent in this respect was Michael Hudson of Market Bosworth, who was also a royal chaplain. He had become Scoutmaster-General of the royalist army in the North and conducted the king from Oxford to Newcastle. After twice escaping from prison Hudson had raised a troop of horse but was eventually killed at the capture of Woodcroft House in Northamptonshire by troops under Lord Grey's command in 1648. The vicar of Sileby, Richard Benskin, had been similarly killed after the storming of Shelford House in Nottinghamshire in 1646 by the forces of Colonel Poyntz and Colonel John Hutchinson.

A number of clergy had sought refuge with the royalist garrisons at Ashby and Belvoir Castles, which was considered by the local parliamentarian committee as active participation. Ferne, Hudson, and Benskin had all had their benefices sequestered, but many others had suffered the same fate for relatively trivial causes. Parliament had appointed County Commissioners to deal with 'scandalous' clergy or ministers who were charged under three distinct headings: i. Delinquency (i.e.attachment to the Royalist cause); ii. Churchmanship (i.e.being of 'papistical' inclinations rather than a 'godly' minister); iii. Moral character (i.e. loose and lax in morality). Charges were often brought under all three headings, so that the unfortunate clergymen had little chance of escape. Some had been allowed to compound for sequestration by paying a fine, and in some cases one fifth of the income was granted in order to support the deprived incumbent's family. Some of the cases from the Committee make interesting, and even occasionally amusing, reading.

Robert Bayley, vicar of Oadby, it was alleged, fought and quarrelled in ale-houses, gave the king's garrison at Leicester - after its capture in June 1645 - a pig, and profaned the Sabbath; while his wife seldom attended church. Edward Heron, rector of Croxton, had joined the Belvoir garrison, and had employed a tanner and a *"drunken wheelwright"* as curates. He claimed that he had been detained at Belvoir against his will, vigorously denied the charges, and escaped with a fine of £70. Royalist sympathies had cost a Clement Bretton the wealthy rectory of Church Langton. He retired to his family home at Uppingham in Rutland where he was to be listed as a suspect in 1655. At Earl Shilton the curate, besides welcoming royalist soldiers, was said to have used old notes as new sermons for the past twenty years. It is not clear which was considered to be the more serious crime in the view of the sober puritans on the committee! The incumbents of Ibstock (Laud's old living), Belton and Hinckley had been active in raising money for the king's cause. All of them were deprived of their livings, though Thomas Cleveland of Hinckley (father of the poet John Cleveland) was reinstated when he compounded and took the Covenant. Most of the clergy produced excuses when accused. The Rector of Kimcote had been charged with *"tippling with Cavaliers"*, which he denied, and with joining the Royal Army at Nottingham. He had replied that *"owing to disorders and private business he was away three weeks, but often home at night"*. Only one accused priest, Thomas Rawson of Hoby, had made no plea, but boldly proclaimed his loyalty to *"Church, King, and the Laws"*. The strangest charge was made against Thomas Bird of Somerby. In addition to being a *"drunkard, swearer and profaner of the Sabbath"* he had been charged with riding after a hare while wearing his surplice and tearing it whilst clearing a gate, so that the parish was forced to *"provide a new surplice for him to read prayers in and to keep the old one for him to hunt in!"* The vicar had maintained in response that his horse had bolted with him when startled by a hare jumping up; what was more, his surplice was not torn and no new one had been bought!

It has been estimated that nearly seventy priests in the county of Leicestershire were deprived of their livings by the Parliamentary sequestrators, which indicates that although puritanism had a strong hold, particularly in Leicester itself, there were many clergy who would not compromise their faith in the name of political expediency. A few even continued to use the traditional forms of worship and defied the Parliamentarian, Commonwealth and Protectoral regimes, remaining undetected, as did Joseph Holt at Stanton Wyville during the 1650s. In several places priests were replaced by Presbyterian or independent ministers without episcopal ordination. In some cases, as happened at Wymeswold, a *"parish register"* of preferred godly preachers was elected by the parishioners.

The newcomers who joined the magistracy and the local committees under the Commonwealth regime were not necessarily religious as well as political radicals. The magistrates of Leicester, for example, who included Thomas Beaumont and the Rump MP Peter Temple, vigorously repressed the local Baptists. Eventually the borough corporation split on religious lines and was unable to appoint without a considerable delay to fill a vacant lectureship following the resignation of John Angel.

With the pro-royalist clergy mostly ejected, it might have been expected that the remaining incumbents could have relaxed. This proved to be far from the case. A priest's or a minister's life was full of pitfalls during this period, *"as if a man did flee from a lion, and a bear met him"*. In 1651-52 the *Oath of Engagement* pledging loyalty to the Commonwealth without King or House of Lords was presented to the clergy. Some of those who had felt able to take the Covenant abolishing episcopacy found this next move more than they could accept and were, in their turn, deprived. Amongst them were Job Grey, the son of the old Earl of Kent who had been rector of Aston Flamville, and John Angel, master and confrater of

Wyggeston's Hospital. John Angel was an influential figure in Leicester, having been confrater and lecturer at St. Martin's Church since 1627. In 1633 he had persuaded the Town Corporation to move the town library from St. Martin's Church [now Leicester Cathedral] to the old Town Hall [now the Guildhall], and had compiled a library catalogue. A leading puritan, he had been admonished by Archbishop Laud in 1634, and was arrested after the capture of Leicester by the royalist army in 1645, but was exchanged for a captive royalist. He had replaced William Chillingworth as the master of Wyggeston's Hospital when the latter had been ejected because of his involvement with royalist forces. A record remains in the Hall Papers of the Borough of Leicester dated 11th February 1651 which is addressed to the Mayor and Aldermen and reads as follows, *"Gentlemen, We doe earnestly desyre that you would be pleased to use your uttermost indeavour* [sic] *that wee may have Liberty to continue in our places at Leicester for the space of two or three monthes : in which tyme wee doubt not but the Lord will cleere* [sic] *his will and our way before us; and wee assure you that our not ingaging* [sic] *hitherto hath not issued out of any principle of opposition; but out of conscyence to Allmighty God. This wee shall take as a favour and shall rest*

> *Youres in the Lord*
> *John Angell*
> *John Price"*[31]

Evidently they did not feel able to take the Oath of Engagement in the event and sometime later in 1651 John Angel left the town he had served so well. He repaid the Corporation in full the £35 it had previously loaned to him. Indeed, both he and John Price were so well thought of that the Corporation paid on 22nd February 1652 for a gallon of sack and a gallon of white wine and sugar when the Mayor and Aldermen took their leave of them in an official farewell. John Angel was later appointed a lecturer at Grantham in Lincolnshire. Here, for some reason, he does not seem to have been required to subscribe to the Engagement. He remained well thought of in Leicester and the Borough Chamberlain's accounts for 1654-55 record a payment of £10 to *"Mr Angell, late Lecturer in this Towne, by order of a Common Hall"*. John Angel died in Grantham in 1655. He was replaced as Lecturer in Leicester in February 1652 by a Mr. Pyke, *"he beinge in such esteeme with the Lord Generall"* [Oliver Cromwell]. [32]

During these same troubled years George Fox, born in the Leicestershire village of Fenny Drayton in 1624, founded the Society of Friends or the 'Quakers' as they came to be known. They received their nickname from one of their early exhortations - *"Tremble and quake in the presence of the Lord!"*. The Quakers felt obliged to protest against *'steeple houses'* (churches) and *'Baal's priests'* (clergymen). They refused to pay tithes or to remove their hats as a sign of submission to higher authority other than God. This refusal of the 'Friends' to conform to expected conduct in religious matters or to show respect for temporal authority or social 'superiors' led to their persecution throughout the Commonwealth, the Protectorate and the Restoration. George Fox had begun preaching in 1649, the year of the king's execution. At his first appearance in Leicester itself as a 'Quaker' Fox caused something like a riot in a church, for which he appears to have escaped unpunished. Later, in 1654, he had a confrontation with Francis Hacker and a fascinating debate ensued. Having failed to persuade the Quaker leader to avoid trouble Hacker sent him up to Cromwell, then Lord Protector, in London. At a personal level the two seem to have got on well together. Fox made some converts in Leicester, who suffered imprisonment and complained of it in letters to the Corporation and the local magistrates.

Arms of the Commonwealth

NOTES

1. Records of the Borough of Leicester - Hall Papers XI, No. 421.
2. Ibid ; Hall Papers XI, No. 451 [17 November 1645].
3. John Vicars, *Magnalia Dei Anglicana*, or *England's Parliamentary Chronicle*, (London 1644 - 1646) Part IV, p. 177
4. Ibid ; Part IV, p. 313.
5. Ibid ; Part IV, p. 361.
6. Bulstrode Whitelocke, *Memorials of the English Affairs*, (London, 1682), p. 192.
7. Vicars, op. cit. 363. [February 7th, 1646].
8. Ibid ; p. 378. [March 4th, 1646].
9. Dugdale, *A Short View of the Late Troubles in England*, pp. 202 - 203.
10. Rushworth, *Historical collections abridged and improved*, Vol. VI, p. 1.
11. Vicars, op. cit., Part IV, p. 444.
12. Journal of the House of Commons, Vol. V., p.620.
13. *State Trials*, Cobbett's Complete Collection, 1810. & Mark Noble, *Memoirs of the Protectoral House of Cromwell*, Vol. I., p.119. Birmingham, 1787.
14. See the copy of the Death Warrant reproduced at the end of this chapter.
15. Lucy Hutchnson, *Memoirs of the Life of Colonel Hutchinson*, Oxford University Press, London, 1973 Edition. p.200.
16. Ibid. Everyman's Library Edition, Dent, London, 1965. p.266.
17. Ibid. p.265.
18. Mark Noble, *The Lives of the English Regicides*, London, 1788. Vol. I p.268.
19. For more details of the role played by Lord Grey of Groby see *Aristocrat and Regicide - The Life and Times of Thomas, Lord Grey of Groby (1623-1657)*, New Millennium. London, 2000, by this author.
20. Clarendon, op. cit. Vol. VI. pp. 521-2.
21. David Underdown, *Royalist Conspiracy in England*, New Haven, Yale University Press, 1960.

22. Records of the Borough of Leicester - Hall Papers XII, 1649.
23. Ibid., Hall Papers XIII, 1651.
24. Ibid.
25. Records of the Borough of Leicester - Chamberlains' Accounts, 1650-51.
26. Calendar of State Papers (Domestic Series), Vol. XXIV; Mar. 1. 1652.
27. William Shakespeare, *Twelfth Night* or *What You Will*, Act II, Scene 3.
28. Calendar of State Papers (Domestic Series), Vol. XX. Dec. 18. 1650.
29. Records of the Borough of Leicester - Chamberlains' Accounts, 1650-51.
30. Ibid.
31. Records of the Borough of Leicester - Hall Papers, XIII, 1651.
32. Ibid., Hall Papers, XIII, 1651-2.

Great Seal of the Commonwealth

S. Prospect.

Prospect of Leicester from the south

The Trial of King Charles I by the High Court of Justice

King Charles I

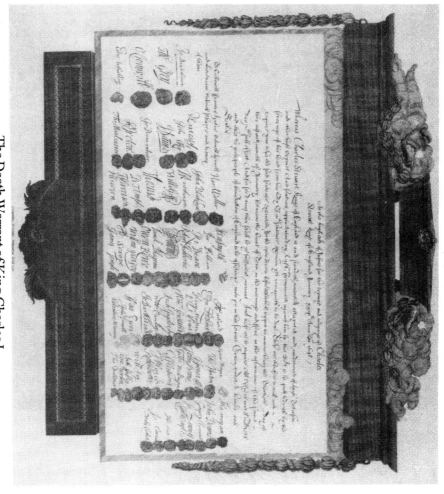

The Death Warrant of King Charles I

The Execution of King Charles I

Thomas, Lord Grey of Groby (1623-1657)

CHAPTER NINE

RESTORATION AND NEMESIS

"And the Lord said unto Samuel, 'Hearken unto the voice
of the people in all that they say unto thee: for they
have not rejected thee, but they have rejected me,
that I should not be king over them'."

(1 Samuel Chapter 8 v.7.)

The wheel of fortune turned again with the collapse of the Republic
and the restoration of the Monarchy, under Charles II. The return
of the House of Stuart seems to have come upon Leicester as
something of a surprise. When the Sheriff of Leicestershire, George
Faunt, presented an address on 30th January 1660 to General Monck
at St. Albans giving the support of the county to his endeavours,
(thought by many to be aiming at the restoration of the monarchy),
the Borough of Leicester cautiously refused to join in. Clearly, they
still favoured the Republic.

In those early days of 1660 General George Monck, a former royalist
officer promoted by Oliver Cromwell, who had been in charge of
the army in Scotland marched it south on the pretext of saving the
Rump Parliament from elements of the army in England. This
followed the confusion after the collapse of the Protectorate under
Richard Cromwell, the son and political heir of Oliver Cromwell.
Upon his arrival in London Monck declared for a *'free parliament'*.
This readmitted the members of the 1640 'Long Parliament' who
had been excluded and secluded since the civil war, and particularly
since 'Pride's Purge' in which Lord Grey of Groby had played a
leading role prior to the king's trial and execution. This Parliament
dissolved itself in March 1660 and the following elections saw the
return of the Convention or 'Cavalier' Parliament in April. From
this point on the restoration of the monarchy became a certainty.
The Rump Parliament and the Army had become too unpopular by
now and the surviving 'Rumpers' had become outnumbered in

Parliament. Old Sir Jacob Astley's prediction, whilst sitting on a drum at Stow-on-the-Wold in March 1646 at the end of the first civil war, had been proved correct at last. King Charles II was proclaimed in London on 8th May.

It was now the time for the settling of scores. The 'Cavalier' Parliament began to consider an Act of Oblivion in mid-May 1660. This would wipe out and excuse all offences committed under the Commonwealth unless the 'crimes' and the individuals had been specifically excepted.

In particular vengeance was sought against those held responsible for the shedding of:- *"... the late king's blood. First the fact was disowned, then all the acts made after it rendered void, then an inquisition made after those that were guilty thereof, but only seven were nominated of those that sat in judgement on that prince, for exemplary justice, and a proclamation sent for the* rest *to come in, upon penalty of losing their estates."* [1]

Thomas, Lord Grey of Groby had died in late April/early May 1657. His son and heir, also named Thomas, and also styled Lord Grey of Groby, was aged about seven years old at the time of the Restoration and would have to wait until his grandfather's death in 1673 to become the second Earl of Stamford at the age of twenty four.

In a letter dated 15th May 1660 a Mr. Ayloffe informs a Mr. John Langley of proceedings in the matter of the Act of Oblivion:- *"... The Act of Oblivion is the thing they are now vigorously upon; wherein their indulgence to except but seven persons (which 'tis said the General* [Monck] *was the occasion of) is much wondered at; though the numbers be resolved, yet I do not hear that the persons are yet established, which perhaps may be kept secret till as many as can be found [i.e. of the regicides] may be secured, and that 'tis thought has made many hide themselves, for there is a stop upon all posts; but 'tis said there are about 20 secured here and fetching up; 'twas moved*

270

that the executioner [of Charles I] *might be enquired out, and the Speaker said that would be known in due time ...*

"... This day 'twas moved to name the seven, to put the others out of terror, but took not; they have ordered bills of Attainder against the late Protector, Bradshaw, Ireton, and Pride for the confiscation of their estates; 'twas moved the Lo. Gray of Groby might ha' been another, but was not. One thought the seven too few, he would have had of all professions, some soldiers, lawyers, courtiers, clergy, but 'twas not seconded; 'tis said divers are run away, as Mildmay, Ludlow, Lo. Mounson, Lisle, and Martin; but they have a plentiful world of these delinquents, enough to hang, enough to confiscate, enough to banish, enough to imprison, and enough to run away. They have secured Thurlow [Thurloe]*; some think rather to squeeze some discovery out of him, than for anything capital."* [2]

The House of Commons resolved on 9th June 1660, *"That the* [late] *Lord Grey of Grooby be not excepted out of the Act of General Pardon and Oblivion as to his Estate."* [3]

The House was probably lenient because the heir's stepfather, Gustavus Mackworth, had died supporting his uncle's (Sir George Booth) rising on behalf of the king in August 1659, while his grandfather, the first Earl of Stamford, had also declared for the king and had been arrested and imprisoned for high treason early in the following month. Despite the record of his own father, therefore, the young Thomas Grey found that his family had now acquired acceptable royalist credentials. Sir George Booth, the Cheshire landowner and husband of Elizabeth, the Earl of Stamford's eldest daughter, was rewarded after the Restoration of the Monarchy by being created Lord Delamere. (This was the man who had written in April 1645 to warn his brother-in-law, Lord Grey of Groby, of the inadequate state of Leicester's defences).

What would have happened had Thomas, Lord Grey of Groby, the aristocratic regicide, still been alive is a different matter. Some bizarre

271

rumours were in circulation concerning his actual role in the matter of the king's death. Some argued that he, rather than Oliver Cromwell, was the prime mover in securing it and the signatures on the Death Warrant. Some went even further.

On 4th June a Dr. Thomas Smith wrote of "[News] *From H* [umphrey] *R* [obinson] *thus - They have one in hold who affirms that Lord Grey of Groby was the executioner of the late King."* [4]

There is little evidence to support this allegation and it does not seem to have been taken any further. It is true that on New Year's Day 1649 Lord Grey of Groby had been active in carrying the ordinance for the king's trial from the House of Commons up to the House of Lords. More significantly, it was alleged that when the Lords rejected the ordinance he had proclaimed that he would himself perform the executioner's office rather than let the King escape from justice. On the day of the king's execution the executioner and his assistant had been not only masked, as was usual, but disguised beyond recognition in thick close-fitting frieze-coats with hair and beards that were evidently not their own. Descriptions of the two executioners differed considerably. An account written at the time describes them in seamen's clothes. One of the witnesses in 1660 said that they wore woollen habits like butchers. There is agreement about the grey hair and beard of the executioner but his assistant is variously described as flaxen and black-bearded. The diminutive stature of Lord Grey is likely to have given him away if he had indeed acted in one of these offices. It is more likely that this allegation merely added to the demonic and fanatical image of him created by his enemies.

Fortunately for the Greys of Groby and Bradgate the Earl of Stamford had been freed from his imprisonment in the Tower of London as a consequence of the Restoration and was able to use his influence to prevent the exhumation and posthumous 'execution' and mutilation of Lord Grey of Groby's body, as happened to the corpses of Cromwell, Ireton, Bradshaw, and some other deceased regicides

272

who had been involved in Charles I's execution. He also managed to save most of his late son and heir's estate from being exempted from the Act of Oblivion .

Reprisals against the Parliamentarians, especially the regicides, began in earnest within six months of the Restoration. In addition to the exceptions to the Act of Oblivion, which in the event numbered far more than the original seven, in November 1660 commissions were appointed *'to inquire of and seize'* the estates of traitors and a list was attached in the case of each of twenty four counties in England and Wales.

There had been in total sixty-nine regicides - the sixty-seven who *'stood up'* at the sentencing of the king, and two others, Thomas Chaloner and Richard Ingoldsby, who were not present then, but who had later signed the Death Warrant. Of the fifty-nine who had signed the Death Warrant eighteen had already died. Of the Leicestershire regicides two were deceased by the time of the Restoration. One, as has been mentioned, was Thomas, Lord Grey of Groby, the aristocratic regicide. The other was Thomas Horton. Horton, from Noseley, had died later in 1649 whilst serving as a colonel of horse in the Army in Ireland. He had bequeathed to Oliver Cromwell his horse, which was called 'Hesilrige' after his former employer and commander!

On 30th January 1661 - the anniversary of Charles I's execution - the corpses of Cromwell, Ireton, and Bradshaw, who had all died before the Restoration, were dug up and exposed all day on the gallows at Tyburn in a grisly spectacle. At sunset the bodies were taken down and buried in a common pit below the gibbet. The heads were cut off and exposed on spikes on the top of Westminster Hall.

Most of those who had been involved in the death of Charles I were, however, still alive in 1660. Of the forty-one survivors sixteen fled the country. Three of these, including Edward Whalley, found sanctuary amongst the puritans of New England. Whalley had been appointed in 1655 the Major-General for the East Midlands district, which included Leicestershire and Nottinghamshire, during Cromwell's Protectorate. He died in Massachusetts in or around 1675. Three others, and the two former clerks of the Court, fled to Switzerland. One, John Lisle, was stabbed and killed by an Irish Royalist one Sunday in Lausanne. The other four lived out their lives in Vevey and were buried there. Five others took refuge in Germany and the Low Countries. Three others escaped to Holland only to be tracked down and betrayed by a former colleague, Cromwell's Scoutmaster-General George Downing (after whom Downing Street is named) who was working his way into the favour of the new regime.

Many of the surviving regicides surrendered, hoping for the mercy promised by the new king to all, but those excepted by the Act of Oblivion, who came in within forty days of his return from abroad. The overwhelming reaction in favour of the re-established monarchy made the regicides scapegoats for the crimes of the nation. Some, such as John Downes, Edward Harvey, and Thomas Wayte (or Waite) pleaded that they had done all they could to save the king; whilst others, including Henry Smith of Rutland, claimed that they had been ignorant, weak, intimidated and misled by the 'arch-criminals' such as Cromwell, Ireton and Lord Grey of Groby. Henry Smith (or Smyth), originally a Leicestershire lawyer from Withcote, was spared execution and, like the others, was imprisoned in the Tower of London. He was released before his death in or about 1668.

Thomas Wayte, the Leicestershire squire and M.P. for Rutland, claimed to have withdrawn from the House of Commons on 12th or 13th December 1648 and to have returned to Leicestershire where he suppressed republican petitions both there and in Rutland. He had returned to London around 25th January. He claimed to have been tricked into attending the Court by a message allegedly from Lord Grey of Groby. He had served under Lord Grey previously in the civil war and had been made by him the Governor of the garrison at Burley-on-the-Hill. Although they had then quarrelled he and Lord Grey were apparently on good terms again at this time. The forged note, purporting to have come from Lord Grey of Groby calling him to the Court on the 27th January 1649, the fateful day of the verdict, had actually been sent by Cromwell and Ireton. According to his story he only attended on Monday the 29th because he had been assured there would be no execution, but he had been forced to sign the death warrant by Cromwell and Ireton who were collecting signatures at the House of Commons. Wayte thus seems to have been deceived twice over. Lord Grey's degree of complicity in the deception is not clear but he certainly seems to have had influence over Thomas Wayte. Wayte appears to have harboured no ill feeling towards Lord Grey of Groby, however, and also must have been trusted by him as he acted as both witness of Lord Grey's will and as joint executor of his estate in 1657.

Colonel John Hutchinson, the former Governor and M.P. for Nottingham, who was respected by all parties, was persuaded in the interests of his family to profess repentance for his part, as a regicide, in the king's death. He thus purchased his liberty, albeit with a very troubled conscience when he saw what happened to many of his ex-comrades; but he was arrested in 1662 on spurious claims of suspicion of complicity in plots against the restored monarchy.

When found guilty, the death sentence on the lesser men was usually remitted to life imprisonment. In some cases this included an annual humiliating appearance, on the anniversary of the king's execution, when they were drawn through the streets on hurdles to Tyburn and back. Amongst those who were to remain in prison until they died were John Hutchinson, Sir Arthur Hesilrige, Peter Temple, and Thomas Wayte. John Hutchinson was kept in prison, untried, finally dying as a result of the conditions in which he was confined at Sandown Castle in Kent in 1664. He was a fine, proud man, of great integrity who would have won much sympathy from spectators in a public trial. Sir Arthur Hesilrige, M.P. for Leicestershire, had been a close colleague of Oliver Cromwell and a firm parliamentarian and republican. He was a man of a fiery temperament and a sense of humour. As a champion of Parliament and the republican Commonwealth he came to oppose Cromwell when the latter made himself Lord Protector. At the Restoration he was imprisoned in the Tower of London where he died of fever in 1661. His epitaph, on the monument he shares with his two wives (one either side of him) in Noseley Chapel in Leicestershire, reads that *"he was a Lover of Liberty and Faithful to his Country. He delighted in sober company."*

Other Leicestershire regicides who were imprisoned for life were Thomas Wayte (or Waite) and Peter Temple. Thomas Wayte was, like the rather better known John Lilburne and Robert Overton, imprisoned in a castle in Jersey. Wayte, or Waite (sometimes even White), was claimed by hostile royalist authors to have been the son of an ale-house keeper at Market Overton in Rutland, but was more likely to have been the son of Henry Waite of Wymondham in east Leicestershire. He had been Governor of the Burley-on-the-Hill garrison during the civil war and M.P. for Rutland. He died in his island captivity in or about 1668. Peter Temple, the former linen draper, Leicester Committee man, Captain of Horse in the militia, M.P. for the Borough of Leicester, and a long time supporter of Lord Grey of Groby, suffered a similar fate. Under the Commonwealth he had been a member of the Council of State (the ruling body of the Republic) and High Sheriff of Leicestershire. After the Restoration his estate at Sibson, near Market Bosworth in west Leicestershire, was confiscated by King Charles II for his brother, James, Duke of York. Temple died in the Tower of London in 1663.

In the end only nine of the surviving regicides suffered the hideous death designed by the law for traitors. This was not the dignified decapitation they had given to Charles Stuart but the following grim and vengeful ritual sequence - drawing on a hurdle or cart to the place of execution, half hanging by the neck, cutting down whilst still alive, castration, disembowelling with the entrails being burnt before the victim's eyes, quartering whilst still alive, and finally decapitation. In addition four men who had not signed the death warrant were also executed in this barbaric manner. Amongst these were John Cook who had presented the case against Charles Stuart at the trial, Hugh Peter the most famous preacher in the New Model Army, and the ubiquitous Francis Hacker who had commanded the soldiers of the guard on the fateful day of Charles I's exeution in January 1649 - as well as the parliamentarian cavalry in the defence of Leicester in the summer of 1645. They were hanged, drawn, and quartered, in the manner described above, in October 1660. During the Commonwealth period Colonel Francis Hacker had kept the death warrant for the king's execution at his home, Stathern Hall, in the Vale of Belvoir, north-east Leicestershire. After his own grisly execution at Tyburn his remains are believed to have been buried in Stathern churchyard. John Cook had no hope of mercy. As Solicitor-General at the time of the trial of Charles I, Cook, from Husbands Bosworth in south Leicestershire, had prepared the charge and conducted the prosecution. He had later said of it, *"I went cheerfully about it, as to a wedding."* Cromwell had made him Chief Justice of Munster in Ireland, where he is reported as being an efficient reformer. Now he conducted his own defence at another political show trial, before bravely facing his own horrible end.

Most of the condemned suffered their dreadful fate with brave resolution. Shortly before he died John Cook wrote to his wife:- *"We are not traitors, nor murderers, nor fanatics, but true Christians and good Commonwealth men, fixed and constant to the principles of sanctity, truth, justice and mercy, which the Parliament and Army declared and engaged for; and to that noble principle of preferring the universality, before a particularity, that we sought the public good and would have enfranchised the people, and secured the welfare of the whole groaning creation, if the nation had not more delighted in servitude than in freedom."* [5]

Lord Grey of Groby was fortunate indeed to die before the Restoration; to be spared the horrible 'live' execution suffered by these regicides or the imprisonment until death of others such as John Hutchinson, Sir Arthur Hesilrige, Peter Temple and Thomas

Wayte; fortunate not to have his body - wherever it was carefully buried away - exhumed and mutilated like those of Cromwell, Bradshaw and Ireton. Like Sir Arthur Hesirige he had fallen out with Cromwell over the dissolution of the Rump Parliament in 1653 and the replacement of the Republic or Commonwealth with the Protectorate. Thomas, Lord Grey of Groby was a committed Commonwealthman. He had been arrested at Bradgate by Francis Hacker in 1655 on Lord Protector Cromwell's orders and imprisoned in Windsor Castle for six months. He died in April/May 1657, aged thirty-five. His place of burial is unknown. [6] This may have been deliberate on the part of his family. It certainly proved convenient under the restored monarchy.

How was the restoration of the monarchy received in Leicester itself? In the elections to the Convention Parliament held on 13th April 1660 a John Gray of London [no relation to the Bradgate family] and a Thomas Armstrong of Burbage had been returned as burgesses for the Borough of Leicester. Following the proclamation of Charles II in London on 8th May *"with great acclamation of Joy"* he was proclaimed king in Leicester on 12th May. Two days later the Mayor wrote to John Gray MP to assure him that the king had been proclaimed three times in *"the most publique and convenient places of the said Burrough"* and that the proclamations had been received *"with greate solemnity and acclamations of the people than any of the like nature that hath in this place preceded them with as greate Joy and unanimity as it hath beene performed in any place of his Maiesties* [sic] *Dominions whatsoever. It is not the least of our Joyes to heare that the house have sent Commissioners to waite upon his Maiesty in order to his returne* [with a vote of £50,000 to be sent to him] *and wee hope that you (before the receipt hereof) have had the happiness to kisse his Maiesties hand, and that we nowe are under the protection of our most gracious Soveraigne Lord Charles, whom God grant longe to live and happily to governe in these his Dominions. Sir this short Accompt* [i.e. account] *I by thadvice* [sic] *of my Brethren thought fitt to give you for your*

278

satisfaccion [sic] *and for the prevencion* [sic] *of any Calumnyes that may be cast on this Burrough which have soe cordially and sincerely declared themselves for his Maiestye, which is all that I shall trouble you withall at present ...* [7]

The true cordiality and sincerity of this previously staunchly parliamentarian corporation may be imagined; but times had changed. Despite the three days of official celebrations held in Leicester, as in the rest of the country, in May 1660, the Restoration was not welcomed wholeheartedly by the Borough. It was only fifteen years, to the very month, since the town had been so ruthlessly stormed and sacked by the army of the new king's father. There were other causes for reluctance too. The Borough had purchased the Castle Mills, as former Crown property, during the Commonwealth period and other Crown property as fee-farm rents. They had now to be surrendered and the Corporation set about raising £300 to secure forgiveness and the re-conveyance of the Mills from the new government.

There was still some spirit of resistance though. In May 1660 information was laid against William Dawes, the son of Hugh Dawes who had been the Borough's Sergeant of the Mace during the Commonwealth. It was alleged that, on 27th May *"betweene 11 and 12 of ye clocke in ye fore noon"* William Dawes upon seeing the King's Arms in paper fixed against the informant Christopher Norris' house end *"did throwe a stone or clott against the said Armes."* This was not all. Another informant, William Allsopp, claimed that he had mentioned to William Dawes and his mother, Jane Dawes, that there was a painter in the church *"setting upp the Kings armes and it would doe her good to see them when they were done; whereunto the said William Dawes answered and said that it would doe the Devill good to see them."* [8]

In a similar spirit the Corporation, which at this time still included such former parliamentarian stalwarts as Arthur Staveley, Richard Ludlam, and Archdale Palmer, had to welcome back to Leicester Lord Loughborough (Henry Hastings) and the former Town Clerk,

William Dawes throwing his clots of earth against the newly
erected royal arms on paper to the horror of his neighbours

Edward Palmer, who they had dismissed for his royalist sympathies. The message was underlined in a letter dated 22nd June 1660 to the Mayor and Aldermen from William Staples MP:- "*... this morning the Lorde of Loughborrow* [sic] *and Edward Palmer your Towne clarke were with mee making greate Complaints that albeit hee bee returned and restored to his place of Towne Clarke yett hee doth not receive the fruits and profitts thereof and that many things are kept and deteyned from him which belongs to his place. And therefore my Lord of Loughborrowe desired mee to write to you and informe you that what Edward Palmer did (for which he was turned out of his place) was by his Comand* [sic], *And hee willed mee to informe you, and gave me notice thereof as I was your Recorder, that if hee doe not enjoy his place and all the profitts beloneing* [sic] *to it as fully as hee had it when he was putt out, he would make the King acquainted with it, and with those that were the putters of him out. And that hee would when you came to renewe your Charter move the King to stopp your desires.*" [9]

With the Restoration Henry Hastings, Lord Loughborough, had been created Lord Lieutenant of Leicestershire. He died in 1666, having spent the last years of his life principally at his London mansion called Loughborough House, in Lambeth, and was buried in the Collegiate Church at Windsor.

Despite the Borough's outward show of loyalty to the new dispensation, and the lack of any obvious immediate reprisals, changes were soon to be made. The towns had been generally strongholds of the parliamentary cause *('The Good Old Cause')* and the restored monarchy did not leave them undisturbed for long. A Committee for regulating Corporations was set up and it got to work in Leicester in the autumn of 1662. The two Companies (i.e. the twenty-four and the forty-eight) were so drastically remodelled that, out of the total of seventy-two members in November 1660, forty were struck off the rolls. Of these forty, fifteen were Aldermen. The leading men who had governed the town during the civil war years were thus forced into retirement. These included Archdale

281

Palmer, Arthur Staveley, William Stanley, Richard Ludlam, Edmund Craddock, William Ward, Thomas Henshaw, and Samuel Robinson. The constitution of the Corporation was further remodelled in 1684 when the franchise was extended to all freemen of the borough.

Matters at Bradgate following the Restoration, however, were in a far better state than in Leicester. King Charles II treated the Earl of Stamford with favour. On the Earl's petition the king reconveyed to him in 1666 Armtree Manor and Wildmere Fen in Lincolnshire, which had been presented by him to the crown in 1637 for the purpose of effecting some abortive improvements through land drainage. Stamford also celebrated his sixty seventh birthday in style in a manner recounted in a letter to his son-in-law, the Earl of Ailesbury.

"January 9th, 1666/7.
Broadgate.

I have heard of all your jollities in your house of Austria upon the new year, I pray God to send you many as merry. Friday last was the day of three score and seven pies, and truly in the great hall of Broadgate we dined all our friends and neighbours with a lusty company of Leicester Corporation, but, in truth, ale was our drink and so our venison was seasoned accordingly." [10]

It seems that the good times had returned after all the years of strife for the Greys of Bradgate and their friends on the Corporation of the Borough of Leicester. It was over twenty years since the siege and bloody storming of the town.

When Celia Fiennes, the traveller and diarist, made her visit to Leicester in 1698 there were still some reminders of those momentous times.

"Ye towne [Leicester] *is old timber building Except one or two of Brick. There is Indeed that they call ye Newark which is Encompass'd with a wall of a good thickness and two great gates with towers, as the town gates are, in which they keep*

The celebration of the Earl of Stamford's sixty-seventh birthday at Bradgate

their arms and ammunition. Ye walls now are only to secure gardens that are made of ye ruin'd places that were buildings of strength. In this Newark which is a large space of ground are severall good houses, some of stone and Brick. [11]

As a granddaughter of the old parliamentarian and puritan leader, William Fiennes, 1st Viscount Saye and Sele (known as 'Old Subtlety'), and the daughter of parliamentarian colonel and Cromwellian supporter, the Hon. Nathaniel Fiennes, she was also happy to record that,

"... Here are a great many descenters [sic - i.e. dissenters] *in this town."* [12]

Perhaps the spirit of Leicester's resolute defiance in 1645 lived on; summed up in the words of the town's proud motto - *Semper Eadem.*

Semper
Eadem

NOTES:

1. Lucy Hutchinson, *Memoirs of the Life of Colonel Hutchinson* op. cit. pp. 319-320.
2. Historical Manuscripts Commission (HMC), Appendix to 5th Report, Folio 72. 1660. May 15., p. 184. *Letter from Mr. Ayloffe to Mr John Langley.*
3. Journal of the House of Commons (C.J.). Vol. VIII, 61., 9th June 1660.
4. HMC. MSS. of S.H. Le Fleming of Rydal Hall. (385) June 4th 1660. (Cockermouth) p. 25.
5. T.B. Howell, ed. *A Complete Collection of State Trials,* (London, 1809-26), Vol. V. p. 1265.
6. John Hollings, writing in 1840, makes a somewhat puzzling reference to how "Lord Grey of Groby, of whom mention is so often made in connection with the Civil War in Leicestershire, ended his restless and turbulent career in 1657 at his seat at Wirthorp, in Northamptonshire." This is the only reference to the place of Lord Grey's death, but it is not a place name familiar to his biography, such as Bradgate or Coombe Abbey, or one of his London residences. The statement is without corroboration. Also, neither this author nor the Northamptonshire County Record Office have been able to identify any such place as 'Wirthorp' in that county. The statement is thus best discounted. John F. Hollings, *The History of Leicester during the Great Civil War,* Printed by Combe and Crossley, Leicester. Published 1840. p.68. (First given as a lecture to the Mechanics Institute, Leicester.1839).
7. Records of the Borough of Leicester. DCXCIII. *Letter from the Mayor to John Gray, MP.* Original Letters, No. 81. 14th May 1660.
8. Records of the Borough of Leicester. DCXCV.
9. Hall Papers. XIV, No. 926. 28th May 1660.
10. HMC, MSS of the Duke of Somerset, (Manuscripts of the Marquis of Ailesbury), *Letter from the Earl of Stamford to the Earl of Ailesbury.* p. 175.
11. Celia Fiennes, *Diary of Celia Fiennes,* (c.1700), (Field & Tuer, the Leadenhall Press).
12. Ibid.

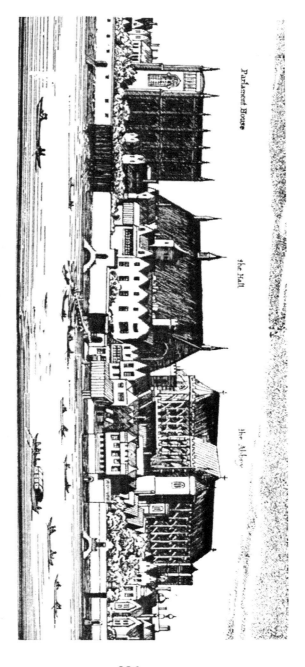

C17th view of the City of Westminster, London, from the river Thames

Parliament House

the Hall

the Abbey

Charles II arriving at Dover

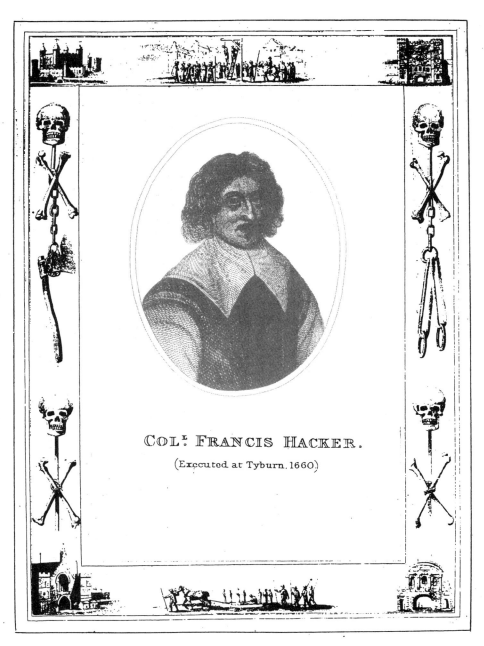

COL? FRANCIS HACKER.

(Executed at Tyburn, 1660)

Colonel Francis Hacker (Engraving)

288

Colonel Francis Hacker (Oil Painting)

PETER TEMPLE, KNT.

Died a Prisoner.

Peter Temple

290

Sir Arthur Hazelrigge (Hesilrige)

George Booth, Lord Delamere

Henry Grey, First Earl of Stamford – (circa. 1673)

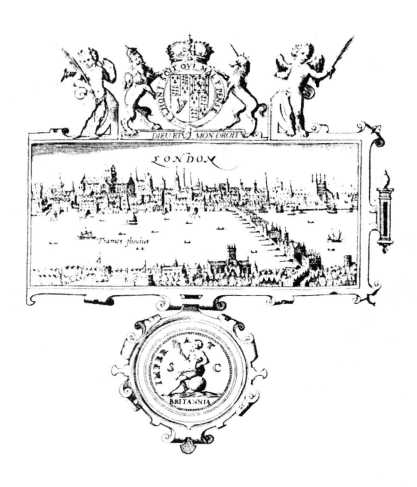

View of London with the Royal Arms of the House of Stuart

CHAPTER TEN

REMAINS AND REFLECTIONS

What evidence remains of the siege in Leicester today and what was its significance?

"Town fortifications in civil war Britain were mostly modelled on principles borrowed from Dutch military engineers. The Dutch system of fortification relied on an *enceinte* formed by an earthen rampart and ditch (preferably wet). Projecting bulwarks and hornworks gave flanking fire along the line of defence. Existing medieval fortifications were utilised where possible, but were often fronted by earthen defences. Walls could also be made more resistant to artillery by raising banks on their inside, as at Chester and Gloucester.

"The extent and location of earthworks about the town [i.e. Leicester] are far from clear. It seems likely that an earthen rampart, possibly palisaded, and ditch stretched around much of the town. The ditch appears to have been continuous, with drawbridges allowing entry into the town. Symonds refers to a hornwork in front of a drawbridge, as well as a flanker on the east side of the town. The flanker was presumably a bastion or bulwark projecting out from the main line of the rampart. The hornwork would have been a detached earthwork lying across the ditch and giving extra protection to the drawbridge. The design of the bastions and the hornworks is uncertain and they may not have been constructed according to the best continental practices of the day, but any defensive work carried out by the [later] royalist and Fairfax garrisons is more likely to have been of a higher standard." [1]

Because of the nature of the ditch and the outworks beyond the town gates and the old town walls little of them has survived from the period. Where they were strengthened by Hastings' garrison and more particularly on the orders of Fairfax after the town's recapture, they were later demolished. One of the earliest and best attempts to identify what they may have been like was by John Hollings in 1838 for his lecture to the Leicester Mechanics Institute. This was later reproduced in his book *The History of Leicester during the Great Civil War* published in 1840.

The following extract is from the Preface to his book:- **"With respect to the 'Plan of Operations against the Town during the Siege', the reader will hardly require to be informed, that the line of defence laid down in it, is in some degree conjectural; it being impossible at the present day [1840] to ascertain the precise situation of works which were demolished soon after their completion, the site of which moreover is now for the most part covered by buildings. That it is not materially inaccurate, however, might be argued from various minute points of evidence, which it would be tedious and little interesting to mention at length. The plan has been prepared by Mr. Lee, from one kindly drawn to scale by Mr. Laurance from the early sketch of [John] Speed and the more accurate map of Stukeley, constructed in 1745."** [2]

This Plan, used by Hollings in his book, is reproduced on page 311, but it contains some errors over names, e.g. Col Leslie for Col. Lisle, Col. Russell is mis-spelt, and he confuses the Grey Friars with the Black Friars. An improved version appears earlier in the main text as 'Map - The Siege of Leicester - 28-31 May 1645' on page 163.

It is hoped that the reader will find the maps on pages 312 and 313 helpful, in conjunction with the narrative in the text, in locating remaining physical evidence from the time of the siege on the ground in Leicester. One is a modern street map of central Leicester. The other shows the area of the old walled town of Leicester as it is today with key historical landmarks identified.

Most of the surviving archaeological remains of the events of the last days of May 1645 were to be found in 1840, as they are today, in the area of the Newarke. This survey begins, accordingly, with the Newarke precinct. A diagram showing the layout of the Newarke and its location may be found on page 314.

Hollings continues in his Preface, **"For the other illustrations of the Lecture the Institute is indebted to the able pencil of Mr. B. F. Scott."** [3] These four sketches, which feature scenes from the Newarke in 1838 or 1840 showing the state of the walls at that time, appear in this book on page 315 and pages 326 to 328.

Hollings adds that **"Mr. Flower** [John Flower, a famous illustrator of Leicester scenes] **has also contributed one of his valuable drawings - a part of Prince Rupert's tower, taken in 1821, of which the woodcut by Mr. Burton at the end of the Lecture is a reduced copy."** [4] This is reproduced on page 316. (Prince Rupert's Tower, now demolished, should not be confused with 'Rupert's (or 'Turret') Gateway (see plan on page 340). Another illustration by John Flower, a lithograph of the Magazine Gateway published in 1826, appears on page 317. A third Flower print depicts the Guildhall where the decision to defy Prince Rupert was taken. This appears on page 332.) A fourth Flower print, of the Blue Boar Inn, is on page 337.

In addition to the illustrations from John Hollings' book I have also included two drawings by S. Read which appear in W. Kelly's *Royal Progresses and Visits to Leicester*, published in 1884. These may be found on pages 318 and 319. One features the Magazine Gateway, but unlike the Flower's lithograph which shows the West Front this shows the view from the East Front. The second view features 'Turret' or 'Rupert's' Gateway, with St. Mary de Castro's church spire in the background. Both of these views remain familiar Leicester landmarks in the twenty-first century which have survived from the time of the siege. A recent photograph of Turret Gateway also looking north into the Castle precinct is included on page 320. A further view, looking south from the town proper towards the Castle precinct, showing the C15th 'Tudor' Gateway with St. Mary de Castro church on the left, appears on page 321.

The walling around the Newarke has gradually been demolished by developments during the 19th and 20th centuries. Only stretches of the walling on the north side, shared with the Castle precinct, still survive. These include a 57m. length of walling behind the Newarke Houses Museum (a-a in the diagram on page 314). The present building has the two adjacent (now joined) 16th century houses at its core; the Chantry House and the white stucco clad Skeffington House (see the photograph on page 322). To the west of these are the buildings of the Trinity Hospital which had been refounded by James I. The walling (about 0.9m. thick) behind these houses has a number of crude roughly circular loopholes hacked through its soft sandstone. These are shown in the photographs on pages 323 to 325. The loopholes are about 30-40 cms. in diameter. The main line of loopholes runs along the same course of masonry and are regularly spaced at about 3m. apart. They would have been suitable for use by musketeers at standing height in the churchyard of St. Mary de Castro. There is a marked drop in the ground level from the churchyard into the Newarke to the south. At the west end of the wall ground level in the garden of the Newarke Houses falls towards the Turret Gateway. At this point there are an additional four loopholes at a lower level. These would have necessitated the defenders lying down in the churchyard in order to fire through the loopholes. At some points there appear to have been another, this time higher, line of musket loopholes lying just below the capping of the wall. If they were indeed used at the time of the siege they would have required ladders or temporary ramparts in order to reach them from the churchyard side. The net effect is to have provided three levels of gun loopholes, as can be seen in the photograph on page 325 which shows a section of the north wall of the Newarke in the Chantry House garden, viewed from the south. This area may have constituted part of 'the Newarke fort'. Yet the field of fire from these loopholes would have been somewhat blocked by the Chantry House and Skeffington House, only 46m. to the south. Perhaps the intention had been at some point to demolish these buildings. If these and the other buildings in the Newarke precinct had been demolished any besiegers who broke through the outer defences and into the Newarke would have been covered by a second line of covering, and flanking, fire from the Magazine Gateway and the Castle precinct through these loopholes.

One of the parliamentarian accounts of the siege referred to in the earlier narrative *(A More Exact Relation, etc.)*, mentions loopholes in the wall on the south side of the Newarke which ran broadly along the line of the modern Mill Lane. [5] These would have been suitable for use by kneeling musketeers or for small cannon. Both the gun embrasures and blocked up breaches in this south wall (marked b-b in the diagram on page 314) were recorded in the 19th century. The line drawings by Mr. B. F. Scott from around 1838-1840 which appeared in Hollings' book are reproduced on pages 326 to 328 and clearly show the extent of damage and in-filling. A pen and wash drawing with front and rear elevations of the same wall prepared by an architect in 1854 also survives and a simplified version is reproduced on page 329. In addition three photographs, probably taken immediately before the demolition of the remains of this south wall of the Newarke, also survive in the care of the Leicester Museum Service. The photograph reproduced on page 330 gives a view of te wall showing embrasures and a sally port from inside the Newarke looking south towards where the attacking royalist battery on the Raw Dykes would have been. The date of the destruction of this wall, which played such a major part in the story of the siege and storming of Leicester, is uncertain but it had disappeared by the time of the publication of the 1886 Ordnance Survey map of Leicester (scale 25 inches to 1 mile). The records relating to this wall show a total of nine embrasures narrowing towards the outer face of the wall (as shown in the drawing reproduced on page 331). These are better constructed and contrast with the crude and probably more hastily made loopholes in the north wall of the Newarke adjoining St. Mary de Castro churchyard which were described in the previous paragraph. There is also a blocked up doorway, or sallyport, in the wall and evidence of breaches blocked up with masonry rubble. The drawings taken from Hollings' book show unrepaired breaches too, though by 1854 these appear to have been filled in with bricks. It is possible that the rubble blocking represents the work of Hastings' short-lived royalist garrison, though the wall was again breached in the second siege after Fairfax ordered an artillery bombardment.

Outside the Newarke precinct, but still inside Leicester's 'Castle Park' area, other remaining buildings which played a part in the events of May 1645 were the Guildhall and the neighbouring St. Martin's Church, both in Guildhall Lane. It was in the Mayor's parlour of the Guildhall that the decision to reject Prince Rupert's surrender terms was made. (The Guildhall remained as Leicester's Town Hall until 1876.) A John Flower print of the exterior of the Guildhall in approximately 1826 appears on page 332. Recent photographs of the exterior of the Guildhall with St. Martin's Church and of the interior of the Guildhall showing the Great Hall appear on pages 333 and 334. St. Martin's Church and its churchyard were the scene of fierce fighting during the last stages of the storming. (Long associated with the civic life of the town, St. Martin's became Leicester Cathedral in 1927 when the Leicester diocese was formed. The appearance of the church had been changed earlier when its medieval structure was extensively restored in the 19th century and the 220ft spire was built in 1867.)

The other main scene of desperate struggle towards the end of the storming was at the High Cross in the Market Place. This was at the junction of High Cross Street and High Street, marking the centre of the old town and the site of the traditional Wednesday (and later Friday) market. (Built in 1557, the Market House had eight pillars supporting a domed roof. It was taken down in 1769. In 1884 the one surviving pillar, with an iron cross on top, was moved to Cheapside, where it stands now next to the current market place, which originated as the Saturday market about 1,000 years ago, just inside the south east corner of the old town walls.) At the point where Highcross Street meets High Street some granite sets are laid into the road in the shape of a cross marking the site of the old High Cross.

The Clock Tower and the Town Hall Square, those focal points in the centre of modern Leicester built in the 19th century, would have been just outside the town walls in 1645 but the ground on which they stand would have been inside the outer defensive line and seen much fighting action during the storming. The town centre has been extended considerably to the east and the south since then. One of the parliamentarian pamphlets (*A Narrative, etc.*) implies that the line of earthen defences was shortened at the Horsefair Leys on the south side of the town shortly before the siege. *"... ..We also began to cut off some superfluous works at the Horsefair Leys and the Friers* [Grey Friars along Friar Lane], *wherein we saved the* [main] *guard of 150 men, and set on labourers to amend the other works where they were in any way defective, ...* [6] This area of ope ground lay to the south of the town wall. It was traditionally used for gatherings and activities such as horse fairs and mustering the trained bands. Its name is commemorated in the present Horsefair Street. In his reconstruction of the defences John Hollings suggested that a large hornwork or bastion had been erected to guard the approach from the 'London Way' from the south into the Horsefair Leys and that this constituted the 'Main Guard' which was attacked by Prince Rupert's Bluecoats under Colonel John Russell. Hollings claimed that this 'Main Guard' would have stood where Welford Place now is; 'London Way' being not the modern London Road but rather the present Welford Road. This would suggest that the Horsefair Leys were still inside the defensive line. Indeed, there is a reference in *A Narration, etc.* to a cannon being removed from the Horsefair Leys during the siege to assist in the defence of the Newarke breach.

The defensive line on the eastern side of the town appears to have taken in the extensive suburban development rather than being centred on the medieval East Gate. This is the impression given by the disputes over the length of the perimeter line which was fixed in the west and north by the river Soar and adjusted in the south to

301

accommodate the Newarke precinct. The length of the line was said to be three miles and there is little recorded evidence of property demolition on the east side of the town. There is also the question of language. The eastern side of the Leicester settlement is said to have been particularly influenced by Danish terms dating back to the days when Leicester was part of the Danelaw. Hence the proliferation of place names containing the word 'Gate' from 'Gota' (Way or Street) rather than its usual English meaning. This explains the references to Wood Gate and Sanvey Gate to the north side and to Church Gate, Belgrave Gate, Humberstone Gate, and Gallowtree (or Galtree) Gate, to name but a few, all along this eastern part of the line. These were not 'gates' as such but passages to be covered from attack. It is perhaps significant that it was on this side that the royalists first broke through the defensive line and into the town beyond. Little physical evidence of the siege and storming remains here, however, apart from St. Margaret's Church (see page 335) and churchyard just outside the north east corner of the old walls, and the ruins of the Abbey Mansion further north and across the Soar. The latter, otherwise known as Cavendish House and the Countess of Devonshire's residence, had been built from stone taken from the old Leicester Abbey which had been destroyed during the Reformation. Now, in turn, it is thought to have been burnt down and destroyed by royalist soldiers after the storming of Leicester. A photograph showing the ruins of the Abbey Mansion appears on page 336.

Some other surviving evidence exists today in the collections of the Leicester Museums Service in the form of cannon balls, grenadoes, and musket balls. Amongst the royalist ordnance captured at Naseby were said to be two demi-cannon, a full culverin, and a mortar, as well as smaller pieces. A number of cannonball finds have been made in Leicester over the years and most of these are shown superimposed on Hollings' 1840 'Plan of Operations, etc.' on page 338. Hollings had noted that cannonballs had been found embedded in the north wall of the Newarke behind the Trinity Hospital, precisely opposite the part of the south wall of the Newarke showing damage.

The cannonballs were said to weigh from 7lb to 12lb. [7] He also states that an angle in the same wall had had a number of holes made of iron shot of small diameter. He suggested that as the two faces were equally marked by them that two batteries had been involved, rather than a single one. Certainly the up-to-date practice on the Continent was to flank the main battery containing the heavy siege guns with lesser batteries on either side in order to give a crossfire when forcing a breach. He also recorded that cannonballs had been found embedded in the timbers of the old East Gate when it was taken down and sold off. The discovery of three cannonballs in Welford Place (see 'Plan' on page 338) seems to support the argument that this may well have been the site of the garrison's 'Main Guard'.

No mention is made in the contemporary accounts of the bombardment of Leicester of the use of mortars, although a mortar was taken from the royalists after Naseby. In those times mortars fired 'grenadoes' filled with incendiary charges. The royalists were probably unable to use their mortars at Leicester due to their high trajectory and relatively limited horizontal range. In sieges it was often necessary to move mortars close up to the defences under cover of prepared earthworks. At Leicester Prince Rupert was in a hurry and moved straight to a storming after a heavy artillery bombardment.

Hand thrown 'grenadoes' did, however, play an important part in the storming. Three ceramic hand grenades in the collection of the Leicester Museums were discovered in the Magazine Gateway in 1854. Three further grenades are also in the collections. (An illustration of two ceramic 'grenadoes', one of which has a wooden 'fusee', may be found on page 339.) Hand 'grenadoes' were often listed in inventories of the day alongside petards (bombs) and firepikes which reflects their role in storming fortifications. The royalist 'fireworker', the Frenchman Bartholomew de la Roche, was based at Oxford during the civil war, but also accompanied Prince Rupert on campaign. He was present at the siege of Bristol in July 1643 when the royalists used hand grenades, firepikes and petards in their assault on the defences. He was very likely present at Leicester too in May 1645. A common use of hand 'grenadoes' filled with incendiary 'wildfire' was to clear earthworks of defenders. This was done most effectively at Belgrave Gate by Col. Bard's men, at Gallowtree Gate by Prince Rupert's Bluecoats, and elsewhere along the perimeter line. The comments of the defenders at both Leicester and elsewhere make it clear that these 'grenadoes' had a devastating effect as close quarter anti-personnel weapons. As the authors of *A Narration of the Siege and Taking of the Town of Leicester, the Last of May, 1645, by the Kings Forces* noted they *"terribly burnt our men and thus gained entry to the town."* [8] No doubt the element of panic spread, like the 'wildfire', amongst the defenders was crucial; especially when they were so inexperienced, exhausted, and outnumbered as was the case at Leicester.

In some ways the siege of Leicester is a misnomer. [9] The late C17th French military engineer Vauban outlined the typical textbook siege with sophisticated Continental defensive works in mind. It would last 48 days before culminating in the storming of the fortified town. The royalist 'siege' of Leicester was a much briefer affair. Langdale and the advance cavalry units arrived to scout, skirmish and burn down mills on 28th May. The following day King Charles, Prince Rupert and the main body of the royalist Horse had arrived and surrounded the town. On the next day the royalist Foot and artillery had arrived and work had begun on the construction of the main battery. The next day, 31st May, the work had been completed and the ultimatum was delivered at midday. Efforts on the part of the defenders to procrastinate and buy time were answered with an artillery bombardment and preparations for a midnight storming of the overstretched and undermanned defences. Classic aspects of siege warfare, therefore, such as mining or tunnelling the defences, the construction of earthworks to give cover to other operations, and the use of incendiary mortars to fire the town were dispensed with. The tactics of the royalists were quite straightforward, given their overwhelming superiority in numbers and ordnance. They trained their large siege artillery on the south wall of the Newarke, left vulnerable to cannon by its lack of earthen banking to the rear and ramparts to the front. (It is not surprising that the *'unlyned'* Newarke wall was easily breached). Smaller calibre artillery may have been more spread out around the defensive line to give covering fire for the various assaults. Using the cover of darkness the royalists launched simultaneous infantry attacks at various spots around the over-extended parliamentarian lines. Bundles of rushes and brushwood faggots were used to fill the ditch which was at least muddy if not filled with water. Ladders were used to climb the defensive bank or to scale against bastions, hornworks or gates. The defenders heroically defended the 'Main Guard' and the breach in the Newarke, displaying conspicuous courage, soldiers and townspeople, men and women. Royalist troops elsewhere, however, stormed the eastern defences with the crucial use of incendiary 'grenadoes' filled with 'wildfire' (a form of Greek fire which burnt the defenders *'terribly'*), causing widespread panic and disorder amongst the outnumbered parliamentarians. Once inside the defences the royalist foot opened the gates and lowered the drawbridges to allow their cavalry to enter the town. Resistance continued for some time within the town, but to no avail.

Amongst the major factors contributing to the fall of Leicester were the smallness of the garrison, the lack of ordnance, the poor state of the defences, and the length of the defensive line. As one parliamentarian pamphlet put it:-

"The greatest defect was want of men, though the Town was not well fortified, nor was there Ordnance to reach from one work to another; it were to be wished that Garrisons of such concernment to the Kingdome might be taken care of, that they might have at least 1,000 foot soldiers in pay, which had this place had, with the help of the Townes-men, in all probability that might have kept out the enemy, and made them pay for their bold attempt. ... ." [10]

The inadequacy of Leicester's garrison, compared with many other Midland towns in terms of numbers, is uncertain though. Indeed, a parliamentarian force of similar size to that in Leicester in 1645 had successfully defended Gloucester in 1643 against a royalist field army until relieved by the Earl of Essex's army, including Lord Grey of Groby and his forces, and the London Trained Bands. It should also be remembered that it has been estimated that over half of both the royalist and the parliamentarian armies in 1645 were tied down by manning the many local garrisons.

The shortage of ordnance experienced at Leicester was also not uncommon throughout the civil war, especially in local garrisons. No doubt the absence of Thomas, Lord Grey of Groby with much of his regiment, and his leadership, during most of 1644 and 1645 contributed to the town's weakness. Grey's roles, firstly as commander of the Midland Association of Counties and then later as an active member nationally of the parliamentarian political leadership meant that his concentration on the locality was diminished. This was in marked contrast to earlier criticism of him by Oliver Cromwell over his concern for Leicester's security. [11] By May 1645, however, as a MP he had been removed from his military command role by Parliament's Self-Denying Ordinance.

Clearly another major point of contention was whether or not the defensive perimeter line at Leicester was too long. Most commentators seem to think that it was and that this was a major factor in the town's capture. Major James Innes, for example, blamed the Militia Committee and especially their apparent reluctance to demolish suburban housing. David Papillon, however, writing in his book *A Practical Abstract of the Arts of Fortification and Absailing, etc.,* shortly after the events argued that the defences of Leicester were unnecessarily short and that recent destruction of the suburbs there had been avoidable. He argued that suburbs should be enclosed in outlying forts which he suggested would strengthen the defences, involve the residents, and require less garrison to defend them. [12]

The accusation was also made, on separate occasions, before and after the fall of the town, by Colonel George Booth and Major James Innes, that it was the Committee's intention to fortify their houses in the Newarke at the expense of the rest of the town. In fact, most of the thirty or so members of the Committee were county men. (A list of the Leicestershire Militia Committee members, which appears in Hollings' book is reproduced on page 341). Indeed, only John Whatton and Edmund Craddock among the members, and Master Thomas Wadland, the committee's awkward clerk, can be shown to have had houses in the Newarke. [13]

Possibly the other members were swayed by Whatton and the three Leicester aldermen on the committee. These were Richard Ludlam, the chandler and ex-Mayor of Leicester, and William Stanley, the *"mercer there by the West Gate,"* [14] in addition to Edmund Craddock.

Whatever the debate about the state of the Newarke's defences; it should be remembered that the royalists first entered Leicester not here, but at Belgrave Gate and other points along the eastern line of defence.

The conscious neglect of Leicester by Parliament implied by some modern commentators (e.g. Everitt, Wilshere & Green, Simmons), and discussed earlier, is not proven and should be rejected. On 26th May Colonel Vermuyden had been ordered to march towards Nottingham and Leicester. At this point the intentions of the king and his army were unclear to Parliament. A letter from Nottingham dated 28th May indicated that the king was within five miles of Leicester and that Colonel Vermuyden was positioned four miles from Nottingham *"in the way of Derby."* [15] Vermuyden indicated his willingness to help Leicester if they were threatened and could hold on. Time, however, appears to have prevented this. Parliament was caught unawares by the rapid movement of the royalist army (as was Captain Peter Temple and his command in the outpost garrison at Coleorton) and their attention was centred on Fairfax's siege of Oxford. There is, however, no indication of lack of commitment to defending Leicester. Prince Rupert was correct to move to a swift storming, realising not only that Leicester was not strongly defended but also that the defenders were trying to play for time and relief from Vermuyden and also Cromwell who was not too far away. Parliament was certainly shocked by the loss of Leicester as the notices to other towns in the area, warning them to defend themselves, demonstrate. Colonel John Hutchinson had earlier used Nottingham Castle in 1643 and 1644 as a citadel whenever the town of Nottingham, whose garrison was in *"a weak and languishing condition,"* was briefly occupied by the enemy. Perhaps if the Newarke had been properly fortified as originally intended by the Committee, *"as a reserve in time of absolute necessity ... . it being a place very easily made a very strong place"* [16], in much the same way it could have held out for a few more days until relief came from a parliamentarian field army.

Conclusion

The siege and storming of Leicester was not a notable affair in the military sense. The defenders, including untried militia and volunteer townsfolk, numbered around 1,000 to 1,500. They had little chance against the full Royalist field army of over 10,000 men, with its experienced soldiers and skilled engineers. The siege was, however, of considerable strategic importance in that it succeeded in drawing the new Parliamentarian field army, the 'New Model Army', into its first major engagement at Naseby which was to prove so decisive. The capture of Leicester by the royalists also contributed, along with other factors, to this defeat by depleting their field army through losses in the storming, desertions after the widespread looting, and the need to leave behind a garrison in the town. Perhaps the resistance and heroism of the defenders of Leicester, be they soldiers or townspeople, men or women, in those last days of May 1645 was not futile after all. They played a significant role in influencing the events that followed two weeks later which were to have profound implications for the course of English history and British constitutional development.

NOTES:

1. Paul & Yolanda Courtney, 'A siege examined : the Civil War archaeology of Leicester' in *Post-Medieval Archaeology,* Vol. 26, 1992, p.60.
2. John Hollings, Preface to *The History of Leicester during the Great Civil War,* 1840, p.iv.
3. Ibid.
4. Ibid.
5. *An Exact Relation of the Siege Laid to the Town of Leicester, 1645.*
6. *A Narration of the Siege and Taking of the Town of Leicester, the Last of May, 1645, by the Kings Forces,* 1645.
7. See William Eldred, *The Gunner's Glasse,* 1646, which lists types of ordnance of the day.
8. *A Narration, etc.* op. cit.
9. This point is well made by Paul Courtney in, *Parliamentarians Divided Or, Fear And Loathing At The Siege Of Leicester, 1645*
   in *The Leicestershire Historian,* Vol. 4, No. 3, 1995. p 3. 10. *A Perfect Relation of the Taking of Leicester,* 1645.
11. Extract from a letter dated 3rd May 1643, from Colonel Oliver Cromwell to the parliamentarian Committee at Lincoln:-
   "... My Lord Grey hath now again failed me of the rendezvous at Stamford ... My Lord Grey sent Sir Edward Hartopp to me, To let me know he could not meet me at Stamford according to our agreement; fearing the exposure of Leicester to the forces of Mr. Hastings and some other troops drawing that way. "Believe it, it were better, in my poor opinion, Leicester were not, than there should not be found an immediate taking of the field by our forces to achieve the common ends. Wherein I shall deal as freely with him, when I meet him, as you can desire. I perceive Ashby-de-la-Zouch sticks much with him ..." [11]
12. David Papillon, *A Practical Abstract of the Arts of Fortification and Absailing, etc.,* London, 1646. pp 10-11.

13. John Whatton lived in Skeffington House and there are records of him leasing additional gardens from Trinity Hospital later, from 1652 during the Commonwealth period. In the same year there is evidence that Thomas Wadland was also still resident in the Newarke. Indeed, after the Restoration (of the monarchy) he was accused of blocking the right of way in Mill Lane, to the south of the Newarke, in 1667, by digging a ditch and constructing a building. At this time he was probably resident within the Newarke at Dean's House, otherwise known as St. Mary's Vicarage. This obstreperous ex-Clerk to the Militia Committee, who had refused to allow the ground adjacent to his property to be dug up and fortified prior to the siege, seems to have survived all political regimes and to have been singularly difficult under all of them!
14. Richard Symonds, *Diary of the Marches of the Royal Army During the Great Civil War*, Camden Society, London, 1859.
15. *A Perfect Diurnall*, May 30, 1645.
16. Letter from the Leicester Committee to the Committee of Both Kingdoms, dated 1st May 1645 cited in John Nichols, appendix to the *History of Leicestershire*, Vol. III; Part II. *The Civil War in Leicestershire*, p. 42.

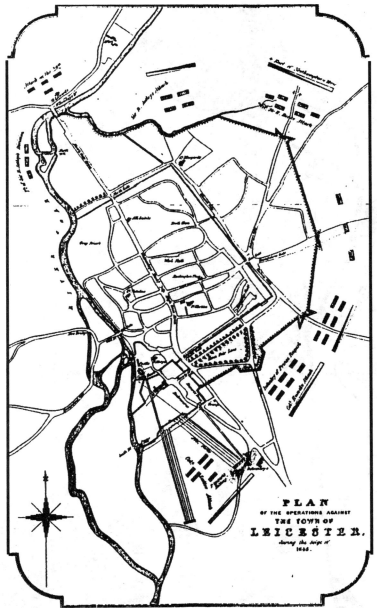

Plan of the operations against the town of Leicester during the
Siege of 1645 (from Hollings)

311

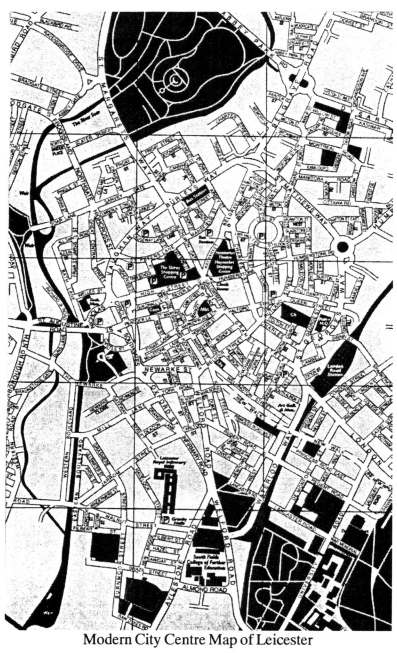

Modern City Centre Map of Leicester

312

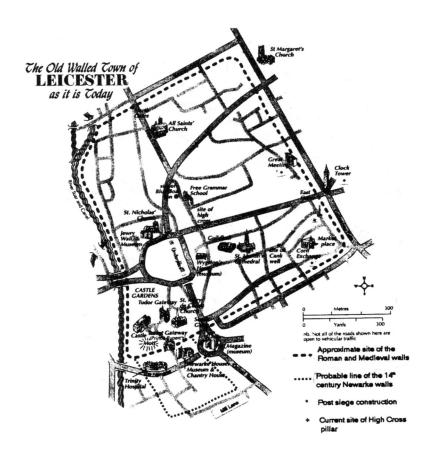

The following text appears within the map image:

The Old Walled Town of
LEICESTER
as it is Today

St Margaret's Church

All Saints' Church

Great Meeting

Clock Tower

Free Grammar School

East G

St. Nicholas' Church

site of high Cross

Jewry Wall Museum

Guild

Market place

St Martin's Cathedral

site of Cank well

Corn Exchange

Wygston's House (museum)

CASTLE GARDENS

Tudor Gateway

St. M Church

Castle Gateway / Prince Rupert's Mott

Magazine (museum)

Newarke Houses Museum & Chantry House

Trinity Hospital

Mill Lane

Metres 300

Yards 300

nb. Not all of the roads shown here are open to vehicular traffic

– – – Approximate site of the Roman and Medieval walls

..... Probable line of the 14th century Newarke walls

* Post siege construction

+ Current site of High Cross pillar

The Old Walled Town of Leicester as it is today (from Stevenson)

313

The Newarke Precinct (from Courtney – based on 1886
Ordnance Survey map)

314

View of Castle Mount (showing the two walls penetrated by shot behind
Trinity Hospital – from Hollings 1840)

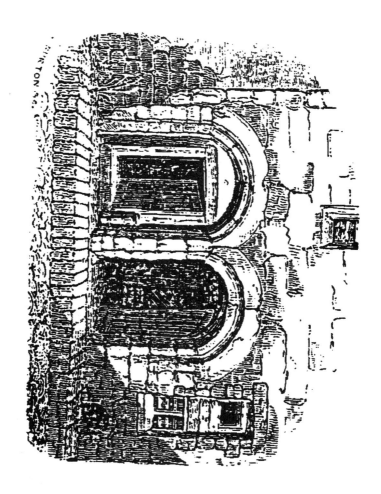

Part of the north front of Prince Rupert's Tower – Flower 1821

316

GATEWAY IN THE NEWARK.

The Magazine Gateway in the Newarke (West Front) – Flower 1826

The Magazine Gateway in the Newarke (East Front) – Read
c. 1880

318

Turret (or Rupert's) Gateway, with St. Mary de Castro's Spire
in the background - Read c. 1880

319

Photograph of *Turret* Gateway leading North into Castle Precinct from the Newarke

Photograph of *Turret* Gateway leading South into Castle Precinct from the Town Proper

Photograph of the North Wall of the Newarke behind Chantry House and Skeffington House from the South

Photograph of the Gun Loopholes in St. Mary de Castro Churchyard Wall from the North

Photograph of the Gun Loopholes in the Chantry House Gardens from the South

Photograph of the three levels of Gun Loopholes in the
Chantry House Gardens from the South

View of the Principal Breach in the South Wall of the Newarke as it appeared in 1838 looking North to the North Wall – from Hollings 1840

View of the South Wall of the Newarke showing the Embrasures and Sally Port – from Hollings 1840

View of the South Wall of the Newarke showing the breaches as hastily repaired and in-filled

— from Hollings 1840

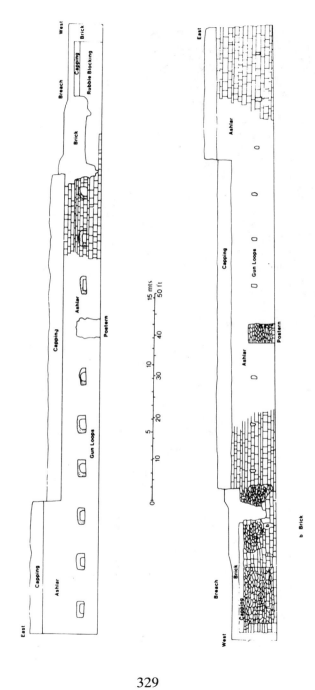

Elevations of the South Wall of the Newarke (after an unpublished original by Thomas Wilson 1854)

329

Photograph (c. 19th) of the South Wall of the Newarke, from the North, showing Gun Loopholes and a Sally Port

As it was now imagined that the principal efforts of the besiegers would be devoted to forcing an entrance into the town, at the quarter of the Newark, the utmost exertions were made to add as much as possible to its strength, the boundary wall on the south side having probably been already pierced with the embrasures for musketry and artillery,[f] of which several may be still observed in that part of it which remains standing.

INTERIOR   EXTERIOR.

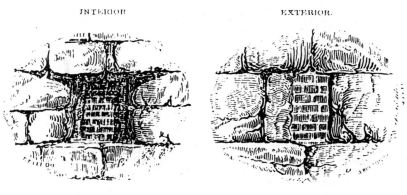

[f] The Committee speak this day of continuing a breastwork already begun within the Newark—perhaps the interior line of defence behind the South wall, completed on the day following under the cannon of the royalists.

This is an extract from page 46 of John Hollings' *The History of Leicester during the Great Civil War'* (1840).

Close-up of Embrasures/Loopholes in the South Wall of the Newarke in extract from Hollings, 1840

The Guildhall (Old Town Hall) – Flower, c. 1826

Photograph of the Guildhall, as it is today, with St. Martin's Church beyond

Photograph of the interior of the Guildhall showing the Great Hall

Photograph of St. Margaret's Church

Photograph of the ruins of Cavendish House, Leicester Abbey Mansion

The Blue Boar Inn – Flower, c. 1826

337

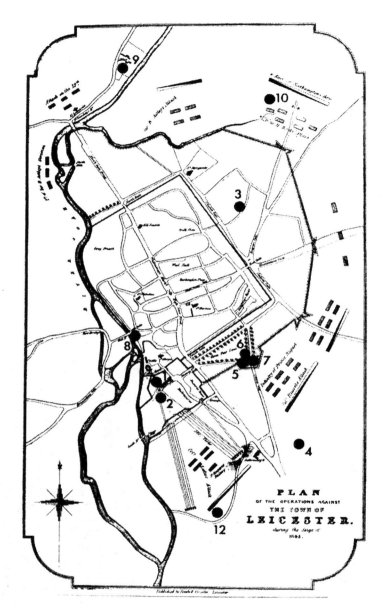

Distribution of Cannon Balls discovered superimposed
on Hollings' 1840 plan of operations map

338

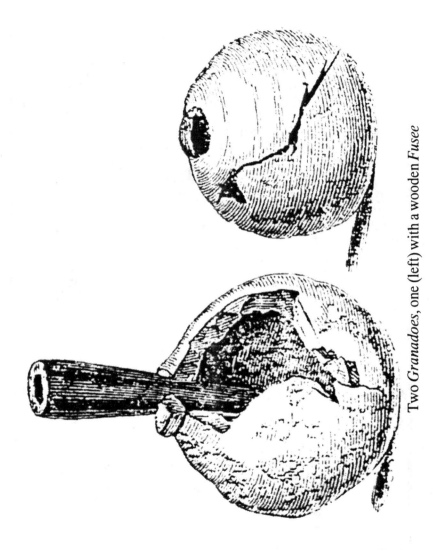

Two Granadoes, *one (left) with a wooden* Fusee

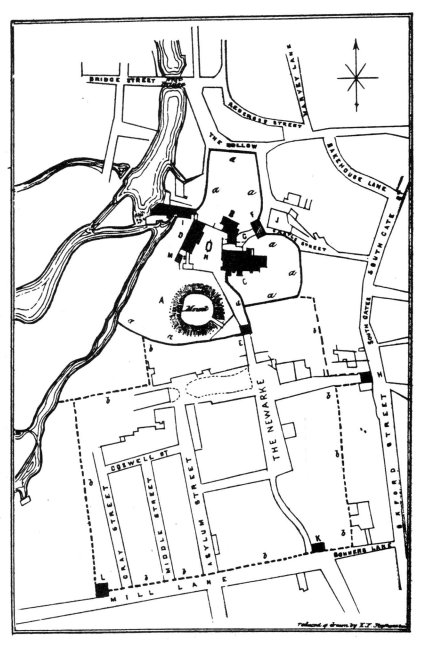

Plan of the Castle and Newarke precincts – from
Thompson, 1859

340

THOS. LORD GREY OF GROOBY,
THEOPH. GREY, ESQRE.
SIR ARTHUR HESLERIGGE, BART.
SIR MARTIN LISTER, KT.
SIR EDWARD HARTOP, JUN. KT.
SIR GEO. VILLIERS, BART.
SIR THOS. HARTOP, KT.
SIR ROGER SMITH, KT.
JOHN ST. JOHN,
THOM. BABINGTON, SEN.
WM. BENBRIDGE,
THOS. BRUDENELL,
JOHN WHATTON,
ARCHDALE PALMER,
PETER TEMPLE,
ARTHUR STAVELEY,
HENRY SMITH,
THOS. HESILRIGGE,
FRAS. HACKER,
JOHN STAFFORD,
JOHN BROWNE,
WM. HEWIT,
JOHN GOODMAN, ESQUIRES,
FRAS. SMALLEY,
JOHN SWYNFEN,
VALENTINE GOODMAN, GENTLEMEN,
        and
Richard Ludlam, [1]
WILL. STANLEY,
EDMUND CRADOCK,
        Aldermen of Leicester

[1] According to Nichols, Richard Ludlam was Mayor of Leicester

List of Leicester Parliamentarian Militia Committee members – from Hollings, 1840

341

DETAILS OF ILLUSTRATIONS

1. EARLY 18th CENTURY ASPECT OF LEICESTER FROM THE NORTH

This engraving by J. Walker (circa. 1715) which appeared in John Throsby's *The History and Antiquities of the Ancient Town of Leicester* (Leicester, 1791) is from a later period but it can still give some idea of the northern prospect of Leicester which would have changed little over the seventy or so years since the Siege of 1645. The picture is reproduced by courtesy of Leicester City Council.

2. QUEEN ELIZABETH I WITH COAT OF ARMS AND MOTTO

This portrait by Crispin Van De Passe (after Oliver) shows 'Good Queen Bess' with the Tudor royal coat of arms and the motto *'Semper Eadem'* which she gave to the Borough of Leicester with its charter in 1589. The portrait is reproduced by courtesy of the National Portrait Gallery, London.

3. JOHN EVELYN

This print of John Evelyn by Robert Nanteuil, from an engraving circa 1650 with its inscription in classical Greek, appeared in an edition of one of the famous diarist's works. In his 1654 *Diary of John Evelyn* he found Leicester *"large and pleasantly seated, but despicably built."* The portrait is reproduced by courtesy of the National Portrait Gallery, London.

4. LEICESTER - 1610 (SPEED)

From John Speed's map of Leicestershire produced in 1610. This 'street map' of Leicester appears in its bottom left corner and includes a shield bearing the arms of the borough.

5. 17th CENTURY MAP OF LEICESTERSHIRE (SELLER)

This map of Leicestershire by Seller in 1695, despite the misspelling of 'Dradgate' for Bradgate and 'Gorby' for Groby, amongst others, gives a good representation of the settlement pattern of the county in the seventeenth century.

6. MAP OF WEST GOSCOTE HUNDRED, LEICESTERSHIRE

In the early years of the civil war much of the fighting between Lord Grey of Groby's parliamentarian forces and the royalist soldiers under Henry Hastings, Lord Loughborough, took place in West Goscote Hundred, which lies to the north-north-west of Leicester. This area includes Bradgate, (Groby is shown close by in neighbouring Sparkenhoe Hundred to the west), Copt Oak, Cole Orton, Ashby-de-la-Zouch, Castle Donington, Birstall, Belgrave, Rothley, Burleigh, Loughborough, and many other places mentioned in this book. This map is reproduced from John Nichols', *The History and Antiquities of the County of Leicestershire.*

7. KING CHARLES I

This portrait of Charles I was painted by Daniel Mytens before the outbreak of the Civil War. It emphasises the king's belief in the majesty and power of the monarchy. The portrait is reproduced by courtesy of the National Portrait Gallery, London.

8. HENRY GREY, EARL OF STAMFORD (circa 1638) AND SIGNATURE

This portrait of the Earl of Stamford from the period around 1638 is by Cornelius Jonson and is reproduced by courtesy of Dunham Massey, The Stamford Collection (The National Trust): photograph Courtauld Institute of Art.

9. HENRY HASTINGS, LORD LOUGHBOROUGH?

Henry Hastings, the second son of Henry, fifth Earl of Huntingdon, was born around 1610. He distinguished himself in the English civil wars by his services in the royalist cause and has been described as the archetypal cavalier. On 16th June 1642 he published the king's first Commission of Array at Leicester, was declared a delinquent by Parliament and formally impeached. In July 1642 he was appointed Sheriff of Leicestershire by Charles I. He raised a troop of Horse which fought at Edgehill and was commissioned as Colonel-General by the king. He established himself at his father's house at Ashby-de-la-Zouch Castle, from where he attacked the parliamentarians in Leicestershire and the neighbouring counties. He was the local rival of Thomas, Lord Grey of Groby, the parliamentarian commander. The hostile parliamentarian press called him " the Grand Rob-Carrier" as he raided the northern carriers on their way to and from London. On 23rd October 1643 the king rewarded him by creating him Lord Loughborough. In the spring of 1644 he took part in Prince Rupert's relief of Newark. In May 1645 he joined in the siege and storming of Leicester and was appointed governor after its capture. On 18th June, following Naseby, he surrendered Leicester to Fairfax on honourable terms. He then held out in Ashby Castle until February 1646, obtaining parliamentary permission to go abroad. In the second civil war he took part in the defence of Colchester, acting as Commissary-General. After the surrender of Colchester he would most likely have been tried for his life, but escaped from imprisonment at Windsor Castle. He joined Charles II's court in exile in Holland in March 1649. With the Restoration of the monarchy in 1660 he was appointed Lord Lieutenant of Leicestershire. He died, unmarried, at Loughborough House, in Lambeth, London, in January 1667, and was buried in St. George's Chapel, Windsor. This portrait by Robert Grinhall is inscribed as Henry Hastings, Lord Loughborough. It is dated 1650, when Hastings was in exile on the continent. It is in private ownership and is reproduced by kind permission of the owner. The sitter is considerably younger than Lord Loughborough would have been at the time, however, and it is thought more likely that this is a portrait of his gifted and learned nephew, Lord Henry Hastings (1630-1649), son of Ferdinando, Earl of Huntingdon, who died at a tragically young age and was mourned and commemorated in ninety-eight elegies published as 'Lachrymae Musarum'. The erroneous inscription appears to have been added later, probably in the C18th. Also, it is almost certain that Lord Loughborough would have been painted in his armour during the period of the civil wars. The portrait is still included because of its intrinsic interest.

10. AN ASPECT OF LEICESTER DURING THE CIVIL WAR, 1642-1645

This map of Leicester as it would have looked in the period 1642-1645 was published in James Thompson's book *A History of Leicester from the time of the Romans to the end of the seventeenth century* (1849). The outworks and hornworks, constructed for the defence of Leicester during the civil war, may be noted and contrasted with their absence from the Speed map of 1610 shown earlier. The royalist artillery was mounted on the north end of the Raw Dykes, pictured at the bottom left corner, during the siege and storming of the town at the end of May 1645.

11. PASS ISSUED BY COLONEL HENRY GREY, GOVERNOR OF LEICESTER

This is a military pass issued by Colonel Henry Grey, in his capacity as Governor of Leicester, and not by Henry Grey, Earl of Stamford as has sometimes been thought. A transcript reads:- *16 of Ap. 1644 Lett the bearer heareof Mr. Thomas Stanford with his horse quiettly passe y[ou]r severall watches scoutes & gardes, & the sight heereof shalbee to you a sufficent warrant. Liecister Hen. Grey Governor.* The original pass is in the care of the Leicestershire Record Office.

12. ENGRAVING OF HENRY GREY, (EARL OF STAMFORD), WITH INSIGNIA AND SIGNATURE

This engraving of Henry Grey, First Earl of Stamford, Second Baron Grey of Groby, Bonvile, & Harington (1599-1673), was based on a portrait by Wenceslaus Hollar. A version of it appears in John Vicars' *England's Worthies*. Although described by W. Mercer in *Anglia Speculum* as *"most courteous and right stately Stanford* [sic]" he appears to have been hot-tempered, haughty and arrogant on many occasions. The Stamford insignia displays in the predominant top left hand side of the shield the white/silver and blue horizontal stripes with the three red spheres which constitute the original Grey family coat of arms (Barry of six, Argent and Azure, in chief three torteauxes Gules, and a label of three points Ermine). The other seven elements displayed in the shield represent the other illustrious families with which the Greys were linked through marriage, including their local rivals, the Hastings, top left of centre. His signature may be compared with that of Colonel Henry Grey (with which it has sometimes been confused) in the previous picture.

346

13. ORDER FOR DEMOLITION OF THE GRANGE HOUSES - WITH SIGNATURES

A transcript of this order appears in the text in Chapter Three. The Grange referred to in the order was the Newarke Grange farm in the South Fields of the town which lay south of the Newarke. It belonged to the Corporation and was leased out to gentlemen farmers residing in the town. Its demolition would deny shelter to any attackers or besiegers. Theophilus Grey's signature (*Theo. Grey*) may be compared to that of Thomas, Lord Grey of Groby (*Thos. Grey*), shown in the following picture, with whom it has sometimes been confused. The original order belongs to the Leicester City Council.

14. THOMAS GREY, LORD GREY OF GROBY (WITH SIGNATURE AND SEAL)

Thomas, Lord Grey of Groby was the eldest son and heir of Henry Grey, first Earl of Stamford. He was the youngest parliamentarian general of the first civil war, having been appointed commander-in-chief of the (East) Midlands Association of Counties by his patron and family friend Robert Devereux, Earl of Essex, and Lord General of the forces raised by the Parliament. Lord Grey of Groby went on to play a leading role in 'Pride's Purge' of the Long Parliament, the trial and sentencing of King Charles I, and was a founder member of the Council of State of the republican Commonwealth. His signature may be compared with that of Theophilus Grey which appears in the previous picture. Lord Grey would have been aged around thirty at the time this portrait was painted. The artist is thought to be Robert Walker. The portrait is reproduced from The Collection at Althorp by permission of the Spencer Estate, Althorp, Northamptonshire and by courtesy of the National Portrait Gallery, London.

15. SIR GEORGE BOOTH

Sir George Booth began the first civil war as a royalist. He had married, as his second wife, Elizabeth Grey, a sister of Thomas, Lord Grey of Groby before he wrote to warn him of the poor state of

Leicester's defences in April 1645. This portrait by Gerard Van Honthorst is reproduced by courtesy of Dunham Massey, The Stamford Collection, (The National Trust): photograph Courtauld Institute of Art.

16. SIR ARTHUR HESILRIGE
He was a Member of Parliament for Leicestershire, and an active Parliamentarian partisan and leader. He had a fiery temper, but also displayed a sense of humour at times. After being Sir William Waller's Lt. General of the Horse early in the first civil war Sir Arthur established himself as Governor of Newcastle-upon-Tyne where his duties caused his absence from the trial of King Charles I. His surname is found spelt in a bewildering variety of ways! His brother, Thomas, was a member of the local parliamentarian Leicester Committee. This portrait, by Robert Walker, is reproduced by courtesy of the National Portrait Gallery, London.

17. LUCY HUTCHINSON
Lucy, the wife of Colonel John Hutchinson, was a firm puritan and an observant commentator on John's contemporaries and current affairs of the day. The child is thought to be her son. This portrait is by Robert Walker and is reproduced by courtesy of the National Portrait Gallery, London.

18. JOHN HUTCHINSON
John Hutchinson, Parliamentarian Governor of, and M.P. for, Nottingham and a fellow regicide with Lord Grey of Groby, was a man of widely recognised integrity. He was committed to the Commonwealth and opposed to Cromwell's Protectorate. Shortly after the Restoration [of the monarchy] he was imprisoned and he died in Sandown Castle, Kent, in 1663. He was then aged forty-nine years. The portrait is also by Robert Walker and is reproduced by courtesy of the National Portrait Gallery, London.

19. WOODCUT OF PRINCE RUPERT AT BIRMINGHAM
This hostile woodcut depicting Prince Rupert and the 'Birmingham Butcheries' comes from a pamphlet entitled *The Bloody Prince,*

348

or a Declaration of the Most Cruell Practices of Prince Rupert and the rest of the Cavaliers, dated 1643. The dog featured with 'Prince Robber' is his pet white large poodle, Boye, which was killed at Marston Moor.

20. SIR ROBERT PYE (Jnr) OF FARRINGDON

Sir Robert Pye, an experienced soldier, appears to have been regarded by most contemporary commentators as the effective leader of the parliamentarian defenders of Leicester. He had only been passing through Leicester to join his cavalry regiment, which was with Colonel Vermuyden, when he was persuaded to assist the town against the besieging Royal Army. This portrait, after Jacob Huysman, is in a Private Collection and is reproduced by courtesy of the Courtauld Institute of Art, University of London.

21. CAPTAIN FRANCIS HACKER

Originally from a Colston Bassett, Nottinghamshire, royalist family, (they were neighbours of John and Lucy Hutchinson at Owthorp, and Francis' brother, Rowland, was with Henry Hastings men at Ashby-de-la-Zouch), Francis Hacker moved to Leicestershire where he became a captain in Lord Grey of Groby's Regiment of Horse. He commanded the garrison at Kirby Bellars and distinguished himself in the defence of Leicester during its siege and storming. One of the officers to whom Charles I's Death Warrant was addressed, he guarded the king and supervised his execution. During the Commonwealth period the Warrant was kept at his home, Stathern Hall in Leicestershire. He was a protégé of Sir Arthur Hesilrige rather than Lord Grey of Groby, however, and under the Protectorate he arrested Lord Grey on Cromwell's orders. This contemporary engraving of Francis Hacker depicts a dour but dependable soldier-saint of the puritan revolution.

22. CAPTAIN PETER TEMPLE

Originally a linen draper and a Leicester Committee man, Peter Temple served as a captain in Lord Grey's Regiment of Horse, commanding the Coleorton garrison in particular. In 1645 he claimed that the royalist advance had been too sudden for him to evacuate Coleorton in time to join in the defence of Leicester. Nevertheless, later that year he was chosen by the burgesses of Leicester to replace Thomas Coke as Leicester's other M.P. alongside Lord Grey of Groby, whose trusted supporter he seems to have been. He was one of the king's judges, signing the Death Warrant, and became a member of the Commonwealth Council of State. Locally he became a landowner and High Sheriff of Leicestershire. This contemporary engraving shows him together with his signature and seal.

23. KING CHARLES I IN ARMOUR
This contemporary engraving of Charles I in armour may give some idea of how he looked "on horseback, in bright armour, in the said town of Leicester" following its storming in 1645. The equestrian engraving [a version of which also appears in colour on the front cover of this book] shows him with his army in formation outside a town, after the style of Wenceslaus Hollar in 1639 and revised in 1644.

24. PRINCE RUPERT OF THE RHINELAND PALATINE
Rupert was the third son of Frederick, the Elector Palatine, and Elizabeth of Bohemia ('The Winter Queen'), sister of Charles I. As a young man he fought for the Prince of Orange in the Thirty Years War in Germany, and at the outbreak of the English Civil War this favourite nephew of the king was given command of the Royalist cavalry at the age of twenty-three. With his tireless gallantry, devotion, dash, and a degree of irresponsibility he initially won a number of brilliant victories. These were followed by the defeats of Marston Moor (1644), and Naseby (1645); and after the surrender of Bristol to Fairfax in 1645 he was summarily dismissed by the king. In December of the same year he went to Oxford and was reconciled to him, but his commissions were not restored. This portrait by Gerard Van Honthorst is reproduced by courtesy of the National Portrait Gallery, London.

25. PRINCE RUPERT SUMMONING THE GARRISON OF LEICESTER TO SURRENDER TO THE ARMY OF CHARLES THE FIRST, MAY 30th 1645

This print appears in John Throsby's *The History and Antiquities of the Ancient Town of Leicester* Vol. III., Leicester., 1791. page 45. It is reproduced by courtesy of Leicester City Council.

26. MAP - THE SIEGE OF LEICESTER - 28-31 MAY 1645

This map is a clearer, modern, and (hopefully) more correct version of the 'Plan of Operations against the town of Leicester during the Siege of 1645' which appears later as No. 60 and is from Hollings' book of 1840. This revised version shows the main features of the defensive situation of Leicester and its fortifications together with the deployment of the main royalist divisions prior to the storming of the town.

27. PRINCE MAURICE

Like his elder brother, Prince Rupert, whom he idolised, Prince Maurice had his first taste of fighting in the Thirty Years War in Germany. In the early days of the English Civil War the two brothers fought alongside each other. Maurice held a number of commands, and in 1644 was commissioned as Lt.-General of the counties south of the Thames. Unquestionably brave and constantly loyal to his brother, he had no gift for strategy and *'understood very little more of the war than to fight very stoutly when there was occasion'*. He was several times wounded. This portrait is by William Dobson (1611 - 1646), and was probably painted in Oxford in 1645. It is reproduced by courtesy of the National Portrait Gallery, London.

28. JAMES COMPTON, THIRD EARL OF NORTHAMPTON

He was the eldest son and heir of Spencer Compton, second Earl of Northampton (killed at the battle of Hopton Heath). One of a large and loyal royalist family, he *'performed many gallant acts in those times of confusion'*; he was at Edgehill and the taking of Banbury, and at Lichfield with Prince Rupert; he commanded the royalist horse at the first battle of Newbury in 1643, and fought at Cropredy Bridge and Lostwithiel. In 1644 he raised the siege of Banbury where his brother was the Governor, but in April 1645 was heavily defeated by Cromwell. During the Interregnum he remained in England and was imprisoned for a time. At the Restoration he was made a member of the Privy Council and Constable of the Tower of London. This portrait is by William Dobson and was probably painted during the period 1644-45 at Oxford. The presence of the dog in the picture is thought to represent fidelity. The portrait is reproduced by courtesy of the National Portrait Gallery, London.

29. SIR WILLIAM COMPTON

Sir William was the third son of Spencer Compton, second Earl of Northampton, and brother of the third Earl. He personifies the type of the youthful, idealistic, and courageous cavalier officer common to novels about the civil war. It is appropriate that Compton whom even Oliver Cromwell was later to call *'the sober young man, and the godly cavalier'*, should be the subject of William Dobson's finest full-length portrait. He enlisted in his father's regiment when only seventeen, and at the taking of Banbury in 1642 *'had two horses shot under him'*; later, as Lt. Governor of the town, he was in his turn besieged by Parliamentary forces, when it is said that he *'countermined the enemy eleven times'* and during the thirteen weeks of siege never went to bed. He was Major-General of the royalist forces at Colchester in 1648. During the Interregnum, as a member of the secret 'Sealed Knot' he plotted the return of Charles II. At the Restoration he was appointed Master of the Ordnance. It is thought that this portrait was painted by Dobson in 1643 when the sitter was eighteen and was knighted by the King at Oxford on 12th December of that year. The portrait is reproduced by courtesy of the National Portrait Gallery, London.

30. COLONEL JOHN RUSSELL

The younger brother of the first Duke of Bedford, John Russell was a colonel of foot in the royalist army and he led Prince Rupert's regiment of Bluecoats at the assault on Leicester, particularly in the attack on the Main Guard on the south side of the town. As may be seen from this portrait he evidently had a high regard for his own appearance and had several portraits painted. During the Protectorate he was an active conspirator, and at the Restoration raised, and for twenty-one years commanded, the King's regiment of Foot Guards. This portrait is one of three of him by William Dobson and is reproduced by courtesy of the Althorp Collection and the National Portrait Gallery, London.

31. SIR RICHARD WILLYS

Sir Richard Willys (or Willis) was the second son of Richard Willys of Fen Ditton in Cambridgeshire. He spent some time in military service with the Dutch and in the so-called 'Bishops Wars' against the Scots. During 1640-42 he was one of Charles I's guards at Whitehall and Hampton Court. Knighted at Shrewsbury on 1st October 1642 he fought at Edgehill. He was commissioned as colonel of a regiment of horse at Oxford in February 1643. In late 1644 he was appointed as Governor of Newark and Colonel-General of the royalist forces in Nottinghamshire, Lincolnshire, and Rutland. It seems that he owed this promotion to his friendship with Prince Rupert. It was in his capacity as Governor of Newark that he and his command took part in the siege and storming of Leicester. Some commentators argue that the arrival during the storming of his reinforcements from Newark under Colonel Page tipped the balance against the exhausted and greatly outnumbered defenders. He was replaced by Lord John Belasye in October 1645 for siding with Prince Rupert over his rift with Charles I. This portrait by William Dobson shows the use of ceremonial blued-and-gilt cuirassier armour and is reproduced by courtesy of the Newark District Council.

32. LORD BERNARD STUART, LORD LICHFIELD

Lord Bernard Stuart, Lord Lichfield and younger son of the Duke of Lennox, is pictured on the right. He was a favourite of his cousin, King Charles I, and commanded a troop of horse in the King's Life Guard of which Richard Symonds (whose account of the siege and storming of Leicester appears in this book) was a member. His elder brother, Lord John Stuart, pictured on the left, was killed at Cheriton in 1644. Lord Bernard was killed, following Leicester and

Naseby, at the battle of Rowton Heath, near Chester, in late September 1645. This double portrait (sometimes known as 'the Darnley Van Dyke'), of the two brothers as archetypal 'cavaliers', by Anthony Van Dyke, was painted before the outbreak of the civil war. It is reproduced by courtesy of the National Gallery, London.

33. SIR RICHARD BYRON

Sir Richard Byron (or Biron), of the Newstead Abbey family in Nottinghamshire, was a royalist and a cousin of the parliamentarian Colonel John Hutchinson. As Lucy Hutchinson explains, *"Sir John Biron, afterwards Lord Biron, and all his brothers, bred up in Arms and gallant men in their owne persons, were all passionately the King's."* Sir Richard was the royalist Governor of Newark before Sir Richard Willys. This portrait is attributed to Cornelius Jonson and is reproduced by courtesy of the National Portrait Gallery, London.

34. JOHN, FIRST LORD BYRON

Sir John (later Lord) Byron (or Biron) was the senior of six brothers who were all royalists and achieved high ranks. He had served in the Netherlands and in Scotland. In 1639 he was appointed Lieutenant of the Tower of London. When war broke out he was one of the first to join the king at Oxford, and was for a time Governor there. He enlisted as many students there as possible into the cavalry. He joined Prince Rupert at Powick Bridge, commanded the cavalry reserve at Edgehill, and fought at Roundway Down and first Newbury. In a nocturnal skirmish with some parliamentarian troops at Burford in January 1643 he received a blow in the face with a pole-axe or halberd. The scar from this wound is visible on his left cheek in the portrait. He was described as a cavalry commander who tended to *'engage the enemy when he needed not'*. He was created a baron on 24th October 1643. He then commanded at Nantwich, served at Marston Moor, and became Governor of Chester. He joined the king for the attack on Leicester when the siege of Chester was lifted. He held out for the king at Chester against Sir William Brereton until 1646. In the spring of 1648, in the second civil war, he attempted to raise Wales for the king, but failed. He died in France at the royalist court in exile in 1652. The portrait, by William Dobson, is reproduced by courtesy of the National Portrait Gallery, London.

35. SIR MARMADUKE LANGDALE

Sir Marmaduke Langdale (later first Baron Langdale), was a professional soldier. He was described as *'brave as a lion, enterprising, judicious, but with an unfortunate temper'*. He was one of the most capable and dependable cavalry leaders of the civil wars with his royalist Northern Horse. He defeated the Scots cavalry at Corbridge in 1644, fought bravely at Marston Moor, relieved Pontefract the following year, frightened and briefly occupied Leicester overnight shortly before its siege and storming, and in his most brilliant exploit he defeated Rossiter at Melton Mowbray. Captured on more than one occasion he always managed to effect an escape. At Naseby he was in command of the left wing royalist horse which was turned by Cromwell's Ironsides. Whilst escorting the king he was engaged and defeated at Rowton Heath. In the second civil war he joined the Duke of Hamilton and fought at Preston. After the civil wars he fought for the Venetians against the Turks. He died at Holme in his native Yorkshire, after the Restoration, in 1661. This contemporary engraving is reproduced by courtesy of the National Portrait Gallery, London.

36. SIR BERNARD ASTLEY

Sir Bernard Astley was the son of Sir Jacob Astley, another prominent royalist commander who was created Lord Astley in 1644. The family home was at Maidstone in Kent and the Astleys were Roman Catholics. Early in the civil war Sir Bernard was made colonel of a foot regiment. His father commanded all the royalist foot at Edgehill. Sir Bernard led a significant counter-attack with his musketeers which broke the initial enemy assault at the second battle of Newbury in October 1644. Earlier that month he had been active in Dorset with Lord Cleveland for the royalist cause. At Leicester he commanded one of the four major foot divisions which covered and assaulted the north side of the town. This contemporary engraving by Van der Gucht after an original oil portrait is reproduced by courtesy of the National Portrait Gallery, London.

37. SIR GEORGE LISLE (Engraving)

Sir George Lisle was the son of a bookseller. He saw action in the Netherlands but returned to England at the outbreak of the civil war. He fought at Cheriton as a colonel of horse and was a brigade commander at the second battle of Newbury in October 1644 where he threw off his buffcoat and fought in his shirt sleeves so that his men could see their leader in the darkness. He became Governor of Faringdon Castle, which post he is alleged to have resigned in order to accommodate his friend Sir Marmaduke Rawdon. He was captured in the second civil war at Colchester where he was shot, alongside Sir Charles Lucas, for (like him) having broken his parole not to take up arms against the Parliament again. He also had commanded one of the four major infantry divisions in the royalist assault on Leicester. His 'tertia' had the difficult task of being the first to attempt to storm the breach in the south wall of the Newarke. This engraving, from the same source as the previous one of Sir Bernard Astley, is reproduced by courtesy of the National Portrait Gallery, London.

38. SIR GEORGE LISLE (Oil Painting)

This portrait of Sir George Lisle (already described above) is included to indicate both the similarities and differences between an engraving and an oil painting of the same sitter of this period. This portrait is by the circle of John Michael Wright (1617-1694) and is reproduced by courtesy of the National Portrait Gallery, London.

39. COLONEL WILLIAM LEGGE

Although a soldier of proven ability, he was chiefly remarkable for his loyalty to Prince Rupert. As a young man Legge had fought in the service of the kings of both Denmark and Sweden in the Thirty Years War in Germany. He served the royalist cause devotedly during the civil war and was Governor of Oxford in 1645 when it is thought that this portrait was painted. He was a straightforward soldier whose *'modesty and diffidence of himself never suffered him to contrive bold councils'*. He was one of those who helped the king to escape briefly in 1647, and during the Interregnum he constantly plotted to restore the monarchy. At the Restoration he refused an earldom but accepted a pension. This portrait by William Dobson is reproduced by courtesy of the National Portrait Gallery, London. I cannot resist the temptation to include here the following example of period humour, based upon a pun involving Colonel William Legge:- *"Sir Arthur Aston was governor of Oxon at what time it was garrisoned for the king; a testy, froward [sic], imperious and tirannicall person, hated in Oxon and elsewhere by God and man alike. Who, kervetting on horsback [sic] in Bullington green bfore certaine ladies, his horse flung him and broke his legge: so that it being cut off and he therefore rendred [sic] useless for employment, one coll. Legge succeeded him. Soone after the country people comming [sic] to the market would be ever and anon asking the sentinell 'who was governor of Oxon?' They answered, 'one Legge'. Then replied they:- 'A pox upon him! Is he governor still'?"* Anthony Wood, *Life and Times of Anthony Wood*, ed. A. Clark, (The Oxford Historical Society, 1891-1900) p.110.

40. COLONEL SIR GEORGE GERARD

The son of a Lancashire landowner, George Gerard was educated at Leyden and in France, and like many royalist officers *'trained in the discipline of war from his youth in the United Provinces'* (i.e. the Netherlands). He commanded a regiment of foot at Edgehill, where his steadiness helped to avert total defeat. At the time of the attack on Leicester in the summer of 1645 he was General in South Wales where he had been notably successful in re-establishing royalist control. He had been summoned by the king to meet him at Leicester during the campaign. It is not entirely clear whether Gerard was present personally at the time of the storming but his own regiment , with its distinctive colours of blue and yellow triangles, certainly formed part of Colonel Sir Henry Bard's division which attacked the eastern side of the town. Later in 1645 he was removed from his command in South Wales because of his harsh treatment of the local people. He was badly wounded at Rowton Heath, near Chester, and retired with the king to Newark. He was present in Oxford at the time of its surrender in 1646. He spent the Interregnum in continental exile plotting. At the Restoration he regained his estates and was created Earl of Macclesfield in 1679. This portrait is by William Dobson and is reproduced by courtesy of the National Portrait Gallery, London.

41. HON. PERSIANA BARD

The Hon. Persiana (or Frances) Bard was considered abeauty of the period. She was the morganatic wife of Prince Rupert, which mean that she retained her former lower status than he and that any offspring of their union would have no claim to his possessions or title. Her brother was the impetuous and licentious Colonel Sir Henry Bard, one time Governor of Campden House, Gloucestershire, which he burned down upon evacuating it to join the king's 'Leicester March'. He also is said to have boasted of ravishing several women during or immediately after the storming of Leicester when he had command of the infantry division which stormed the eastern side of the town. In the absence of a portrait of him this one of his sister appears. This portrait is by Sir Peter Lely and is reproduced by courtesy of the National Portrait Gallery, London.

42. THE SIEGE AND SACKING OF MAGDEBURG, GERMANY - 1631

The notorious siege, storming and pillage of Magdeburg in 1631 is depicted here. Although the participants in this engraving are shown wearing C18th costume (e.g. note the tricorn hats), this incident, which resulted in the massare of the civil population by Imperial troops (note the Imperial eagle on the flags), became a byword for the horrors of war - especially civil war. In the heated atmosphere immediately following the fall of Leicester some parliamentarian pamphleteers drew comparisons between the behaviour of the Imperialists and the Royalists. The long term result of the reaction to what happened at Magdeburg was the 'limited war' concept of the late seventeenth and early eighteenth centuries. This engraving is reproduced by courtesy of the Staatsbibliothek Preussischer Kulturbesitz, Berlin.

43. SIR THOMAS FAIRFAX, LORD GENERAL OF THE NEW MODEL ARMY

Sir Thomas Fairfax, later third Baron Fairfax of Cameron, was Lord General of the New Model Army. He commanded the victorious parliamentarian army at Naseby and the recapture of Leicester, but he declined to participate in the trial and execution of the king later. The Fairfax arms are borne on the horse's breastplate. Beneath Fairfax and his mount bodies of horse and foot are shown in battle array with a small encampment to the right. This engraving is by Engleheart, after an earlier portrait by Bowers, and is reproduced by courtesy of the York City Art Gallery.

44. LT. GENERAL OLIVER CROMWELL

This portrait miniature of Oliver Cromwell is attributed to Samuel Cooper. It shows Cromwell as he looked in the 1648/9 period and is reproduced by courtesy of the National Portrait Gallery, London.

45. THE BATTLE OF NASEBY - JUNE 1645

Streeter's engraving of the battle of Naseby from Joshua Sprigge's *Anglia Rediviva* shows the parliamentarian right commanded by Cromwell; Rainsborough's regiment forms part of the reserve directly below the hill on which a group of locals have gathered to watch. The Royalists are shown at the top and the Parliamentarians are facing them from below with Okey's dragoons lining the Sulby hedges in the top left. This engraving skilfully conceals the inequality of numbers between the two opposing forces. The numerical superiority was with the Parliamentarians. This engraving is reproduced by courtesy of Cambridge University Library Syndics.

46. MAP - THE CAMPAIGN OF THE KING'S 'LEICESTER MARCH' - 1645

This map shows the movement of both the main royalist army and the parliamentarian 'New Model' army during the spring and summer of the king's so-called 'Leicester March' which included the siege and storming of Leicester and culminated in the crucial battle at Naseby.

47. PROSPECT OF LEICESTER FROM THE SOUTH

This view of Leicester from the south comes from Thomas Roberts' map of Leicester dated 1741. Although this is from an eighteenth century print it is unlikely that, apart from the advanced disappearance of the old town walls, the view would have changed much since the time of the siege. The continued use of windmills is very noticeable. In 1743 Samuel Buck produced a print showing the same prospect in greater detail. Buck identified certain landmarks and buildings which can be seen in both prints. In the Roberts print shown in this book the five parish churches of Leicester are displayed, including from left to right, St. Mary's de Castro (large spire) in the Newarke on the far left, the Magazine is shown just to the right, then St. Nicholas' (smaller spire), St. Martin's (large spire) in the centre, All Saints' (smaller tower), and St. Margaret's (larger tower) centre right. The remains of Leicester Abbey may be seen further right. In the background, on the horizon, certain high points are indicated in Buck's print. These include the Field Head, (or Markfield Knowle), and Bradgate, (including *the Earl of Stamford's House*' and particularly the high point now known locally as 'Old John'), both of which are described as being upon Charley (Charnwood) Forest and are topped by windmills in the Buck print. In the Roberts print the Field Head is to the left of centre and 'Old John' is just to the right of the St. Martin's spire in the centre. This print is reproduced by courtesy of Leicester City Council.

48. THE TRIAL OF KING CHARLES I BY THE HIGH COURT OF JUSTICE

The trial of King Charles I from a contemporary print. The Commissioners or Judges face the solitary figure of the king. John

Bradshaw presides and the arms of the soon to be declared 'Commonwealth' are displayed at the back of the court. This print is reproduced by courtesy of the Ashmolean Museum, Oxford.

49. KING CHARLES I - WITH SIGNATURE
This contemporary engraving shows the king in armour as he would have been during the siege and storming of Leicester rather than as he appeared as a lone civilian figure at the time of his trial

50. THE DEATH WARRANT OF KING CHARLES I
Thomas, Lord Grey of Groby, was one of the first and the principal signatories of the death warrant of Charles I. His signature appears as the second one, between those of Lord President John Bradshaw and Oliver Cromwell. The signatures of Peter Temple, Thomas Horton, Henry Smyth, and Thomas Wayte from Leicestershire also appear. The warrant is addressed to Colonel Francis Hacker of Leicestershire, amongst others. This print is reproduced by courtesy of the National Portrait Gallery, London.

51. THE EXECUTION OF KING CHARLES I
This contemporary Dutch print of the execution of the king on the afternoon of 30th January 1649, on the black draped scaffold outside his splendid Banqueting House was very popular. Unfortunately it contains several inaccuracies, including the height of the block which was lower than depicted here. This print is reproduced by courtesy of the Ashmolean Museum, Oxford.

52. THOMAS, LORD GREY OF GROBY
Lord Grey of Groby played a leading role in the Army/Independent 'junta' which carried out 'Pride's Purge' of the Long Parliament and the trial and sentencing of King Charles I. He was a founder member of the Council of State of the republican Commonwealth. He fell out with Cromwell over the latter's dissolution of the Rump Parliament, however, and was in opposition to the Protectorate. He died in 1657 before the restoration of the Stuart Monarchy which he had done so much to end. He was thus spared the savage

retribution which befell many of his former comrades. This portrait by J.M. Wright is reproduced by courtesy of Dunham Massey, The Stamford Collection, (The NationalTrust): photograph: Courtauld Institute of Art.

53. CHARLES II ARRIVING AT DOVER - 1660

In 1660 after General Monck had marched south from Scotland and called a 'free Parliament' the eldest son of Charles I was invited to return to England and take the throne. Charles II arrived at Dover where he was met by Monck and the mayor of the town. The eleven year experiment with the English Republic - in both its Commonwealth and Protectorate forms - was over and the Stuart Monarchy was restored. This nineteenth century impression is after Benjamin West (1738-1820) and is reproduced by courtesy of the Mary Evans Picture Library.

54. COLONEL FRANCIS HACKER (Engraving)

With the Restoration in 1660 Colonel Hacker's major involvement in the death of Charles I led to his imprisonment in the Tower of London. He was hanged at Tyburn in 1660 and his remains are believed to lie in Stathern churchyard. This Restoration period engraving from *Rebels no Saints* portrays in its borders the grisly fate of the regicides.

55. COLONEL FRANCIS HACKER (Oil Painting)

This portrait of Colonel Francis Hacker is by an unknown artist. It more likely reflects his appearance towards the later part of his life than that shown in the previous picture which is clearly a reduced version of the engraving of 'Captain Francis Hacker' as featured at the end of Chapter Four. The portrait is reproduced by courtesy of the National Portrait Gallery, London.

56. PETER TEMPLE

After the Restoration Peter Temple was imprisoned in the Tower of London for life. He appears to have been knighted before this; presumably during the Protectorate period. His estate at Sibson, near Market Bosworth in west Leicestershire, was confiscated by Charles II for his brother, the Duke of York. Peter Temple died in the Tower in 1663. Again, this contemporary engraving from *Rebels no Saints* displays in its borders the vengeance and retribution meted out to the regicides.

57. SIR ARTHUR HAZELRIGGE (HESILRIGE)
As a prominent republican and Commonwealthman Sir Arthur was imprisoned in the Tower of London after the Restoration. He died in the Tower in 1661. His epitaph in Noseley Church states that *'He was a Lover of Liberty & Faithful to his Country. He delighted in sober company'*. This portrait, by an unknown artist from Dr. Williams' Library, is reproduced by courtesy of the National Portrait Gallery, London.

58. GEORGE BOOTH, LORD DELAMERE
Booth was the husband of the Earl of Stamford's eldest daughter, Elizabeth Grey. Imprisoned under the English Republic for his part in the abortive royalist rising (based mainly in his home area of Cheshire) named after him in 1659, he was released in 1660 upon the Restoration and was created first Baron Delamere by Charles II in 1661. This portrait by J.M. Wright is reproduced by courtesy of Dunham Massey, The Stamford Collection (The National Trust): photograph Courtauld Institute of Art.

59. HENRY GREY, FIRST EARL OF STAMFORD - (circa. 1673)
This portrait of the Earl of Stamford was painted after the Restoration and shows him later in life. It is dated 1673, the same year as his death, and is attributed to J.B. Gaspars. The portrait is reproduced by courtesy of Dunham Massey, The Stamford Collection (The National Trust): photograph Courtauld Institute of Art.

60. PLAN OF THE OPERATIONS AGAINST THE TOWN OF LEICESTER DURING THE SIEGE OF 1645
This plan appears in John Hollings' book, *The History of Leicester during the Great Civil War* (1840), and was "prepared by Mr.

Lee, from one kindly drawn to scale by Mr. Laurance, from an early sketch of Speed and the more accurate map of Stukeley, constructed in 1745" (from the Preface to the book, page iv). An improved version appears in this book as 'Map - The Siege of Leicester- 28-31 May 1645' on page 163.

61. MODERN CITY CENTRE MAP OF LEICESTER

62. THE OLD WALLED TOWN OF LEICESTER AS IT IS TODAY

This is a slightly amended version of a guide taken from page 47 of *Leicester Through The Ages* by Joan Stevenson (see Bibliography), to whom I am grateful for permission to use it here. The post-siege constructions, e.g. the Clock Tower, are marked with an asterisk, thus *.

63. THE NEWARKE PRECINCT

This is based on a 1886 Ordnance Survey map and is reproduced, with kind permission of Paul and Yolanda Courtney, from *A siege examined : the Civil War archaeology of Leicester* (see Bibliography). It shows the layout of the Newarke precinct in relation to the Castle precinct, the South Gate and the main town walls.

64. VIEW OF CASTLE MOUNT

This lithograph, the first of a series of four by B. F. Scott entitled *Nature & on Stone*, appears on page 52 of John Hollings' *The History of Leicester in the Great Civil War* (1840). This view is from the south, in the Newarke, and shows the two walls penetrated by shot behind Trinity Hospital. The church spire of St. Mary de Castro dominates the skyline beyond the Castle Mount and part of the ruins of the old Leicester Castle may be seen.

65. PART OF THE NORTH FRONT OF 'PRINCE RUPERT'S TOWER'

This print is from page 73 of Hollings' book. The woodcut by a Mr. Burton is a rduced copy of an original drawing by John Flower (a famous illustrator of Leicester scenes) in 1821. Prince Rupert's Tower (not to be confused with 'Rupert's Gateway' or 'Turret Gateway' - see 68 and 69 below) has, unfortunately, long since been demolished.

66. THE MAGAZINE GATEWAY IN THE NEWARKE (WEST FRONT)

This is a lithograph by John Flower which was published in 1826. It shows the main gateway into the Newarke which acted as the arms store and county 'magazine' where gun powder was stored for the trained bands, militia, and town garrison during the periods before, during, and after the civil war. This view is from the west side, i.e. from inside the Newarke.

67. THE MAGAZINE GATEWAY IN THE NEWARKE (EAST FRONT)

This engraving by W.J. Palmer of a drawing by S. Read appears in W. Kelly's *Royal Progresses and Visits to Leicester* (1884). The Magazine remains intact today, although on an island surrounded by traffic. It may be accessed by a pedestrian subway and houses the museum of the former Leicestershire Regiment ('The Tigers'). This view is from the east side, i.e. outside the Newarke, from the direction of Newarke Street.

68. 'TURRET' (OR 'RUPERT'S') GATEWAY, WITH ST. MARY DE CASTRO'S SPIRE IN THE BACKGROUND

This engraving by W. J. Palmer of a drawing by S. Read appears in W. Kelly's *Royal Progresses and Visits to Leicester* (1884). The view looks north from the Newarke into the Castle precinct showing the church of St. Mary de Castro and its spire.

69. PHOTOGRAPH OF 'TURRET' GATEWAY

This photograph, as with the illustration described above, looks north into Castle precinct or yard from the Newarke. The Gateway has also been known locally since the time of the siege as 'Rupert's Gateway'. This is unfortunate as it can cause confusion with 'Prince

Rupert's Tower' (see 65 above) and is thus best avoided and the name Turret Gateway preferred. (From J. Stevenson, op. cit.)

70. PHOTOGRAPH OF 'TUDOR' GATEWAY

This photograph shows the C15th 'Tudor' Gateway leading south into the Castle yard or precinct from the town proper. This view is taken from the north and St. Mary de Castro church can be seen on the left. (From J. Stevenson, op. cit.)

71. PHOTOGRAPH OF THE NORTH WALL OF THE NEWARKE BEHIND CHANTRY HOUSE AND SKEFFINGTON HOUSE FROM THE SOUTH

This photograph shows a view of the north wall of the Newarke in the gardens of the Newarke houses (Chantry House on the left and Skeffington House, with white stucco cladding, on the right) from the south. Turret Gateway is to the left (west) of the wall and St. Mary de Castro church and churchyard lies beyond. (From P. & Y. Courtney, op. cit.)

72. PHOTOGRAPH OF THE GUN LOOPHOLES IN ST. MARY DE CASTRO CHURCHYARD WALL FROM THE NORTH

This photograph clearly shows the gun loopholes which were cut into the wall of the churchyard and which faced south into the Newarke precinct. (From P. & Y. Courtney, op. cit.)

73. PHOTOGRAPH OF THE GUN LOOPHOLES IN THE CHANTRY HOUSE GARDENS FROM THE SOUTH

This photograph clearly shows the gun loopholes cut into the north wall of the Newarke at the rear of the Chantry House gardens when viewed from the south. Note how the ground falls away to the left (west) where the wall adjoins the Turret Gateway which leads into the Castle precinct. In this area there is both an additional upper and lower course of loopholes. (See 74 below). (From P. & Y. Courtney, op. cit.)

74. PHOTOGRAPH OF THE THREE LEVELS OF GUN LOOPHOLES IN THE CHANTRY HOUSE GARDENS FROM THE SOUTH

This photograph shows the three levels of gun loopholes cut into the north wall of the Newarke at the rear of Chantry House gardens towards its west end. The highest level holes are just under the coping or ridge tiles on the top of the wall. (From P. & Y. Courtney, op. cit.)

75. VIEW OF THE PRINCIPAL BREACH IN THE SOUTH WALL OF THE NEWARKE AS IT APPEARED IN 1838 LOOKING NORTH TO THE NORTH WALL

This second lithograph from a series by B.F. Scott entitled *Nature & on Stone*, is dated 1838, and appears on page 54 of Hollings' book *The History of Leicester during the Great Civil War* (1840). The central spectator is gazing in the direction of the north wall of the Newarke and the spire of St. Mary de Castro church beyond.

76. VIEW OF THE SOUTH WALL OF THE NEWARKE SHOWING THE EMBRASURES AND SALLY PORT

This third lithograph by B.F. Scott appears on page 46 of Hollings' book where it is entitled 'Embrasures & Sally-Port in the garden of Thos. Dabbs Esq., Newarke'. The gun loopholes here were much better constructed than those in the north wall and constituted embrasures where the defenders could 'lean in' under cover to fire (see 80 below). The sally-port would be useful for launching quick sorties and raids on the besiegers. This south wall, which is also featured in illustrations 75, 77, 78 & 79, was the scene of some of the fiercest fighting of the siege and storming. Unfortunately the wall, which followed the line of the present Mill Lane, was destroyed by late 19th century development.

77. VIEW OF THE SOUTH WALL OF THE NEWARKE SHOWING BREACHES AS HASTILY REPAIRED AND INFILLED

This fourth lithograph by B.F. Scott appears on page 50 of Hollings' book and is dated 1840. The breaches are shown filled with bricks, stones and masonry rubble.

78. ELEVATIONS OF THE SOUTH WALL OF THE NEWARKE

These elevations of the south wall of the Newarke were produced by architect Thomas Wilson in 1854 from an original pen and wash drawing before the wall was destroyed later in the 19th century. The gun loops are clearly identified, as are the blocked up postern gate or sally-port and the main breach towards the west end of the wall. (From P. & Y. Courtney op. cit.)

79. PHOTOGRAPH (19th century) OF THE SOUTH WALL OF THE NEWARKE, FROM THE NORTH, SHOWING GUN LOOPHOLES AND A SALLY-PORT

This photograph of the south wall of the Newarke gives a perspective of the elevation from inside the Newarke. It also shows the sally-port and the well prepared embrasures used by the parliamentarian defenders during the siege and storming. This is one of three photographs taken, it is believed, shortly before the destruction of the wall which occurred between 1854 and 1886. (From P. & Y. Courtney op. cit.)

80. CLOSE-UP OF EMBRASURES/LOOPHOLES IN THE SOUTH WALL OF THE NEWARKE

This is an extract from page 46 of John Hollings' *The History of Leicester during the Great Civil War* (1840). The print of the interior and exterior views of the embrasures or loopholes, as they were in 1840, is from woodcuts by a Mr. Burton.

81. THE GUILDHALL (OLD TOWN HALL)

This view of the Guildhall (or old Town Hall), where the Borough Corporation met, is by John Flower, circa 1826.

82. PHOTOGRAPH OF THE GUILDHALL AS IT IS TODAY, WITH ST. MARTIN'S CHURCH BEYOND

This photograph shows the Guildhall, as it is today, in Guildhall Lane with neighbouring St. Martin's Church (now Leicester Cathedral) beyond. Both buildings played major parts in the story of the siege and storming of Leicester. (From J. Stevenson op. cit.)

83. PHOTOGRAPH OF THE INTERIOR OF THE GUILDHALL SHOWING THE GREAT HALL

This photograph shows the Great Hall inside Leicester Guildhall. In the adjoining Mayor's parlour the decision was taken, effectively, to defy Prince Rupert and the might of the main Royalist field army in May 1645. (From J. Stevenson op. cit.)

84. PHOTOGRAPH OF ST. MARGARET'S CHURCH

This photograph shows St. Margaret's Church. Construction of the present building had begun in 1168, but it had been substantially rebuilt in the C15th with the addition of its impressive soaring tower. Although built outside the old city walls it was a key defensive position within the outworks during the siege. (From J. Stevenson op. cit.)

85. PHOTOGRAPH OF THE RUINS OF CAVENDISH HOUSE, LEICESTER ABBEY MANSION

This photograph shows the ruins of Cavendish House or the Abbey Mansion, the home of the Dowager Countess of Devonshire, a relative of Henry Hastings, at the time of the siege. It had been built in the grounds of the former Leicester Abbey from the stones of the Abbey itself after the Reformation. King Charles I stayed in the House the night after the capture of Leicester. Ironically, whilst Thomas, Lord Grey of Groby, the local parliamentarian commander, had been forbidden by the House of Lords to cause it any damage, it seems that it was burnt down by royalist soldiers after the king's departure. (From J. Stevenson op. cit.)

86. THE BLUE BOAR INN – (FLOWER, c.1826)

The Blue Boar Inn was famous in Leicester as the place where King Richard III spent the night before the momentous battle of Bosworth Field. Prior to his death in that battle it had been known as the 'White Boar Inn', after his livery badge. The building survived until it was pulled down by a speculative builder in 1836. It is included in this book because it gives a good impression of the sort of structure which existed in Leicester at the time of the siege and storming. This picture is from an engraving by John Flower, circa 1826.

87. DISTRIBUTION OF CANNON BALLS DISCOVERED SUPERIMPOSED ON HOLLINGS' 1840 PLAN OF OPERATIONS MAP (From P. & Y. Courtney op. cit.)

88. TWO 'GRENADOES', ONE (LEFT) WITH A WOODEN 'FUSEE'

These are two grenades of the revelant period in a collection of the Leicester Museums Service. They were found in a room in the Magazine Gateway. (From P. & Y. Courtney op. cit.)

89. PLAN OF THE CASTLE AND NEWARKE PRECINCTS – (THOMPSON, 1859)

This plan of the Castle and Newarke precincts is included because it shows the perimeter walls of both (a and b respectively) and their relationship to each other. It also shows the location of buildings which have since been demolished such as the Castle Mills (I), the Angular Tower (L), and the Tower called "Prince Rupert's Tower" (K); as well as remaining features such as the Magazine Gateway (H), the Turret (or Ruperts) Gateway (E), the 'Tudor Gateway' or Porter's Lodge (G), and St. Mary de Castro Church (C). Most of the southern part of the Newarke precinct is now occupied by buildings of the De Montfort University. The Plan is reproduced from James Thompson's *An Account of Leicester Castle*, published by Crossley and Clarke in Leicester in 1859. This small book was based on a paper he presented to the Annual Meeting of the Leicestershire Architectural and Archaeological Society in 1856. As he states on the adjacent page 34 in his book, "This plan was obligingly supplied by Mr. Stephens, Borough Surveyor, whose son drew it out from the town plan, specially prepared for public purposes."

90. LIST OF LEICESTER PARLIAMENTARIAN MILITIA COMMITTEE MEMBERS

This list is reproduced from page 70 of John Hollings' book, *The History of Leicester during the Great Civil War* (1840), and is, in turn, taken from the pamphlet *An Examination examined, being a full answer to Major Innes' Relation of the taking of Leicester* (1645).

BIBLIOGRAPHY

A. Manuscript Sources

<u>Leicester Museum Archives</u>

Letter to the Mayor of Leicester from Prince Rupert - 6th September 1642

Letter to the Mayor of Leicester from King Charles I - 8th September 1642

Receipt written by Prince Rupert - 9th September 1642

Pass issued by Colonel Henry Grey, Governor of Leicester - 16th April 1644

George Booth's letter to Thomas, Lord Grey of Groby - 12th April 1645

Letter ordering the demolition of the Grange Houses, with signatures - 19th April 1645

Letter from the parliamentarian Committee of Leicester to Lord Grey of Groby - 1st May 1645

Letter from the Mayor of Leicester to John Gray M.P. - 14th May 1660

Also, <u>Quart Manuscripts in the British Museum</u>

B. Contemporary Pamphlets and Newspapers/Newsletters

<u>Pamphlets/accounts, including some of the siege</u>

Horrible News from Leicester!, June 1642
Remarkable Passages from Leiceter, 1642
Terrible News from Leicester, 1645
A Perfect Relation of the Taking of Leicester, etc., 1645 (a more neutral parliamentarian account)
A Narration of the Siege nd Taking of the Town of Leicester, the Last of May, 1645, by the Kings Forces, 1645 (a pro-Committee account)

Present Passages of each day's Proceedings in Parliament, 1645
An Examination of a Printed Pamphlet, entituld (sic) *A Narration of the Siege of Leicester,* by Major James Innis
A More Exact Relation of the Siege Laid to the Town of Leiester, 1645 (said to be the account related to the House of Commons by Colonel Pye and Major Innes)
An Examination Examined, Being a Full and Moderate Answer to Major Innes' Relation Concerning the Siege and Taking of the Town of Leicester, 1645 (another pro-Committee account)

Newsletters

Mercurius Aulicus (Royalist newsletter)
Mercurius Brittanicus (Parliamentarian newsletter)
Mercurius Rusticus (Royalist newsletter)
Mercurius Veridicus (Parliamentarian newsletter)
The Moderate Intelligencer (Parliamentarian newsletter)
The Parliament's Post (Parliamentarian newsletter)
The Parliament Scoute (Parliamentarian newsletter)
A Perfect Diurnal (of some passages in Parliament)
(Parliamentarian newsletter)

Others

Carte's Manuscript concerning the Proceedings of the Leicestershire Committee of Sequestrators, 1645
Hall Papers (Common Hall) - see Records of the Borough of Leicester Town Chamberlains' Accounts - see Records of the Borough of Leicester

C. Other Contemporary Printed Matter

John Corbet, *A true and impartial History of the Militarie Government of the Citie of Gloucester,* London, 1647
John Dryden, *Cymon and Iphigenia*

Sir William Dugdale, *A Short View of the Late Troubles in England*, Oxford, 1681

William Eldred, *The Gunne's Glasse*, London, 1646

James Heath, *Heath's Chronicle - A brief Chronicle of the late Intestine Warr*, 1663

David Papillon, *A Practical Abstract of the Arts of Fortification and Absailing, etc.*, London, 1645/6

Joshua Sprigge, *Anglia Rediviva; England's Recovery* (parliamentarian publication), London, 1647

John Vicars, *God in the Mount, Or, England's Remembrancer*, London, 1642

John Vicars, *Magnalia, Dei Anglicana, Or, England's Parliamentary Chronicle*, London, 1644-1646

Sir Edmund Walker, *Historical Discourses upon Several Occasions*, London, 1705

Nehemiah Wallington, *Historical Notes of Events Occurring Chiefly in the Reign of Charles I*, Republished London, 1869

R. Ward, *Animadversions of Warre*, London, 1639

Bulstrode Whitelocke, *Memorials of the English Affairs*, London, 1682

D. Later Publication of Contemporary Diaries, Correspondence, Histories, Memoirs, Official Documents, Records and other works

Robert Baillie, *The Letters and Journals of Robert Baillie*, ed. David Laing., Edinburgh, 1841-1842

Robert Bell, ed. Fairfax Correspondence - *Memorials of the Civil War*, London, 1849

John Birch, *Military Memoirs of Colonel John Birch*, ed. J. & T.W. Webb, Camden Society, 1873

Borough of Leicester - see Records of the Borough of Leicester Calendar of State Papers (Domestic Series) 1641-3

Clarendon, (Earl of), *The History of the Great Rebellion and Civil Wars in England*, Publ. 1702-1704

Cobbett's Complete Collection, *State Trials*, 1810

Commons, (House of) - see Journal of

John Evelyn, *Diary of John Evelyn*, (1654); ed. H.B. Wheatley, Bickers & Son, London, 1906

Celia Fiennes, *Diary of Celia Fiennes*, (c.1700), Field & Tuer, the Leadenhall Press

Historical Manuscripts Commission (HMC) : Hastings Collection

Historical Manuscripts Commission (HMC) : Appenix to 5th Report, 15th May 1660 – Letter from Mr. Ayloffe to Mr. John Langley

Historical Manuscripts Commission (HMC) : MSS of S.H. Le Fleming of Rydal Hall, June 1660

Historical Manuscripts Commission (HMC) : MSS of the Duke of Somerset (Marquis of Ailesbury) - Letter from the Earl of Stamford to the Earl of Ailesbury, 9th January 1667

Denzil Holles, *Memoirs of Denzil Holles*, London, 1815

T.B. Howell, (ed.) *A Complete Collection of State Trials*, London, 1809-1826

Lucy Hutchinson, *Memoirs of the Life of Colonel Hutchinson*, Everyman's Library 317, Dent, London, 1965 <u>and</u> Oxford University Press, London, 1973

Edward Hyde, Earl of Clarendon, *History of the Great Rebellion*, ed. W.D. Macray, 1888

Journal of the House of Commons (C.J.) - various volumes

Journal of the House of Lords (L.J.) - various volumes

David Laing, (ed.),*The Letters and Journals of Robert Baillie*, Edinburgh, 1841-1842

Leicester (RBL) - see Records of the Borough of Leicester

Leicestershire Museums Service - Archive Teaching Unit No. 1., 1979, *Bloodie Rebellion - Leicestershire and Rutland in the Civil War.*

Lords, (House of) - see Journal of

Sir Samuel Luke, *Letter Books of Sir Samuel Luke* (1644-45)

D. Parsons, *The Diary of Henry Slingsby,* London, 1836

Records of the Borough of Leicester (RBL) : 1603-1688, (ed. Helen Stocks, Cambridge,1923) incl. Hall Papers, Original Letters, Town Chamberlains Accounts.

John Rushworth, *Historical Collections of Private Passages of State.*

John Rushworth, *Historical Collections abridged and improved.* Shropshire Gentleman (and Royalist Officer), *The History of the Civil Wars in Germany from 1630 to 1635; also Genuine Memoirs of the Wars in England in the unhappy Reign of King Charles the First. Written by a Shropshire Gentleman, who personally served under the King of Sweden in Germany; and on th Royal Side during the unhappy Contests in England.* Newark, 1782. (Cited n John Nichols)

Henry Slingsby, *The Diary of Heny Slingsby* - see D. Parsons above

Richard Symonds, *Diary of the Marches of the Royal Army During the Great Civil War,* ed. C.E. Long. Camden Society, Vol. LXXXIV., 1859

Thomas Vaughton, *Tales of Sutton Town and Chase,* incl. the song *The Armourer's Widow.* Cited by Roy E. Sherwood, *Civil Strife in the Midlands, 1642-1651,* Phillimore, London & Chichester, 1974

E. Warburton, *Memoirs of Prince Rupert and the Cavaliers,* London, 1849

Anthony Wood, *Life and Times of Anthony Wood,* ed. A. Clark, The Oxford Historical Society, 1891- 1900

E. Secondary and General Sources

John Adair, *A Life of John Hampden - The Patriot (1594-1643),* Macdonald and Jane's, London, 1976.

Paul Courtney, *Castle Park - A Souvenir Guide,* Leicestershire County Council, 1995.

Paul Courtney, *Parliamentarians Divided, or, Fear and Loathing at the Siege of Leicester,* 1645', article in *The Leicestershire Historian* Vol. 4., No. 3., 1995

Paul & Yolanda Courtney, *A Siege examined: the Civil War archaeology of Leicester* article in *Post-Medieval Archaeology* No. 26, 1992, pp. 47-90.

Alan M. Everitt, *The Local Community and the Great Rebellion,* Published by the Historical Association, 1969. (G.70).

Susan Green, - see Jonathan Wilshere

John Hollings, *The History of Leicester during the Great Civil War*, Combe & Crossley, Leicester, 1840. (from a lecture given to the Mechanics Institute in Leicester, 1839)

W. Kelly, *Royal Progresses and Visits to Leicester*, 1884.

John Morrill, *The Revolt of the Provinces - Conservatives and Radicals in the English Civil War, 1630-1650*, Longman, New York, 1980.

Bob Moulder, *Cavaliers & Roundheads*, Tarquin Publications, Diss, Norfolk, 1997.

John Nichols, *The History and Antiquities of the County of Leicester*, Leicester, 1788-1804 - several volumes, particularly Vol. III., Part II., & Appendix IV., 1804. *The Civil War in Leicestershire*.

Mark Noble, *Lives of the English Regicides*, London, 1798.

Mark Noble, *Memoirs of the Protectoral House of Cromwell*, Birmingham, 1787.

Alison Plowden, *Women All On Fire - The Women of the English Civil War*, Sutton Publishing, Gloucester, 1998.

Jeff Richards, *Aristocrat and Regicide - The Life and Times of Thomas, Lord Grey of Groby (1623-1657)*, New Millennium, London, 2000.

Roy E. Sherwood, *Civil Strife in the Midlands, 1642-1651*, Phillimore, London & Chichester, 1974.

Jack Simmons, *Leicester - The Ancient Borough to 1860*, Alan Sutton, Gloucester, 1983.

Joan Stevenson, *Leicester Through the Ages*, Kairos Press, Newtown Linford, Leics. 1995.

James Thompson, *The History of Leicester*, Leicester, 1849.

James Thompson, *Leicester Castle,* Crossley & Clarke, 1859 (facsimile, Sycamore Press, Leicester, 1977)

John Throsby, *The History and Antiquities of the Ancient Town of Leicester*, Vol. III. Appendix. 1791.

John Throsby, *Select Views of Leicestershire - from original drawings - containing seats of the nobility and gentry, town views and ruins, accompanied with descriptive and historical relations.* Leicester 1789.

John Throsby, *Supplementary Volume to the Leicestershire Views - 'Excursions,* Leicester, 1790.

Victoria County History of Leicestershire, Vol. II. (1954) & Vol. IV. (1958),- ed. W.G. Hoskins & R. A. McKinley. [Key chapter by J.H. Plumb].

E. Warburton, *Memoirs of Prince Rupert and the Cavaliers,* London, 1849

C.V. Wedgwood, *The Historian and the World,* (1942), - republished in *History and Hope* - C.V. Wedgwood's collected essays. Fontana, London, 1989.

Jonathan Wilshere & Susan Green, *The Siege of Leicester - 1645,* (- A 325th Anniversary History), Published by Leicester Research Services, Leicester. 1970, & 1972.

INDEX OF PLACES

Edgehill, battle of - see also Kineton, Warwickshire 48, 49, 51, 52, 54, 55, 59, 236, 345, 352, 353, 354, 356, 357
Edmundthorpe, Leicestershire 243
Evesham, Worcestershire 82, 103, 195

Fawsley Park, Northamptonshire 206
Fenny Drayton, Leicestershire 260
Framland Hundred, Leicestershire 5, 28
France 4, 124, 237, 355, 356

Garendon Abbey, Loughborough, Leicestershire 31
Gartree Hundred, Leicestershire 5, 28
Germany 57, 189, 274, 350, 351, 357, 358
Gloucester 23, 45, 57, 138, 159, 199, 200, 222, 295, 306
Gracedieu, Leicestershire 90
Grantham, Lincolnshire 260
Great Glen, Leicestershire 205, 210
Great Yeldham, Essex 89
Guilsborough, Northamptonshire 206
Guthlaxton Hundred, Leicestershire 5, 27

Hartlebury, Staffordshire 238
Hawkesley House, Worcestershire 84
Hereford 49, 57, 84, 212, 213, 220, 221, 222, 223, 224, 226, 233
Hinckley, Leicestershire 5, 61, 257
Hoby, Leicestershire 257
Holland - see Netherlands 42, 274, 343
Holmby (or Holdenby) House, Northamptonshire 206, 239
Horsefair Leas, Leicester 24, 27, 138
Hugglescote, Leicestershire 27
Hull (or Kingston-upon-Hull), Yorkshire 12, 13, 24, 39
Humberstone, Leicestershire 111, 115, 123, 216, 217, 302
Huntingdonshire 58
Husbands Bosworth, Leicestershire 243, 277

Ibstock, Leicestershire 27, 257
Ireland 11, 12, 82, 122, 210, 273, 277

Jersey, Isle of 10, 276

Kibworth, Leicestershire 27, 28
Kidderminster, Worcestershire 212
Kimcote, Leicestershire 257
Kineton, Warwickshire (see also Edgehill, battle of) 49, 52, 54
Kingston-upon-Hull, Yorkshire - see also Hull
Kirby Bellars, Leicestershire 61, 109, 197, 349
Kislingbury, Northamptonshire 206

Langport, battle of 223
Leipzig, Germany 189
Leicester (town or borough) 1, 2, 3, 9, 10, 14, 21, 24, 48, 62, 63, 79, 91, 104, 155, 157, 201, 205, 213, 214, 225, 231, 240, 259, 261, 262, 269, 276, 278, 282, 286, 297, 304, 309, 343, 350, 351, 364, 372, 373, 374, 375, 377
Leicester Abbey 40, 43, 61, 138, 144, 184, 189, 190, 194, 302, 360, 369
Leicester Forest 5, 6, 247
Leicestershire 4, 5, 7, 8, 9, 11, 14, 15, 21, 27, 29, 31, 38, 39, 42, 43, 44, 49, 51, 55, 56, 58, 59, 61, 63, 71, 74, 85, 86, 88, 90, 91, 92, 106, 107, 110, 158, 159, 183, 207, 208, 211, 221, 225, 233, 234, 236, 243, 245, 246, 256, 258, 260, 269, 273, 274, 276, 277, 281, 285, 307, 309, 310, 344, 345, 346, 348, 350, 361, 363, 365, 373, 375, 376, 377
Lichfield 182, 212, 213, 233, 234, 238, 352
Lichfield Cathedral, Staffordshire 56
Lincolnshire 58, 222, 247, 260, 282, 353
London (town/city) 2, 5, 11, 12, 31, 38, 42, 52, 54, 62, 70, 71, 74, 75, 77, 80, 82, 84, 85, 86, 88, 89, 108, 190, 192, 194, 195, 196, 198, 214, 224, 237, 243, 244, 245, 248, 250, 260, 269, 270, 274, 278, 281, 285, 345
London, Tower of 7, 195, 272, 274, 276, 352, 354, 363

Loughborough, Leicestershire 5, 29, 31, 32, 33, 61, 90, 116, 344

Loughborough House [Lambeth, London] 281, 345

Low Countries – see Netherlands

Ludlow, Shropshire 84, 238, 271

Lutterworth, Leicestershire 5

Magazine Gateway, Leicester 29, 79, 297, 299, 303

Magdeburg, Germany 189, 359

Market Bosworth, Leicestershire 5, 38, 256, 276, 363

Market Drayton, Shropshire 85

Market Harborough, Leicestershire 5, 205, 206, 243

Market Overton, Rutland 276

Marston Moor, battle of 62, 82, 347, 351, 355

Medbourne, Leicestershire 105, 256

Melton Mowbray, Leicestershire 5, 27, 28, 61, 72, 73, 355

Middlesex 15

Morley, Derbyshire 234

Mountsorrel, Leicestershire 32

Munster, Ireland 277

Naseby, [Northamptonshire] battle of 207, 208, 211, 212, 213, 221, 223, 224, 233, 236, 303, 308, 345, 351, 354, 355, 359, 360

Netherlands 12, 354, 356, 358

Newark-upon-Trent, Nottinghamshire 72, 73, 89, 110, 111, 129, 130, 139, 183, 184, 185, 191, 194, 206, 215, 218, 237, 242, 243, 246, 253, 254, 277, 362, 371, 372, 373

Newarke [The], Leicester 70, 76, 77, 79, 86, 115, 116, 118, 123, 130, 132, 133, 137, 138, 139, 140, 142, 146, 149, 151, 184, 188, 193, 196, 198, 199, 212, 214, 216, 217, 237, 253, 297, 299, 300, 302, 303, 305, 307, 308, 310, 347, 356, 360, 365, 366, 367, 368

Newarke Fort 115, 149, 151, 155, 299

Newarke Gate – see also Magazine Gateway, Leicester 29, 79

Newarke Grange Farm 347

Newarke Houses 116, 298, 366
Newarke Houses Museum 298
Newbury [Berkshire], battle of 82, 352, 355, 356
Newcastle-upon-Tyne 237, 243, 348
Northampton 43, 45, 58, 69, 86, 113, 116, 135, 194, 196, 212, 220, 232, 261, 358
Northamptonshire 56
Noseley, Leicestershire 243, 273, 276, 364
Nottingham 3, 21, 24, 39, 43, 44, 47, 48, 57, 58, 61, 69, 78, 86, 89, 107, 108, 110, 111, 214, 221, 256, 257, 275, 307, 308, 348
Nottingham Castle 78, 308
Nottinghamshire 61, 151, 205, 220, 223, 233, 237, 242, 243, 256, 273, 349, 353, 357

Oadby, Leicestershire 257
Oxford 54, 55, 63, 81, 84, 89, 104, 105, 108, 120, 132, 190, 192, 194, 199, 200, 205, 206, 223, 224, 226, 231, 232, 236, 237, 238, 256, 261, 304, 308, 351, 353, 354, 357, 358, 361, 373, 374, 375
Oxfordshire 4

Packington, Leicestershire 89
Preston, Lancashire 214, 240, 355
Prestwold, Leicestershire 90

Queniborough, Leicestershire 5, 27, 28, 47
Quorn (or Quorndon) Leicestershire 32

Ravenstone, Leicestershire 27, 211
Raw Dykes, Leicester 28, 29, 31, 33, 132, 184, 299, 346
Rockingham Castle, Northamptonshire 61
Rothley, Leicestershire 32, 51, 109, 344
Rutland 4, 44, 57, 58, 61, 116, 155, 184, 240, 243, 257, 274, 276, 353, 375

Billars, William 86, 129, 132, 219
Birch, Colonel John 226, 373
Bird, Thomas [of Somerby] 257
Biron - see Byron 354
Blackstone, Sir William 121
Blithe, Francis 86
Blunt, Thomas [Commissary] 77, 108
Booth, Colonel George [later Lord Delamere] 75, 76, 89, 116,
196, 271, 307, 347, 363, 371
Bradshaw, John 242, 251, 252, 271, 273, 278, 361
Bradshawe, Robert 254
Brereton, Sir William 75, 82, 84, 236, 355
Bretton, Clement [of Church Langton] 257
Broughton, Colonel Robert 122
Brown, Humphrey 155, 184, 240
Brown, John 77
Browne, John 80, 81, 252
Browne, Major General 84, 192
Brudenell, Thomas 252
Buckingham, Duke of, [George Villiers] 7, 9
Bunnington, Major 146
Burrowes, Mistress 189
Burton, Casibilian 252
Burton, Mr. 297, 365, 368
Byron, Lord [see Byron, Sir John] 223, 236, 354
Byron, Sir John [later Lord Byron] 84, 121
Byron, Sir Richard 121, 354

Cambridge, Owen 235
Carew, Mr. John 62
Cary, [or Carey] Colonel Horatio 89, 121
Chaloner, Thomas 273
Chambers, John 29, 31, 33, 34, 35, 37, 38, 63
Chapman, Thomas 252
Charles I, King 5, 6, 7, 8, 10, 12, 22, 38, 43, 47, 64, 82,
84, 89, 90, 91, 103, 104, 116, 120, 130, 137, 138, 155, 184,
189, 190, 206, 210, 222, 223, 232, 233, 237, 238, 239, 240,

242, 243, 244, 256, 271, 273, 276, 277, 301, 304, 344, 347, 348, 350, 351, 353, 360, 361, 362, 369, 371, 373, 375

Charles II, King 254, 269, 270, 276, 278, 282, 352, 362, 363

Charles, Prince of Wales [see Charles II, King] 39, 40, 43, 278

Chesterfield, Earl of 90

Chillingworth, William 259

Clarendon, Earl of [see Edward Hyde] 14, 44, 52, 55, 56, 59, 63, 64, 69, 92, 146, 159, 187, 201, 205, 223, 225, 226, 246, 261, 373, 374

Cleveland, John 257

Cleveland, Lord 355

Cleveland, Thomas [father of the poet John Cleveland] 257

Commons, House of 6, 9, 10, 11, 12, 14, 15, 22, 24, 42, 61, 62, 64, 86, 91, 104, 110, 194, 214, 215, 216, 225, 232, 240, 261, 271, 272, 274, 275, 285, 372, 374

Compton, James [3rd Earl of Northumberland] 120, 351

Compton, Sir William 120, 352

Compton, Spencer [2nd Earl of Northumberland] 351, 352

Cook, John 243, 277

Cooke [Cook or Coke], Thomas 9, 231, 232, 242

Corbet, John 63, 372

Cotes, Henry 35

Cotton, Thomas 71, 74

Craddock, Edmund 71, 77, 282, 307

Cromwell, Oliver 75, 84, 108, 206, 207, 210, 211, 212, 214, 240, 242, 243, 245, 249, 251, 252, 253, 254, 260, 261, 269, 273, 274, 275, 276, 277, 278, 306, 308, 309, 348, 349, 352, 355, 359, 361, 376

Cromwell, Richard 269

Dalison, Sir Robert 221

Danvers, Henry 252

Danvers, William 71, 74, 252

Davis, Lieutenant 113

Dawes, Hugh 253, 279

Dawes, Jane 279

Dawes, William 279

Gaunt, John of 3
Gell, Sir John 55, 56, 89, 205, 234
Gerard, Sir Charles 85, 206, 212
Gerard, Sir George 357
Goddard, Thomas 71, 74
Goodman, John 71, 252
Goodman, Valentine 77
Goodwin, Arthur 110
Goring, Lord John [later Lord Norwich] 82, 84, 85, 206, 212, 236
Gouge, Captain 84
Gray, John 278, 285, 371
Green, Master 114
Green, Susan 124, 307, 376, 377
Gregory, Under-Sheriff 28, 31
Grey, Anchitel [son of the Earl of Stamford] 45
Grey, Anne [daughter of the Earl of Stamford] 45
Grey, Captain Edward 61
Grey, Colonel Henry 59, 81, 86, 109, 111, 115, 121, 144, 197, 346, 371
Grey, Diana [daughter of the Earl of Stamford] 45
Grey, Elizabeth [daughter of the Earl of Stamford] 45, 75, 271, 347, 363
Grey, Henry - first Earl of Stamford, second Lord Grey of Groby 7, 9, 344, 346, 347, 363
Grey, Henry - Lord Ruthin [later Earl of Kent] 9, 15, 24, 28, 29, 85, 86, 103, 111, 197, 252
Grey, Jane [daughter of the Earl of Stamford] 45
Grey, Job [Rector of Aston Flamville and son of the Earl of Kent] 195, 259
Grey, John [son of the Earl of Stamford] 45
Grey Lady Jane [The Nine Days Queen] 9
Grey, Leonard [son of the Earl of Stamford] 45
Grey, Mary [daughter of the Earl of Stamford] 45
Grey of Groby, Lord - see Thomas Grey, [third] Lord Grey of Groby 7, 9, 10, 28, 45, 51, 56, 57, 58, 59, 61, 62, 64, 70, 71, 75, 76, 80, 88, 106, 115, 121, 138, 194, 196, 198, 211,

231, 240, 242, 243, 245, 250, 251, 255, 261, 269, 270, 271, 272, 273, 274, 275, 276, 277, 278, 285, 306, 345, 346, 348, 349, 350, 361, 369, 371, 376

Grey, Theophilus 71, 72, 80, 103, 111, 197, 347

Grey, Thomas [fourth] Lord Grey of Groby & Second Earl of Stamford 270

Grey, Thomas [third] Lord Grey of Groby, son of the first Earl of Stamford – see Grey of Groby, Lord [above]

Hacker, Francis [Captain, later Colonel] 71, 80, 81, 109, 116, 121, 129, 140, 144, 179, 181, 184, 185, 197, 219, 220, 244, 252, 254, 260, 277, 278, 349, 361, 362

Hacker, Rowland [Captain] 219

Halford, Andrew 33

Halford, Sir Richard 27, 33, 35

Hampden, Anne [daughter of John Hampden] 110

Hampden, John [Colonel] 8, 54, 110, 124, 243, 375

Harley, Sir Edward 124

Harley, William 218

Hartopp, Sir Edward 71, 74, 309

Hartopp, Sir Thomas 71

Hartoppe, William 252

Harvey, Edward 274

Hasbridge, Thomas 252

Hastings, Henry - also Lord Loughborough 11, 12, 27, 28, 29, 31, 32, 33, 34, 35, 38, 39, 40, 42, 44, 49, 55, 56, 59, 60, 61, 69, 74, 90, 146, 193, 212, 220, 236, 280, 281, 344, 345, 349, 369

Hastings, Lord Ferdinando - see also Huntingdon, sixth Earl of 12, 38, 49, 52, 54, 55, 235

Hastings, Lord Henry 343

Hastings of Ashby-de-la-Zouch 7, 9, 26, 29, 40, 44, 47, 106, 346

Hastings, Walter 33, 34, 37

Hastwell, William 152

Hawley, Lord 85

Henrietta Maria, Queen 11, 189

Henshaw, Thomas 282

Heron, Edward [Rector of Croxton] 257

Hesilrige, [also Hesilrigg & Heselrigge, etc.] Sir Arthur 9, 15, 24, 29, 31, 51, 63, 71, 75, 104, 106, 108, 110, 121, 198, 242, 244, 275, 278, 348, 349, 363

Hesilrige, Thomas 71, 77

Hewett [or Hewitt], William 71, 104, 252

Holles, Denzil 57, 64, 372

Hollings, John 132, 133, 135, 137, 146, 158, 185, 197, 199, 201, 202, 214, 285, 296, 297, 299, 301, 302, 307, 309, 351, 363, 364, 367, 368, 369, 376

Holt, Joseph 258

Hopton, Sir Ralph [later Lord] 122, 236

Horton, Thomas 243, 273, 361

Howard, Colonel Thomas 121

Hudson, Lieutenant-Colonel 85

Hudson, Michael [Vicar of Market Bosworth] 256

Huntingdon, fifth Earl of - Henry Hastings [father of Ferdinando & Henry Hastings] 7, 8, 9, 11, 12, 27, 55, 56, 235, 344

Huntingdon, sixth Earl of - see Ferdinando, Lord Hastings 345

Hurst, Captain 144, 196, 197

Hutchinson, Colonel John 21, 24, 63, 78, 91, 220, 226, 244, 256, 261, 275, 278, 285, 308, 348, 349, 354, 374

Hutchinson, Lucy 21, 63, 91, 108, 200, 202, 224, 226, 244, 261, 285, 348, 349, 354, 374

Hyde, Sir Edward [later Earl of Clarenden] 14, 55, 63, 64, 374

Ingoldsby, Richard 273

Innes, Major James 88, 89, 110, 111, 113, 114, 115, 121, 129, 135, 149, 152, 182, 185, 194, 195, 197, 198, 199, 214, 306, 307, 372

Ireton, Henry 206, 207, 249, 271, 273, 274, 275, 278

Loughborough, Lord [see Henry Hastings] 61, 69, 89, 121, 122, 192, 194, 210, 211, 212, 213, 220, 231, 236, 280, 281, 344, 345
Lovelace, Lord 33
Loveton, John 27
Lucas, Sir Charles 354
Lucas, Sir Gervase or Jarvis 44, 233
Ludlam, Richard 39, 60, 71, 104, 280, 282, 307
Ludlow, Edmund 271
Luke, Sir Samuel 75, 205, 208, 225, 374
Lunsford, Captain 38

Mackworth, Gustavus 271
Manchester, Earl of 58, 75
Markham, Captain Henry 72
Markham, Henry 253
Massey, Colonel Edward 45, 103, 222, 223
Maurice, Prince 120, 121, 207, 223, 351
Middleton, Sir Thomas 75
Midland Association of Counties 56, 61, 75, 306, 347
Mildmay, John 271
Miller, G [Printer] 214, 225
Milton, John 255
Monck, General George 269, 270
Montague, Colonel 207
Montrose, Marquis of 81, 222
Moore, Rev. John [Minister of Shearsby] 248
Morrill, John 15, 124, 376
Motley, Francis 152
Mounson, Lord 271

Needham, Colonel John 220, 235, 236
New Model Army 46, 75, 85, 110, 205, 206, 208, 222, 237, 239, 242, 277, 359
Newark, Lord 24
Newdigate, Richard 252
Newton, Mr. of Houghton, Leicestershire 105

396